Ulrike Ernst

From Anti-Apartheid to African Renaissance

Anglistik

Amerikanistik

Band 7

LIT

Ulrike Ernst

From Anti-Apartheid to African Renaissance

Interviews with
South African Writers and Critics
on Cultural Politics
Beyond the Cultural Struggle

LIT

Cover Picture: "The Gumboot Dance" by Ulrike Ernst

Die Deutsche Bibliothek – CIP-Einheitsaufnahme

Ernst, Ulrike:
From Anti-Apartheid to African Renaissance : Interviews with South African Writers and Critics on Cultural Politics Beyond the Cultural Struggle / Ulrike Ernst. – Hamburg : LIT, 2002
 (Anglistik/ Amerikanistik ; 7)
 ISBN 3-8258-5804-9

© LIT VERLAG Münster – Hamburg – London
 Grindelberg 15a 20144 Hamburg Tel. 040 - 44 64 46 Fax 040 - 44 14 22
 e-Mail: hamburg@lit-verlag.de   http://www.lit-verlag.de

Distributed in North America by:

Transaction Publishers
New Brunswick (U.S.A.) and London (U.K.)

Transaction Publishers
Rutgers University
35 Berrue Circle
Piscataway, NJ 08854

Tel.: (732) 445 - 2280
Fax: (732) 445 - 3138
for orders (U.S. only):
toll free (888) 999 - 6778

For Ulrike Kistner
a critical spirit, brilliant teacher and great friend

Contents

Acknowledgements	9
Preface	11

Introduction *by Ulrike Ernst*

Is There a Happy End to the 'Cultural Struggle'? – Some Remarks on Cultural Politics in South Africa in a Time of Transition.   13

Peter Horn	*"The Counter-Rotating Fate of Writers"*	36
Mandla Langa	*"The Arts Start to Play Second Fiddle"*	50
Stephen Gray	*"History Is Invented the Morning After"*	66
Michael Chapman	*"There Is No Essential Africanness"*	78
Ari Sitas	*"Art Should Nation Build and the Idea Cracked"*	90
Nise Malange	*"To Understand the Gumboot Dance"*	108
Nadine Gordimer	*"Writers Need Readers"*	134
Mongane W. Serote	*"Ordinary People - Creators of African Culture"*	148
Jeremy Cronin	*"The Cinderella Department"*	164
Ulrike Kistner	*"Underrated - A Critical Poetics of Knowledge"*	184

Highlights of Interviewees' Literary-Political Contexts	193
Abbreviations/Acronyms	203

Acknowledgements

I would like to express my gratitude to the interviewees for their participation in the project and willingness to discuss some rather provocative issues with openness and creativity.

I thank the Friedrich-Ebert-Foundation (Bonn/Berlin), Adalbert Schlag, for their generous funding, which enabled me to pursue this project in different South African cities, Dr Ulrich Golaszinsky of the Friedrich-Ebert-Foundation (Johannesburg), Sigrid Thomsen of the Heinrich-Böll-Foundation (Johannesburg) and the Goethe-Institute who were always very supportive. The University of the Witwatersrand, Johannesburg, provided the base for my investigations. I am especially grateful to Professor Reingard Nethersole, and Professor Carlotta von Maltzan. I thank my 'doctor-mothers', Professor Dr Christina von Braun (Cultural Studies) and Professor Dr Flora Veit-Wild (African Studies) at the Humboldt-University, Berlin for accepting this détour of my doctoral thesis. I was fortunate enough to have found Veit D. Hopf of LIT Publishers who has a deep interest in African issues. I thank Margot Pakendorf for the careful transcriptions of the interviews, Peter Deiter for his proofreading of the final version and Ulrike Bossler and Ilaria De Biasi for their layout advice.

Special thanks to my scattered friends, who pressed for the publication of the interviews, and despite my commuting between Europe and Africa, still followed the project closely over long distances. My long time friend Makhosazana Nizimande (Durban/Texas) raised my original interest in the South African transformation. Elinor Kern (Johannesburg) helped with valuable suggestions and corrections. Judith Kalk's (Johannesburg) meticulous attention and her knowledge of the publishing procedures were very welcomed. I received valuable criticism from Ronja Kempin (Berlin/Paris).

Most of all I have benefited from numerous challenging conversations with Dr Ulrike Kistner (Johannesburg) - who made me ask questions - beyond the traditional boundaries of learning.

A special mention goes to my parents, Ursula Ernst und Peter Ernst, for their support and encouragement. This project would neither have come into being nor to an end without Michèle Auga.

Berlin - Johannesburg - Bamako, 2001   Ulrike Ernst

Preface

Back in Berlin from a lengthy sojourn in Johannesburg and in the process of preparing this book for printing, a friend sent me the following e-mail: "Dear Ulrike, In the suggested title you write *'From Anti-Apartheid to African Renaissance. Interviews with South African Writers and Critics on Cultural Politics After the End of the 'Cultural Struggle''* - this is not quite accurate. I do not think one should speak of the 'end of the 'cultural struggle''. It's too final and it's not over yet, use another more neutral term, such as 'after 1990', or something of that nature."

In fact, in South Africa, I often met with laughter when I inquired about cultural politics after the 'end of the struggle'. Had the use of 'culture as a weapon' in the struggle not been denounced in 1989 amidst a lively public debate? Why then did the end of apartheid not signal the end of the struggle in the eyes of those who would eagerly abolish 'revolutionary culture'? It turns out that many of those who nowadays advocate 'struggle aesthetics' have themselves become part of the new political establishment. The complexity of these basic questions, I felt, could only be tackled through interviewing people.

This book wants to explore the role of the writer/intellectual in South Africa during the period of transition (that is between 1990 to 2000) within the historical, social, and political context.

The focus of this collection is cultural politics, especially the cultural and literary policy of the former anti-apartheid alliance (African National Congress, South African Communist Party and Congress of South African Trade Unions). Three shifts are noted: the end of apartheid (1990), the alliance's accession to power (1994), and the change of presidency from Nelson Mandela to Thabo Mbeki, including the introduction of the neo-liberal *'Growth, Employment and Redistribution'* strategy (GEAR).

The investigation both assumes and stresses the importance of the role of writers and intellectuals in political and societal transformation processes. These processes have a tendency to destroy the agency that initially set them in motion. Startling revelations are being made, which highlight the emptiness of much rainbow nation sloganeering. Statements are recorded here that are otherwise seldom heard. Although public debate, including a critical stance towards the ANC in government, is desperately needed, it is only slowly becoming acceptable and is still associated with manifold political risks.

The interviews attempt to address a number of frequently asked questions: Why does the ANC post-apartheid cultural politics strike one as being so confused? What was the real reason for the collapse of the Congress of South African Writers? Why is the Nobel Prize winner for literature, Nadine Gordimer, less well received in her own country than abroad? What was Thabo Mbeki's motivation for developing the African Renaissance? Is this a concept for overcoming political, social, and cultural conflicts in South Africa? What is behind a neo-traditional Africanism? Why is the notion of 'national culture' especially problematic in South Africa?

At some points I could not resist asking some questions that are related to my interest in the role of the writer/intellectual in the (East) German Transition.

This book is composed of interviews with ten writers and/or critics, all of whom have been important voices in the cultural-political scene of the old and the new South Africa. I deliberately selected people who have been members of the ANC, COSATU or the SACP, or who were anti-apartheid activists, but not part of the 'mainstream opposition', or who have played a critical role as non-aligned public intellectuals.

For my investigation I chose writers and critics who publish in English. In order to facilitate comparisons, and to gauge the range and scope of the responses, core questions for each interview were composed. These were supplemented with questions relating to the specific expertise of the particular interviewee. The interviews were not restricted to cursory moments of passing interest. The interviews took place in three major South African centres, namely Johannesburg, Durban and Cape Town, between January 2000 and April 2001. The reader will probably find a certain improvement in the interviewer's skills over time. This will become evident when the interviews are being read in sequence. Each piece can also be read individually. I personally like illustrated books - I have therefore included photographs that I took of the respondents.

Given the different positions and perspectives of the interviewees, the understanding of and responses to the questions differed widely. The introductory essay *"Is There a Happy End to the 'Cultural Struggle'?"* is my answer to the question as to why I decided to (almost) retain the disputed title of this collection.

Conducting the interviews has been an astonishing experience, a little spark of which will hopefully reach the reader. Responses are very welcome.

To be continued.   Ulrike Ernst

Introduction

Is There a Happy End to the 'Cultural Struggle'? - Some Remarks on Cultural Politics in South Africa in a Time of Transition.

1. Roots of the Cultural Politics of the Apartheid Mainstream Opposition.

If one wants to talk about cultural politics as part of the anti-apartheid struggle, it is necessary to point out its theoretical background. Concepts of race, class and nation were the subject of discussions between the various wings of the anti-apartheid movement from the very beginning.[1]

The South African Communist Party (SACP founded 1921 as CPSA) was the driving force in establishing a revolutionary socialist strategy for South Africa. One of the issues persistently debated was the question as to the link between the socialist struggle and the struggle against national oppression.[2] After the VI Comintern Congress (1928), the dominant position was that socialism in South Africa could only be achieved after the end of the national oppression. This found expression in the theory of a two-stage revolution. First, a multiracial 'Native Republic' would be established in a national democratic revolution, in which an alliance was to be forged with the black petite bourgeoisie. The socialist revolution was to follow as the second stage. Communists were to work together with national liberation movements like the African National Congress (ANC).[3] The two-staged struggle was systematically elaborated in the theory of a 'Colonialism of a Special Type' (CST):

> "South Africa combines the worst features both of an imperialism and colonialism in a single national frontier; indeed 'Non-White South Africa' is the colony of 'White South Africa'. The indigenous population experiences the features of a colony: national oppression, poverty, exploitation [...]. This fosters strong national identity (and the SACP held that there were no [...] antagonistic class divisions among the African peoples)."[4]

The understanding of oppression as national oppression was upheld by the ANC, including the rather questionable definition of nationalities. Despite the colonial and apartheid legacies that spawned the infamous South African ethnogenesis, the ANC coined its own version of ethnicity, based on Stalin's understanding of nationhood, namely the 'Four Nation Thesis'.[5] The ANC Youth League Policy Manifesto of 1948 elaborated:

> "South Africa is a country of four chief nationalities, three of which (the Europeans, Indians and Coloureds) are minorities, and three of which (the Africans, Coloureds and Indians) suffer national oppression"[6], underlining: "that we are oppressed not as a class, but as a people, as a Nation."[7]

To fight what was understood as 'national oppression', the formation of a 'national identity' was required. This was to become the domain of cultural work, in opposition to the 'dominant culture' of the oppressor. This oppositional 'national culture' was simplistically equated with 'resistance culture' or 'revolutionary culture' (Ulrike Kistner).[8]

During periods of a 'war of position', oppositional cultural production had been neglected or generally seen as part of education; the ANC Youth League's 1948 Manifesto gave cultural policy its own place, and also prescribed the task of art: "African works of art [...] should reflect [...] the present phase of the national libratory struggle [and the League] supports the cultural struggle of the African people".[9] The ANC Programme of Action (1949) promptly followed with the goal "to unite the cultural with the educational and national struggle".[10]

After the repression that followed the uprising of 1976/7 (Soweto), a shift occurred in the legitimating and organising discourse of the ANC. Now, non-racialism was emphasised in contrast to the exclusivism of Steve Biko's Black Consciousness Movement. The ANC emerged as the liberation movement with broadest support base, which resulted in the popularisation of the Freedom Charter. Cultural work was intensified, and complementary cultural strategies were developing.[11]

Cultural work also played an important role in the trade unions. The Federation of South African Trade Unions (FOSATU) had a syndicalist orientation. These syndicalists, or workerists, saw cultural work within the trade unions as a direct contribution to the formation of class-consciousness. The notion of the 'cultural worker' developed.[12]

When the Congress of South African Trade Unions (COSATU) was founded in 1985, it took a charterist position from the beginning. With this change in the ideological landscape of the trade unions, the independent left in the country suffered a backlash. (However, Ari Sitas argues that the shift from workerism to populism was not that crass, and one should rather talk of 'wopulists'.[13]) The United Democratic Front (UDF) that formed itself as an international wing of the national liberation movement in 1984, (because the ANC was then illegal) had underlined the national momentum before class differences. In subscribing to the principles of the Freedom Charter, COSATU became the trade union of the ANC. Consequently, the cultural work of COSATU (besides the thesis of the exceptionalism in Natal) and that of the UDF were also close to the ANC's cultural work. The fact that COSATU had its own Cultural Unit, the UDF its own Cultural Desk and the ANC its own Cultural Department in exile (1983) made no difference.[14]

The cultural conferences of the 1980s were milestones and manifestations of the notion of culture then prevalent in the movement. In 1982, over 800 cultural workers gathered at a conference entitled Culture and Resistance in Gaborone and resolved that cultural work was part of the struggle for freedom in South Africa.[15] Another high point of 'cultural struggle' was the Conference for Another South Africa (CASA) in Amsterdam in 1987. The resolutions of the conference read as follows:

> "Cultural activity and the arts are partisan and cannot be separated from politics. Consequently a great responsibility devolves on artists and cultural workers to consciously align themselves with the forces of democratic and national liberation in the life and death struggle to free our country from racist bondage."[16]

Cultural workers were asked to organise themselves into useful structures at all levels (local, regional, international) for collective action[17] and work on the basis of a collectivist aesthetics.[18]

In 1989, the special issue *'Ten Years of Staffrider'*, entitled *'Worker Culture'*, was published. The introductory comment noted that in the last five years "the militancy of the working class has made a powerful mark in the struggle against apartheid [...]. When we talk of resistance, we are at the same time talking about cultural expression".[19]

2. The Njabulo S. Ndebele and Albie Sachs Debate.

'The most sensational bit of literature to have hit the cultural scene' in South Africa was Albie Sachs' paper entitled *"Preparing Ourselves for Freedom"*. It had originally been prepared as an ANC-in-house seminar paper to be presented to some comrades in Lusaka late in 1989.[20] When it became widely accessible with its publication in *'The Weekly Mail'* in 1990, it caused a heated debate.[21] The outrage was not caused only by the content, but also by the context[22], the timing[23] of the publication, and the "popularising presentational style".[24] Overall, the theses "gained their salience precisely from the fact that it was Sachs who was speaking, and not some unregistered or unauthorised voice".[25]

Sachs, who had up to that point supported the 'cultural struggle', now proclaimed: "our members should be banned from saying that culture is a weapon of struggle".[26] This turn about became necessary, Sachs pointed out, because the former notion "result[ed] in an impoverishment of our art. Instead of getting real criticism, we g[ot] solidarity criticism"[27]. "The cultural question which [has] remain[ed] central to the ANC, [has been] shaping its identity."[28] According to Sachs, the movement had developed its own special culture. "Our culture, the ANC culture, [...] has a real character and dynamic on its own" and its members could produce a dynamic national culture out of a diversity of traditions.[29] Furthermore, Sachs postulated that cultural politics should restrain from being prescriptive and that "the Constitutional Guidelines should not be applied to the sphere of culture".[30] The emphasis of cultural work, he maintained, must be put on "building national unity".[31] This led Sachs to the pronounced differentiation "between leadership and control" in the ANC: "we want to give leadership to the people, not exercise control over them".[32] Finally, he emphasised the requirement "to write better poems and make better films and compose better music".[33] Programmes of affirmative action were to be applied in the sphere of culture.[34]

Njabulo S. Ndebele's broader intellectual critique appeared in a sequence of essays. In *"Turkish Tales"*, Ndebele criticised contemporary black fiction for its stereotypical roles, symbols and its bare aesthetics of recognition.[35] Furthermore, he attacked creative writings' "obsessive emulation of journalism".[36] Because the African resistance movement had not been in control of information management, it was, according to Ndebele, easy for sloganeering, defined as superficial thinking, to develop:

> "The psychology of the slogan [...] is the psychology of intellectual powerlessness. [...] The slogan is the substitution of the gut response for clarity of analysis based on systematically acquired information."[37]

Ndebele demands self-criticism from writers. He advocates a mode of storytelling whose processecuality transforms the reader.

Tony Morphet circumscribes Ndebele's 'ordinary' (of *'The Rediscovery of the Ordinary'*) as "the place where the cultural and the political encounter each other as 'realities' rather than through the meshes of pre-constructed concepts or slogans or symbols".[38] Or in Ndebele's own words "the ordinary lives of people should be the direct focus of political interest because they constitute the very content of the struggle, for the struggle involves people, not abstractions".[39] Literature thus has the task "to provide an occasion within which vistas of inner capacity are opened up".[40]

In *"Redefining Relevance"* (1989), Ndebele again speaks out against unreflective rhetoric or writing of protest. He introduces one new category with which he wants to crack open the closed structures of thought: "The challenge is to free the entire social imagination of the oppressed from the laws of perception that have characterised apartheid society".[41] The term 'social imagination', which reappears in Sachs' paper as 'cultural imagination', demonstrates his indebtedness to Ndebele (Peter Horn).

Their important shared contribution to the understanding of the relation between politics and art in a society in transition was not a call for the separation of the two - as some wanted to interpret the import of their writings - but for an end to the notion of art in the service of political struggle. Both demand an improvement of the formal quality of art through variety of skills. Being radical humanists, they stress the need for a culture that supports a democratic society.[42] Their critics caution against the danger that their humanism "denies its own structures of power".[43] The difference in their positions lies in the different resistance traditions that they align themselves with.[44] Sachs' does not question the hegemony of the ANC, whereas Ndebele focuses on the Black oppressed.

Eve Bertelsen put a question to Albie Sachs in an open letter: "Could it be possible that two decades of radical cultural debate (the politics of language, discourse and power, postcolonial culture) have somehow slipped your attention?"[45] In her opinion, Sachs was offering dated common-sense views on art "now resurrected as a curious hybrid, shot through with personal sentiment and party slogans"[46]; he "remains wedded to a naturalist/realist aesthetic".[47] Critics commented on his dated European realist apperception of fiction and on his idea that "mastery over one's craft allows one to return to social and political issues with far greater freedom, understanding, insight and comprehensiveness".[48] There were also broader responses to the Sachs debate from cultural workers and organisations, who or which felt their art discredited.[49] The conservative-liberal wing saw its chance to reinstate the notion that art should be separated from politics.

3. From Liberation to Emancipation? 1990-1994.

In the process of these debates, it emerged that there were severe limitations to the democratising potential of the national liberation movement and its cultural politics. While some theorists advocated a truly post-liberation discourse, cultural organisations lagged behind in their willingness to undergo necessary changes. This resulted in the rise of independent cultural organisations and the fall of insufficient aligned ones, which indicates the cultural power battles that were fought in the period between the 'Sachs debate' and the first free elections in 1994.

In the ensuing post-apartheid euphoria, the aim was to bring the cultural discourses more closely in the line with the radically changed political terrain. This was only partly - if at all - achieved.[50]

One of the responses to the political challenge of art was the attempt to mobilise the notion of 'resistance culture', for a 'theory of reconstruction': "[T]he idea of 'revolution' is being broadened [...] and made to accommodate the idea of an ongoing evolutionary drive towards a complex, modernising future".[51] Michael Chapman envisages the blur between literary and cultural studies, the contribution of criticism to social change, and a greater service of the universities to the wider community.[52]

Stephen Gray's elaborations in *"An Authors Agenda"* (1991) might serve as an example of the renewal of form.[53] He carefully distinguished his own style from the "self-evident-political truths" that he sees at work in Nadine Gordimer's writings and from Njabulo S. Ndebele's notion of the dialectical relation between politics and arts. He questions the pertinence of their realism and calls for a drastic revision of inherited canonical forms in order to deliver new messages in a 'post-everything' phase. Gray sees no possibility of inventing new forms and therefore suggests "reviewing older forms" or "choosing non-canonical forms to challenge the hegemony of received ideas".[54]

The important development of this period (1990-1994) was the fact that artists and cultural organisers cut themselves loose from the Congress Alliance, and from the ANC's Department for Arts and Culture (DAC) in particular.

After the return of the ANC from exile, the internal Mass Democratic Movement-based cultural organisations (MDM) backed down from confrontations with the ANC's DAC.

In 1990, clashes had occurred between the UDF's Cultural Desk and the DAC over the interpretation of the cultural boycott in a time of transition[55], and over the participation of DAC head Barbara Masekela in the mainly 'white' Grahamstown Festival, where she gave an address.[56]

The United Democratic Front/MDM Cultural Desk was dissolved. Cultural structures of the MDM could be maintained, but only as 'more-or-less autonomous organisations', which were expected to be 'accountable' to the 'parent organisation'. Mzwake Mbuli[57], known among other things for challenging the ANC's authority, gave in. He publicly conceded that "The DAC is the parent which bore our people's organisation and now has established itself inside the country; we look for its leadership".[58]

Differing positions found their common foe - the provincial Performing Arts Councils[59], which came under pressure to focus more on the representative, non-white-elite South African community and to get rid of their past support of so called 'high arts'.[60] Individual artists came to speak out more critically and vociferously against a felt dependence on the ANC. "With horror, we watch again as the arts are sacrificed on the altars of political expedience, held ransom by the egos of political commissars, conscripted by party political agendas".[61] The perhaps well-meant mothering role of the DAC was indeed a control system, based on the old centralist party discipline.

In December 1992, the National Arts Initiative (NAI) was launched as a politically independent representative organisation of arts practitioners and administrators with Mike van Graan as general secretary. (Njabulo S. Ndebele became its honorary president in 1993). The ANC in turn tried to slander the NAI as a National Party initiative and to block it wherever possible.[62]

The ANC tried to prove that it would support principles of artistic freedom with the Culture and Development Conference in Johannesburg in April 1993, which installed a board of trustees to independently administer a Foundation for Arts and Culture. But critics found that the conference reproduced the clichés of the past, and that the board of trustees served as controlling instance.[63] Overall, many delegates felt that the conference was a strategy to bring artists behind the ANC's electoral campaign.[64]

The number of arts' practitioners who were refusing the ANC's 1980's cultural desk style control of the arts was increasing, as the Conference of Politicians, Teaching and the Arts (Institute of Race Relations) showed. Nise Malange, then director of the Cultural and Working Life Project in Durban and acclaimed cultural worker, told the 'cultural parents' off, saying that they must learn to let go:

> "Let us see for ourselves what future policies we want [...]. Since 1990 we've experienced self-censorship. There's been a fear: if you become critical of the ANC you might be marginalized, you might be eliminated."[65]

When the DAC responded by saying that they only tried to facilitate the development of arts and culture and not to control them, it became a semantic battle over 'facilitation' or 'domination'.[66]

At the end of 1993, a National Arts Convention took place in Durban. It was organised by the NAI, which transformed itself into the independent National Arts Coalition. With 300 delegates who represented 120 000 artists from diverse interest groups, every future government would have to take this cultural lobby seriously. With the convention taking place shortly before the election, the ANC was under pressure to respond to their demands. The resolutions that were passed were thought to be guidelines for the future government's cultural policy. Central points were: the political independence of arts, a radically new direction in arts education, which would include the recognition of the non-formal arts. The demand for the dissolution of the provincial Performing Arts Councils was closely connected with that of the distribution of funding through a new funding policy, because up until then, the Performing Arts Councils received nearly all the state expenditure on arts and culture.[67] But there were also two main weaknesses. Firstly, there was a noticeable chasm between grassroots cultural organisations, including rural artists, and the rest. Secondly, the non-aligned stance was put into question when it appeared that the steering committee was dominated by pseudo-independent organisations like the ANC's Congress of South African Writers (COSAW).[68]

The centre of power in arts administration in the period 1990-1994 lay in the management of arts funding. Who would receive money or support from whom and for which projects? The ANC/DAC, mainly in the persona of Mongane Wally Serote[69], knew how to capitalise on this situation, forming different cultural organisations which received funds to administer them, for example Arts and Culture South Africa, Dorkay House Trust, South African Music Education Trust or the National Film Trust of South Africa.[70] The formation of these organisations seemed to be a way to distribute resources. But since the relevant discipline-based organisations were not consulted in the process, it effectively meant a channelling of power.[71]

Why were there crises, including financial problems, in arts initiatives and cultural organisations? Several cultural centres had to be closed for financial reasons. Three main reasons can be identified: a) After 1990, the patterns of international funding shifted (e.g. Kagiso Trust, US Aid). This happened because their funding focus had never been on the arts, but on the community centres established in the 1980s. The community centres were some of the few anti-apartheid projects that international forces were able to support under the then given political circumstances. b) The cultural centres were no state initiatives and therefore had to find private financing. c) Many cultural projects never appropriately administered their resources. Irregularities were found in their financial accounting.[72]

COSAW came under fire for such irregularities. In 1990, COSAW had received R3.5-million from the European Community. In 1993, the organisation was going into liquidation, due to "inadequate social and financial accountability, top-heavy bureaucratic structures"[73] and the drying up of international funds.[74] (Mandla Langa was the last chairperson of COSAW.) What cultural organisations lacked were professionalism and efficiency, accountability and transparency in terms of procedures of consultation and debate, and in terms of financial administration. It was "no longer sufficient (if it ever was) simply to ascribe democratic tendencies to organisations which happen to have an anti-apartheid, or 'majority' political pedigree".[75]

4. The Cultural Policy of the New Government. 1994-1996.

In January 1994, the Tripartite Alliance adopted the *'Reconstruction and Development Programme'* (RDP) in preparation for the April elections. The RDP offered a special section on "Arts and Culture" under the rubric of "developing our human resources".[76] It underlined the importance of arts and culture permeating all aspects of society, social and economic. The policies aim to affirm the "diverse expressions of South African culture"[77] on the one hand, and to "promote the development of a unifying national culture"[78] on the other. In the process of making arts and culture available to all, "priority must be given to those [...] previously denied access".[79] The arts as part of education received a special mention. A language policy that supported "all the languages of Africa"[80] was to be implemented. The RDP policies aimed to "link culture [...] to areas of national priority such as health, housing, tourism, etc., to ensure that culture is entrenched as a fundamental component of development".[81] In this connection, "a reading and learning culture" was to be promoted.[82]

Some RDP recommendations relating to cultural structures were bound to raise trouble. Besides a Ministry of Arts and Culture, national and regional Arts Councils were to be established. Existing structures, such as the Performing Arts Councils, it was stated, "must be democratised [...] and complete the task of transformation within two years".[83]

The National Arts Coalition wanted the complete dissolution of the Performing Arts Councils in favour of more competitive funding structures. Furthermore, it questioned the ideological transformation capacity of these institutions. But with some trickery involving the DAC, the Performing Arts Councils survived.[84]

After the first free elections in April 1994, the new Department of Arts, Culture, Science and Technology (DACST) was established in line with the recommendations contained in the RDP. This independent department took over functions previously belonging to the Department of National Education and that of the Department of Trade and Industry. The separation from the Education Department was to be read as appreciation of the role of culture and its aspiration to professional quality. The main reasons for the conjunction of the branches of arts and culture, and science and technology were said to be threefold.

a) Both are compatible because "the creative abilities of people are very important".

b) "In both fields it is true that the State should not play a large active role. This means that the State acts as a facilitator of arts and culture and science and technology".

c) "Because they are fields in which freedom and creativity are so important, they must be managed remotely".[85]

A Council of Culture Ministers was established, consisting of the Minister and Deputy Minister of DACST and the Provincial Members of Executive Councils (MEC) responsible for Arts and Culture. Minister of the new Arts, Culture, Science and Technology Department became the Inkatha Freedom Party (IFP) member Dr Baldwin Sipho Ngubane. Many questions remain open about the tactical background to his appointment. Did the appointment of a person with no cultural profile assure that no prior private alliances would interfere? Did the government, in giving the cultural department over to the IFP, consider cultural affairs of lesser importance than other portfolios? Or was it a matter of ceding part of the terrain of culture - that concerning the role of tradition, traditional leaders, or ethnic conflicts - to the IFP? Was it that a moderate IFP minister, who was more or less working in line with the ANC, was considered potentially useful?

The minister appointed a representative Arts and Culture Task Group (ACTAG) to formulate democratic arts and culture policies. It "was the beginning of a process to arrive at a new culture dispensation consistent with the new constitution". Within half a year, the astonishing *'ACTAG Report'* of 400 pages was drafted. After being publicly discussed and adopted at a National Conference, it was handed over to the Minister in June 1995.[86] This comprehensive report marked some important achievements. In line with the RDP, the programme was to be based upon the understanding that development is rooted in culture.[87] It was noticeable that the report started with definitions of 'art', 'the artist' and 'culture', - categories that had usually been used interchangeably or in an undefined manner.[88] The report set itself the task to try to "provide a philosophical basis for arts and culture as integral components of reconstruction and development" and "in their own right".[89] To describe and to "ensure that the State and Political Parties are not directly involved in the selection and evaluation of arts and culture activities", the principle of 'arms-length' was introduced. 'nation-building' was seen as one among other principles for a democratic policy. It was to "foster a sense of pride and knowledge in all aspects of South African culture, heritage and the arts", "encourage mutual respect and tolerance and intercultural exchange between the various cultures and forms of art to facilitate the emergence of a shared cultural identity constituted by diversity".[90]

However, the former cultural power battles that were fought between 1990-1994 seemed to have died out. The protests calmed down for several reasons. With the establishment of the new government, the cultural work of the ANC and COSATU had been cut down, as many members took on governmental posts (Jeremy Cronin). On the other hand, independent critics like the NAC were involved in the preparation of contributions to the *'ACTAG Report'*, which kept them busy and gave them the sense of being consulted. As for the question of the Performing Arts Councils, ACTAG recommended the "phasing out" within an "appropriate timetable", with redeployment of resources and staff.[91] The overall priorities and targets were also timetabled and differentiated into immediate ones for 1995, intermediate 1996-2000 and long-term priorities[92], which would give the department time in the face of criticism and the call for 'delivery'.

Critical voices could be kept at bay for some time to come, while waiting for the Minister's *'White Paper on Arts, Culture and Heritage'*.[93] It took the department one year to shrink the *'ACTAG Report'* and to blend it in with their own sentiments, to finally come up with a draft *'White Paper'* in June 1996. The democratising efforts of ACTAG were echoed in the draft *'White Paper'* in much more generalised ways. The same principles were repeated, such as the principles of 'arms-length' and 'nation-building'. The paper differed in terms of the Performing Arts Councils. They were not to be dissolved but to be transformed so as to lose influence. The overseer of this process was to be the National Arts Council, which in the future was to play the role of the arms-length connection with funding administration responsibilities.[94]

It was striking that in the draft *'White Paper'* the notions of 'arts and culture' were more strongly differentiated from 'heritage', which found greater appreciation from the start. This might have been the first reflection on the shift in overall government strategy that was underlining economic values. The statements of Deputy Minister Brigitte Mabandla gave hints of an early elaboration of the notion of the African Renaissance. She stated:

> "We believe that indigenous South African art forms can and will reach a standard of excellence, and if anything, can set new and even higher standards [...]. This renaissance in South Africa's art will depend on a policy that ensures equity and [...] diversity. Through this document, we are laying a basis to reclaim our heritage".[95]

Would it not be too ironic if the idea for the notion of the African Renaissance announced by Thabo Mbeki was introduced through the term 'South African Arts Renaissance', which served as a means for an IFP minister to celebrate 'Zulu' heritage sites? This marketing strategy clearly served the interests of government as a whole.

5. Cultural Policy in the Times of the *'Growth, Employment and Redistribution Strategy'* (after 1996).

While the Department of ACST was preparing its future policy, the government of national unity had to cope with the 'morning after'. The goals set out in the ANC's *RDP* in early 1994 were confronted with the economic realities of the country. The *'White Paper on the RDP'* came into being as the government's strategy for transformation in September 1994. It stressed the "interdependence of the objectives of reconstruction and development on the one hand, and growth on the other". It was stressed that the Government's RDP activities should "not be seen as a new set of projects, but rather as a comprehensive redesign and reconstruction of existing activities".[96] The paper set out "key change management strategies [...] and guidelines on areas of particular importance for change".[97] It focused on the introduction of a viable market economy. As the central term 'growth' suggested, the *'White Paper on the RDP'* is the link between the RDP and the *'Growth, Employment and Redistribution Strategy'* (GEAR) that was introduced in 1996. What about arts and culture? Nothing much was left of the developmental goals of the RDP. Under the headline "Culture of Learning" a school rebuilding project is being mentioned.[98] But the document contains three lines on tourism: "The percentage of GDP generated by tourism must increase".[99]

The macro-economic policy GEAR does not mention arts and culture at all. Although it found that "South African investment in human resource development is inadequate", it did not consider whether its own narrow understanding of development - only as immediate cash paying capacities - might be a hindrance to emancipated citizenship.[100]

The DACST made its own contribution to GEAR, with the establishment of a Cultural Strategy Group who prepared the report *'Creative South Africa. A Strategy for Realising the Potential of the Cultural Industry'*.[101] The study is a strategy analysis for 'industry' to make recommendations on music, film, publishing and crafts industry. The aims were to: "maximise investment opportunities", "highlight areas for government participation", "identify potential private sector initiatives", "leverage in multiple funding sources" and "benefit all stakeholders and practitioners within the industry and the economy as a whole".[102] The role of culture is to add value, socially and politically:[103]

> "Cultural activities, both traditional and new, create 'meaning' and thus are concerned with and embody the identity and values of a country. They can communicate both the heritage of South Africa as well as the idea of what it means to be South African in the 21st century. The cultural industries thus provide an avenue for creating

a South African identity that is essential for nation-building and political transformation."[104]

These suppositions have been waiting for their elaboration. After the declining role of arts and culture in the transformation process (as evidenced in the *'White Paper on the RDP'* and in GEAR), the *'Creative South Africa Report'* at least broadened the view again, but in a much more pragmatic way than the *'ACTAG Report'*.

6. The African Renaissance. New Sloganeering?

For many, the notion of the African Renaissance seemed just a new slogan to market the new South Africa globally and to enhance the profile of Thabo Mbeki as successor to the more charismatic Nelson R. Mandela.[105] But the slogan has snowballed, so that one cannot ignore the ways in which it plays itself out in cultural politics.

A strong correlation can be noted between the notion of the African Renaissance and the commodification of culture. The prologue of the Cultural Strategy Group's document argues "that the cultural industries can play an important role in the African Renaissance".[106]

When Thabo Mbeki, in his *"I Am an African"* speech to the Constitutional Assembly on 8th May 1996, initialised his concept of the African Renaissance, he was referring to a consciousness building process. For Mbeki, Africans are those who truly view the continent as their home.[107] Nevertheless, the slogan rang with essentialist notions of African identity, empty phrases on 'African thought' initiatives and on collating 'indigenous knowledge systems'.[108]

With the circulation of the African Renaissance slogan, yet another bureaucratic structure was built. In 1998, over 470 African participants spent time at a conference, among them Thabo Mbeki, discussing the African Renaissance. In 1999, The African Renaissance Institute was founded. The Institute is structured into three levels: a council of elders, the national chapters and provincial structures. The South African Chapter was founded in Johannesburg at the African Renaissance Conference in April 2000. According to its constitution, it is a non-governmental organisation. It has set up its own headquarters and 12 working commissions.

As regards the content of the work of these structures, it is instructive to look at the preamble of the South African Chapter: "a need has been identified to facilitate initiatives that develop mankind in relation to Africa". The Chapter "seeks to establish [...] diverse traditional African values and in particular ubuntu

[...]".[109] The proceedings of the 1998 African Renaissance conference[110] are not much more enlightening. In most of the articles, the concept is not clearly defined; it veers between an old-style pan-Africanism or a romanticised African history or philosophy.[111]

The subtitle of the proceedings is eye-catching: "The New Struggle". Indeed, there are more indicators for a perceived continuation of the liberation movement's struggle. Some sessions of the South African Renaissance Conference in April 2000 deal explicitly with 'Liberation Culture' (Dansokho) or 'Liberation Struggle' (Pityana). The convenor of the 2000 conference was Mongane Wally Serote, praised for his organisation of the Culture and Resistance Conference (1982) and the Culture in Another South Africa Conference (1987), and blamed for his undemocratic practices after his return from exile. All these indications mount to a danger of repeating the shortcomings of 'struggle' culture and to provide merely a haven for 'struggelati': sloganeering, thin content, populism, and bureaucratic structures. Can party-political credentials substitute expertise?

An alternative, historical-critical notion of the African Renaissance was formulated by Mahmood Mamdani. For him, a Renaissance must be a reawakening of thought. This means that processes of intellectual production, and thought systems would need to be challenged. The driving forces of change include the formation of a new identity to which intellectuals are central and which brings together the spheres of knowledge and culture.[112]

South African intellectual production is - despite and because of colonialism and apartheid - marked by two racialized assumptions: the notion of South African exeptionalism, and the presumption of the sameness and backwardness of the rest of Africa.[113]

Therefore is "[t]he deracialisation of intellectual production [...] the key challenge and constitutes an African Renaissance."[114] Mamdani's conclusions:

1) There can be "no renaissance without an intelligentsia to drive it".
2) An African Renaissance "requires an Africa-focused intelligentsia".
3) South Africa "lacks an Africa-focused intelligentsia in critical numbers".
4) "State action can change the institutional context of knowledge production".[115]

7. Some Considerations for the Future.

According to Mamdani, post-apartheid South Africa undertook a process of political 'deracialisation' without a corresponding process of 'detribalisation'. As a result, democratisation is severely curtailed. Should it not be the task of the institutions of cultural politics to dare to take on this challenge? Is not the task of institutions of learning also the task of institutions of culture? As one cannot dictate intellectual processes, one cannot dictate artistic or cultural outcomes. One can, however, create enabling conditions. Since detribalisation remains a task to be tackled, economic interests in tribal tourism and tribal arts products should be assessed for their political and historical appropriateness and artistic value. In the same way, the notion of 'tradition' must be scrutinised.

But post-apartheid cultural politics has not, until now, provided the conditions for such critical work. With or without a call for the completion of the second stage of the revolution, there is little sense in a continuation of the *old* kind of 'cultural struggle'. It should be made to not miss its chance to happily end in time.

References

[1] Wolpe. 1988.
[2] See Cronin. 1986: 73.
[3] Davies/O'Meara/Dlamini. 1988. Vol. 2: 292.
[4] Quoted in Bundy. 1989: 4. See also SACP. 1981.
[5] See Stalin. [1913] 1945^3. For cultural politics and ethnogenesis in South Africa, see Schmidt. 1996.
[6] ANC. 1948. In: Karis/Carter (eds.). 1987. Vol. 2: 329.
[7] ANC. 1948. In: Karis/Carter (eds.). 1987. Vol. 2: 330.
[8] Kistner. 1989.
[9] ANC. 1948. In: Karis/Carter (eds.). 1987. Vol. 2: 326.
[10] ANC. 1948. In: Karis/Carter (eds.). 1987. Vol. 2: 339.
[11] See Jolly/Attridge. 1998: 2.
[12] See Meintjes/Hlatshwayo. 1989.
[13] See Sitas interviewed by Ernst. 2000.
[14] See COSATU. 1989.
[15] See Serote. 1990: 17.
[16] Campschreur/Divendal. 1989. CASA Resolution 2: 215.
[17] Campschreur/Divendal. 1989. CASA Resolution 3: 216.
[18] Campschreur/Divendal. 1989. CASA Resolution 4: 217. See also Kistner. 1991: 217-227 and Devenney. 1994: 35.
[19] Meintjes/Hlatshwayo. 1989: 3.
[20] de Kok/Press. 1990: 19-29.
[21] de Kok /Press. 1990. See also Brown/van Dyk. 1991.
[22] One may add that in the same time Joe Slovo's influential essay "Has Socialism Failed?" appeared (see Slovo. 1990.).
[23] It was published exactly on the 2 February 1990, the day political organisations were unbanned by the de Klerk government.
[24] Pechey. 1994. In: Ndebele. 1994^2. Introduction: 4.
[25] de Kok/Press. 1990: 139. See also Bertelsen. 1990: 130.
[26] Sachs. 1989: 19.
[27] Sachs. 1989: 20.
[28] Sachs. 1989: 22.

[29] Sachs. 1989: 22.
[30] Sachs. 1989: 23.
[31] Sachs. 1989: 24.
[32] Sachs. 1989: 27-28.
[33] Sachs. 1989: 28.
[34] Sachs. 1989: 29.
[35] Ndebele. [1984] 1991: 27.
[36] Ndebele. [1984] 1991: 24.
[37] Ndebele. [1984] 1991: 25.
[38] Morphet. 1992: 133.
[39] Ndebele. [1986] 1991: 55.
[40] Ndebele. [1986] 1991: 56.
[41] Ndebele. 1989: 65.
[42] See Sole. 1993: 91.
[43] Sole. 1993: 92.
[44] See Morphet. 1990: 139-140.
[45] Bertelsen. 1990: 133.
[46] Bertelsen. 1990: 133.
[47] Parry. 1992: 125.
[48] Ndebele. 1988: 343.
[49] See de Kok/Press. 1990.
[50] Petersen. 1991: i. See also Boehmer/Chrisman/Parker. 1994.
[51] Chapman. 1991 [1990]: 9.
[52] Chapman. 1991 [1990]: 11.
[53] Originally, the paper was prepared as a discussion position for a panel with Mongane Wally Serote and others (see Gray interviewed by Ernst. 2000).
[54] Gray. 1991: 27. "If the message is not friendly towards the ruling albocentric, patriarchal, capitalist, fascist, heterosexual, etc., order, so the form cannot be taken from there uncritically" (Gray. 1991: 27.).
[55] When, in 1987, Oliver Thambo declared the cultural boycott 'selective' rather than 'blanket', he caused a chaos in which Mongane Wally Serote's word, being head of the DAC in exile, "became boycott law" (Bauer. In: Mail & Guardian. 9-15 Nov. 1990: 10).
[56] Masekela. 1990: 38-40.
[57] The 'peoples' poet' served as a leading member of the UDF Cultural Desk.
[58] Powell. In: Mail & Guardian. 7-13 Sept. 1990: 7.
[59] The Cape Performing Arts Board (CAPAB), the Natal Performing Arts Council (NAPAC), the Performing Arts Council of Transvaal (PACT) and the Performing Arts Council of the Orange Free State (PACOFS) were established by the nationalist government in 1963 to serve the cultural interests of the white population with European art.
[60] Steinberg. In: Business Day. 27 Dec. 1993.
[61] van Graan. In: Mail & Guardian. 7-13 May 1993.
[62] van Graan. In: Mail & Guardian. 7-13 May 1993.
[63] Among the members of this board was ANC member Nadine Gordimer, who asked in an interview about the board, preferred not to talk about this matter (see Gordimer interviewed by Ernst. 2000).
[64] Gevisser. In: Mail & Guardian. 7-13 May 1993.
[65] Gevisser. In: Mail & Guardian. 1-7 Oct. 1993 (see also Malange interviewed by Ernst. 2000).
[66] Gevisser. In: Mail & Guardian. 1-7 Oct. 1993.
[67] Powell. In: Mail & Guardian. 10-16 Dec. 1993.
[68] The Congress of South African Writers had close links with the ANC since its establish-

ment in 1987.

[69] Mongane Wally Serote also came under fire for trying to set up a relationship between the ANC's DAC and Sun International by establishing a joint arts foundation. This would give an unfair advantage to Sun International. Even worse, the ANC's DAC interfered directly with the work of the local ANC in Bophutatswana who was at the time still struggling against a repressive regime that supported the Sun business. ANC Bop found any formal relationship with Sun International intolerable (see Gevisser. In: Mail & Guardian. 30 Jul.-5 Aug. 1993.).

[70] The irregularities were topped with a false Oliver Thambo letter in support of NAFTSA. Serote stepped down as this trust's chairperson.

[71] Powell. In: Mail & Guardian. 25 Feb.- 3 March 1994.
[72] Powell. In: Mail & Guardian. 3-9 Sept. 1993.
[73] Sole. 1994: 7.
[74] See Gordimer interviewed by Ernst. 2000.
[75] Sole. 1994: 7.
[76] ANC. 1994: 69-72.
[77] ANC. 1994: 69-72. Section 3.4.3.1.
[78] ANC. 1994: 69-72. Section 3.4.3.2.
[79] ANC. 1994: 69-72. Section 3.4.3.3.
[80] ANC. 1994: 69-72. Section 3.4.3.7, Section 3.4.10.
[81] ANC. 1994: 69-72. Section 3.4.3.6.
[82] ANC. 1994: 69-72. Section 3.4.3.8.
[83] ANC. 1994: 69-72. Section 3.4.6.
[84] Powell. In: Mail & Guardian. 28 Jan. - 3 Feb. 1994.
[85] See DAC. Annual Report. 1994. Introduction: i-ii.
[86] Arts and Culture Task Group. June 1995.
[87] Arts and Culture Task Group. June 1995: 11.
[88] Arts and Culture Task Group. June 1995: 5.
[89] Arts and Culture Task Group. June 1995: 5-6.
[90] Arts and Culture Task Group. June 1995: 9.
[91] Arts and Culture Task Group. June 1995: 344-347.
[92] Arts and Culture Task Group. June 1995: 12-14.
[93] Department of Arts, Culture, Science and Technology. 1996.
[94] On a national level, the Business and Arts South Africa (BASA) was also empowered to coordinate funding.
[95] Department of Arts, Culture, Science and Technology. 1996: 3.
[96] Government of National Unity. 1994: i.
[97] Government of National Unity. 1994: 53.
[98] Government of National Unity. 1994: 57.
[99] Government of National Unity. September 1994: 36.
[100] Government of National Unity. 1996: 19.
[101] Cultural Strategy Group. 1998. Additionally the DACST started in 1997 to publish 'The Arts, Culture and Heritage Guide to South Africa' on a regular basis.
[102] Cultural Strategy Group. 1998: 5. The public-private Cultural Industry Development Agency (CIDA) was supposed to be in the centre of the furthering of the recommendations.
[103] Cultural Strategy Group. 1998: 52.
[104] Cultural Strategy Group. 1998: 12-13.
[105] Lodge. 1999: 96-109.
[106] Arts and Culture Task Group. June 1995: 6. For the commodification of culture see also Ernst. 2001.
[107] Mbeki. 1996.
[108] See Serote interviewed by Ernst. 2000.

[109] SACAR. 2000: 1.
[110] See Makgoba. 1999.
[111] See Lodge. 1999: 105-8.
[112] Mamdani. 1999: 130-131.
[113] Mamdani. 1999: 132.
[114] Mamdani. 1999: 133. See also Sole. 1997: 116-154.
[115] See Mamdani. 1999: 134.

Bibliography

African National Congress. 1948. "Basic Policy of Congress Youth League". Manifesto Issued by the National Executive Committee of the ANC Youth League. In: Karis/Carter (eds.). 1987. Vol. 2: 323-331.

African National Congress. 1949. "Programme of Action". Statement of Policy Adopted at the ANC Annual Conference, December 17. In: Karis/Carter (eds.). 1987. Vol. 2: 337-339.

African National Congress. 1994. The Reconstruction and Development Programme. A Policy Framework. Johannesburg.

Arts and Culture Task Group. 1995. Report to the Minister of Arts, Culture, Science and Technology. Pretoria.

Attridge, Derek/Jolly, Rosemary (eds.). 1998. Writing South Africa. Literature, Apartheid, and Democracy 1970-1995. Cambridge.

Attridge, Derek/Jolly, Rosemary. 1998. "Introduction". In: Attridge/Jolly (eds.). 1998: 1-13.
Bauer, Charlotte. "Poet Meets Paradox. Mongane Wally Serote Is Home Again". In: Mail & Guardian. 8-15 Nov. 1990.

Biko, Steve. 1978. I Write What I like. London.

Bertelsen, Eve. 1990. "Phasing the Spring. Open Letter to Albie Sachs". In: Pretexts 2 (2): 129-136.

Boehmer, Elleke/Chrisman, Laura/Parker, Kenneth (eds.). 1994. Altered State? Writing and South Africa. Sidney et al.

Brown, Duncan/van Dyk, Bruno. (eds.). 1991. Exchanges. South African Writing in Transition. Durban.

Bundy, Collin. 1989. "Around which Corner? Revolutionary Theory and Contemporary South Africa". In: Transformation 8: 1-23.

Campschreur, Willem/Divendaal, Joost (eds.). 1989. Culture in Another South Africa (CASA). London.

Chapman, Michael. 1990. "The Critic in a State of Emergency. Towards a Theory of Reconstruction (after February 2)". In: Petersen/Rutherford (eds.). 1991: 1-13.

Congress of South African Trade Unions. 1989. "Report on Culture and Media". In: Staffrider 8 (3&4): 58-60.

Cronin, Jeremy. 1986. "The National Democratic Struggle and the Question of Transformation". In: Transformation 2: 73-78.

Cultural Strategy Group. 1998. Creative South Africa. A Strategy for Realising the Potential of the Cultural Industries. A Report to the Department of Arts, Culture, Science and Technology. Pretoria.

de Kok, Ingrid/Press, Karen (eds.). 1990. Spring is Rebellious. Arguments about Cultural Freedom by Albie Sachs and Respondents. Cape Town.

Davis, Robert/O'Meara, Dan/Dlamini Sippho. 1988^2. The Struggle for South Africa. A Reference Guide to Movements, Organizations and Institutions. London.

Department of Arts, Culture, Science and Technology. 1994. Annual Report. Pretoria.

Department of Arts, Culture, Science and Technology. 1996. White Paper on Arts, Culture and Heritage. Pretoria.

Department of Arts, Culture, Science and Technology. 1999. Five Year Report. Pretoria.

Devenney, Mark. 1994. The Fictions of Radical Democracy. MA Thesis. University of the Witwatersrand. Johannesburg.

Ernst, Ulrike. 2001. "Cultural Politics in South Africa in Transition. Or, Multiculturalism and the Logic of South African Macro-Economics". Paper presented at the conference 'Africa and Europe: Myths, Masks and Masquerades'. Johannesburg (Forthcoming).

Gevisser, Mark. "The War of the Cultural Workers". In: Mail & Guardian. 7-13 May 1993.

Gevisser, Mark. "ANC Tries for Place in the Sun". In: Mail & Guardian. 30 Jul.-5 Aug. 1993.

Gevisser, Mark. "Cultural Parents 'must learn to let go'". In: Mail & Guardian. 1-7 Oct. 1993.

Government of National Unity. 1994. Reconstruction and Development Programme. White Paper. Discussion Document. Pretoria.

Government of National Unity. 1996. Growth, Employment and Redistribution. A Macro-Economic Strategy, Pretoria.

Graan, Mike van. "We Want Culture, not Commissars". In: Mail & Guardian. 7-13 May 1993.

Gray, Steven. 1991. "An Author's Agenda. Re-visioning Past and Present for a Future South Africa". In: Petersen/Rutherford (eds.) 1991: 23-31.

Karis, Thomas/Carter, Gwendolen M. (eds.). 1987 [Vol. 1-4 paperback reprint of 1972-77;

Vol. 5, 1997, Pretoria]. From Protest to Challenge. A Documentary History of African Politics in South Africa 1882-1990. Stanford.

Kistner, Ulrike. 1989. "Literature and the National Question". In: Journal of Literary Studies 5(3/4): 302-314.

Kistner, Ulrike. 1991. "The Politics of Canon Formation in Literary Theory - for example: Realism and the Popular Front". In: Journal of Literary Studies 7(3/4): 217-227.

Lodge, Tom. 1999. South African Politics since 1994. Cape Town/Johannesburg.

Makgoba, Malegapuru William (ed.). 1999. African Renaissance. The New Struggle. Prologue by Thabo Mbeki. Cape Town.

Mamdani, Mahmood. 1996. Citizen and Subject. Contemporary Africa and the Legacy of Late Colonialism. Cape Town.

Mamdani, Mahmood. 1999. "There Can Be no African Renaissance Without an Africa-focused Intelligentsia". In: Makgoba (ed.). 1999: 125-134.

Masekela, Barbara. 1990. "We Are not Returning Empty Handed". In: Suid-Afrikaan (8): 38-40.

Mbeki, Thabo. 1996. "I Am an African". Reprinted in: Mbeki, Thabo. 1998. Africa, the Time Has Come. Cape Town.

Meintjes, Frank/Hlatshwayo, Mi et al. (eds.). 1989. Worker Culture. Special Issue of Staffrider 8 (3/4). Johannesburg.

Meintjes, Frank/Hlatshwayo, Mi. 1989. "Comment". In: Meintjes/Hlatshwayo et al (eds.). 1989: 3-7.

Morphet, Tony. 1990. "Cultural Imagination and Cultural Settlement. Albie Sachs and Njabulo Ndebele". In: de Kok/Press (eds.). 1990: 131-144.

Morphet, Tony. 1992. "Ordinary-Modern-Postmodern". In: Theoria 80.

Ndebele, Njabulo S. 1984. "Turkish Tales and some Thoughts on South African Fiction". In: Ndebele. 1991: 11-36.

Ndebele, Njabulo S. 1986. "The Rediscovery of the Ordinary. Some New Writings in South Africa". In: Ndebele. 1991: 37-57.

Ndebele, Njabulo S. 1989. "Redefining Relevance" [revision of "Beyond Protest"]. In: Ndebele. 1991: 58-73.

Ndebele, Njabulo S. 1991. Rediscovery of the Ordinary. Essays on South African Literature and Culture. Johannesburg.

Ndebele, Njabulo S. 1994^2 [extended edition of 1991]. South African Literature and Culture. Rediscovery of the Ordinary. Introduction by Graham Pechey. Manchester/New York.

Oliphant, Andries Walter. 1988. "Njabulo S. Ndebele. The Writer as Critic and Interventionist". In: Oliphant/Vladislavi´c (eds.). 1988: 341-346.

Oliphant, Andries Walter/Vladislavi´c, Ivan (eds.). 1988. Ten Years of Staffrider 1978-1988. Special Issue of Staffrider 7(1).

Parry, Benita. 1992. "Culture Clash". In: Transition 55: 125-34.

Pechey, Graham. 1994. "Introduction". In: Ndebele. 1994[2]: 1-16.

Petersen, Kirsten Holst. 1991. "Introduction. An Altered Aesthetics?" In: Petersen/Rutherford (eds.). 1991: i-viii.

Petersen, Kirsten Holst/Rutherford, Anna (eds.). 1991. On Shifting Sands. New Art and Literature from South Africa. London et al.

Powell, Ivor.. "Cultural Politics and the Return of the ANC". In: Weekly Mail. 7-13 Sep. 1990.

Powell, Ivor. "Cultural Oases, but the Wells Have Run Dry". In: Mail & Guardian. 3-9 Sep. 1993.

Powell, Ivor. "The Shape of the Arts to Come". In: Mail & Guardian. 10-16 Dec. 1993.

Powell, Ivor. "A New Site for an Old Cultural Battle". In: Mail & Guardian. 28 Jan.-3 Feb. 1994.

Powell, Ivor. "Showdown in the Culture Corral". In: Mail & Guardian. 25 Feb.-3 March 1994.

Sachs, Albie. 1990 (1989). "'Preparing Ourselves for Freedom'. ANC In-House Seminar Paper on Culture". In: de Kok/Press (eds.). 1990: 19-29.

SACP. 1981. South African Communists Speak. London.

Schmidt, Bettina. 1996. Creating Order - Culture as Politics in 19th and 20th Century South Africa. Nijmegen.

Serote, Mongane Wally. 1990. On the Horizon. Fordsburg.

Slovo, Joe. 1990. "Has Socialism Failed?". In: The African Communist (2): 25-28.

Sole, Kelwyn. 1993. "The Role of the Writer in a Time of Transition". In: Staffrider 11(1/2/3/4): 90-98.

Sole, Kelwyn. 1994. "Democratising Culture and Literature in a 'New South Africa'. Organisation and Theory". In: Current Writing 6(2): 1-37.

Sole, Kelwyn. 1997. "South Africa Passes the Posts". In: Alter Nation 4(1): 116-154.

South African Chapter of the African Renaissance. 2000. Constitution. Johannesburg.

Stalin, Josef W. 1945³ [Russian 1913]. Der Marxismus und die nationale Frage. Moskau.

Steinberg, Carol. "Arts Councils Must Strive to Shed their Apartheid Pasts". In: Business Day 27 Dec. 1993.

Wolpe, Harold. 1988. Race, Class and the Apartheid State. London.

Peter Horn

Peter Horn interviewed by Ulrike Ernst
on 17 February 2000 in Cape Town

"The Counter-Rotating Fate of Writers"

Ulrike Ernst: *In his essay "The Rediscovery of the Ordinary", Njabulo Ndebele (1986) criticised the stereotypification of the political struggle in literature. He spoke out against the 'struggle symbolism' in the literature emanating from ANC cultural activism. What Ndebele endorsed, instead, was critical literature of 'the ordinary', at a time when this had not been fashionable.[1] The debate sparked by this intervention culminated in Albie Sachs' paper "Preparing Ourselves for Freedom" (1989/90), which called for the abandonment of the notion hitherto upheld by ANC cultural activists, that 'culture' should be wielded as a 'weapon in the struggle'.[2]*

How do you perceive the development of South African literature and its impact on society after the end of apartheid?

Peter Horn: I take Albie Sachs' for an epigone because he doesn't say anything other than what Njabulo Ndebele had said previously. Albie Sachs was only important because he was a political figure, and in that way he gained an effect that Njabulo Ndebele possibly didn't have. The whole issue is, of course, highly complicated - not only from a literary or literary-theoretical point of view but also from a literary-political point of view. After Albie Sachs' pronouncements, those who had always said that political literature was bad felt somehow vindicated and made a great show saying that that was what they had always said. Njabulo Ndebele didn't say that we should no longer write political literature. He only spoke out against very special forms of political literature, which were basically nothing else than versified catch phrases and slogans. There was nothing to be said against that, but how it was understood - that was problematic.

The other point which, I believe, one has to consider is that it meant that the role of the Congress of South African Writers (COSAW) was being questioned. As a result, the self-perception of COSAW was undermined, and that exactly at a time where funding from abroad stopped flowing in. That meant that within a few years, around 1992-1994, the Congress of South African Writers nearly stopped to exist as a Congress. There was still a central office and there were a few people in Johannesburg who continued for a while; but the publishing house, COSAW Publishing, disappeared from the scene and it was practically impossible to find COSAW publications. That was a terrible defeat and a defeat especially for young black writers who didn't have connections to established publishers, who didn't have connections to any cultural environment and who suddenly were left alone. I experienced it here in Cape Town, where we tried several times so far as it was possible, without financial means. We found that again and again, young, promising black writers at some stage suddenly gave up, saying 'what for'. I am sure that Albie Sachs' intervention contributed immensely to the destruction of a very interesting cultural undertaking.

Some people like Andries Oliphant and Mike van Graan tried to establish something new by way of organisational political transformation. But that was not so much to the benefit of the great number of black writers, as it was to a few chosen ones who were already established anyway.

If any young black poet approaches me today and asks, where shall I publish, I must simply brutally answer, I do not know. There is no publishing house that would publish what you do. The established publishers keep to the people who are already known anyway, and other publishing houses don't exist. Well, that is the situation.

Ulrike Ernst: *Maybe you could elaborate on the developments within the Congress of South African Writers and explain how you see the role of other literary and cultural organisations in the context of the changes in the political landscape.*

Peter Horn: The Congress of South African Writers practically ceased to exist. So one cannot say that COSAW gave any meaningful impulses to the establishment of a new South Africa. Individual people, of course, did.

Mandla Langa, the last president of COSAW, is presently deeply involved in cultural and media politics. There he is influential not so much through theoretical inputs as through his practical involvement in the organisation. Njabulo Ndebele was - for a short period of time - discussed as a chairperson within South African TV and Radio broadcasting. He was pushed aside, but he is still playing an important role. Other people have been sidelined, if I read that correctly. It is a bit difficult because from here it is not easy to get the whole picture. Ari Sitas and Astrid von Kotze were participating substantially in the establishment of trade union-based theatre and literature in Natal. If I understand it correctly, they are isolated and have virtually no means to continue this work that they have started.

I would say that individual writers - but nearly all people who were known before COSAW was founded - continued to be influential after 1994, but the most interesting voices, like Jeremy Cronin, were practically completely submerged in national politics. He still published a collection of poems, but these were mainly all pieces that he had written before 1994. Ari Sitas has written pieces during the last years, but nobody has published them. Then there is Kelwyn Sole who has published a very interesting poetry collection; but with a very small and unknown publisher. The people who were really active in COSAW - with the exception of a few who participate in the new political structures as organisers - are left outside, they are no longer asked for.

I can illustrate this with my personal experience. During the 80s and the early 90s, I had not only a literary function but, as a writer, also a political function, especially in collaboration with the trade unions, the Congress of South African Trade Unions (COSATU). So it was as a matter of course that I was invited to May Day celebrations to perform something. That stopped in 1994. The need simply wasn't there any more. I think this happened not only to me, but to many others as well. I know about Keith Gottschalk, who was very closely affiliated to the ANC and who had a role within the ANC similar to the one I had within COSATU. For him too, this has come to an end. I can remember that I was at one of the last big happenings, a birthday party of the ANC, around 1993. So it was just before the new South Africa. There was a huge gathering on the Parade in Cape Town - the same place, where Nelson Mandela had spoken when he had been released from prison. Both Keith and I had been invited to contribute to the birthday party. That was about the end of political poetry.

The problem is of course that on the other side there is a group of young traditional artists so-called 'izimbongi'. They are praise-singers who perform praise songs in Xhosa, Zulu or Sotho. To them belongs a friend of mine, Victor Kamize, who also belongs to my group, the Western Cape branch of COSAW. From time to time he is asked to perform a poetical ornament and to utter a praise song at the opening of Parliament.

What is less and less asked for - and one can see this very clearly in the fate of Jeremy Cronin - is critical poetry, a loyal-critical opinion towards the government. One-and-a-half years ago Jeremy Cronin was given hell by Mbeki, not because of his poems, but because of his otherwise critical standpoint; because at the same time Cronin had a function in the Communist Party and the Communist Party and the trade unions do not completely agree with some things in government. That means that such critical voices, be it as poets or as political thinkers, have difficult times. There are problems. The conflict is exactly about the ways of constructing the new. There are basically two concepts, the original concept of *'Reconstruction and Development'* (RDP) that the ANC launched at the beginning, and now the call to create black capitalists, a black class of capitalists, which is part of the vision of the *'Growth, Employment and Redistribution Plan'* (GEAR). This conflict, if the ANC in Government were to have its way, should ideally not take place publicly. Critical intellectuals who bring this into the public, are immediately neutralised as traitors of party discipline, to say it bluntly. Of course, when you ask about intellectuals from COSAW, there are those who in their present position identify completely with the ANC.

Ulrike Ernst: *You have already mentioned examples of the cultural political discourse of the ANC and some conflicts. How would you evaluate the cultural political discourse or the cultural politics of the ANC after its accession to power?*

Peter Horn: Totally confused. On the one hand, the large and basically Eurocentric institutions, for instance the national symphony orchestra and opera house and state theatre etc. are being dissolved, perhaps rightly so. One would expect that on the other hand alternative cultural institutions would be installed with the money that was saved in closing down those operations that have previously catered mainly to white interests. But nothing like that happens. That is the problem.

In the Western Cape branch of COSAW (that goes also for other provinces, but I can describe it here best from my own experience), we tried out the idea of establishing cultural centres in those areas which so far have never had any cultural infrastructure, libraries and cultural places, where people can gather and can do all sorts of cultural activities together, like music, theatre, and film etc. In Montagu, we installed a library and a small cultural centre for the people. But unfortunately it stopped when money ran out in 1993-1994. Here in Athlone, COSAW had not only offices, but also rooms, libraries, etc. for the coloured and the black townships. People could go there; there were books that were usually not accessable. That was our idea. I had expected that consequent cultural politics in special support of the communities would have been a priority of the government. But that has, as far as I can see, not taken place. Well, I have to add something to that. One can understand that the government inherited incredible liabilities from the debts of the former regime, that the money is unbelievably scarce, and that there are thousands of other priorities, like building and equipping hospitals and schools. What perturbs me is that we don't see any initiative from the Department of Arts and Culture (DACST), and that they do not follow up in a plan the initiatives coming from writers and artists. There is a real problem, and it is not only one of money. Of course, money is always very nice, but with some imagination and creativity one can do a lot. There should be a clear plan of the government's side about what to achieve in 5 years, and in 10 years. Then we could see where we were going. I can't see any direction in our Department of Arts and Culture. That seems to be one of our weakest departments.

Ulrike Ernst: *To come back to literature itself: the ANC is trying to transform itself from an anti-apartheid into a post-apartheid movement. Do you see any analogy in literature?*

Peter Horn: First of all, I would say that there is no clear direction in South African literature at the moment. There are all sorts of approaches. What Kelwyn Sole did in his last poetry collection, for example, does go into this direction, but in a very critical manner, as it should be in my opinion. There are some others, there has certainly been a very interesting literature since 1994. Slowly, something is coming up, but a clear line parallel to the other development I can't see.

Ulrike Ernst: *You have already said that the economic policies of the new government have changed. That became evident when Thabo Mbeki became Nelson R. Mandela's successor as president. Do you find this reflected in current literature?*

Peter Horn: Only in so far as a good deal of current literature turns away from the political scene, not only among white, but also black writers. Let us do something completely different, they seem to say. That is somehow normal. During the anti-apartheid struggle - I emphasised that over and over again - one could not live as a writer and pretend the struggle was not there. Therefore one had to be engaged. When today the government says we are directed towards an ordinary democratic state, people might say: OK, in an ordinary democratic state I as a writer don't need to take on any political role. When I want to take upon a political role, I become a politician. That is the opinion of many people, and not only of Whites.

On the one side - despite Ndebele and despite Sachs - there is a continuation of struggle literature, à la Mzwakhe Mbuli etc. There are endlessly many clones - when you go to some celebration or funeral or something like that in the townships, you will still see these people. That simply continues. That is like the Afrikaans-speaking Whites in this country who have still not forgotten that they were defeated by the English in 1902. There are still, within Afrikaans literature, some elements of the anti-British struggle, even after one hundred years. Of course that is no great literature, and it is not being circulated widely. Perhaps it appears in small magazines.

Then there are people who write very much out of their own experience, out of their township. They write poems and prose and novels and drama, like Zakes Mda, which are political in an indirect sense. That means, they start with the daily life-experience of people and show what is wrong there. I think that is part of the most interesting literature at the moment.

Then there is, of course, such interesting and great literature of people like JM Coetzee and Nadine Gordimer and André Brink, who are not apolitical, but political in a very different way.

To come back to the question: I believe that the diversity and the disparity of literature make it impossible to speak of one homogeneous movement or even one overriding kind of support of governmental policy or of the state literature parallel to state politics.

Ulrike Ernst: *Now I would like to move to a more theoretical level. The characterisation of art or literature in non-democratic societies is retrospectively often connected with the notion of an 'aesthetics of conviction'. In your short story "The Greenhouse Effect" (1999), you elaborate on the pejorative reception of cultural expressions of current South African artists.[3] How do you theoretically analyse the political importance of literature?*

Peter Horn: The first point is of course that a poet is not a politician. That means that the poet does not assume that he or she will achieve direct political effects with his or her poetry. What some of the 1968 generation in Germany believed in, that one could make a revolution with literature, that was for us clearly nonsense throughout the time of the struggle. Revolutions are made by politicians and by the masses.

Politics comes into literature or is part of literature because of two reasons: The first reason is that I live in a society and when I as a writer reflect on this society, then politics finds its way unavoidably into writing. And this time not as advocacy, not saying you have to do that or the other, but simply as a reflection of the reality I live in. That is the first stage.

In a situation of National Socialism in Germany, or apartheid in South Africa or similar dictatorial conditions, the writer is connected with politics in a more far-reaching way, for two further reasons. Firstly, as a writer, he tries to gain the freedom to be able to say what he thinks. That is a kind of professional interest, an ethos of profession, to create a space in which he can speak. And secondly, the writer is also a human being, who is interested in his political freedom.

In devaluing this kind of writing as 'aesthetics of conviction' certain power groups attempted to declare this kind of writing as substandard, as of only of inferior value. It is very interesting to consider Njabulo Ndebele here - where such writing uses simplifying forms so that it becomes mere slogan poetry. Unfortunately that was often the case during the anti-apartheid struggle. They uttered some rhymed sermons. One has to face that.

The function of the writer is - and I think Njabulo is right here - the critical analysis of the situation, of what is going on. And out of this situation, he can make political suggestions of what to do. But he makes these suggestions not in form of a political speech - for that I don't need to be a writer - but in an imaginative form, that shows what one can do or that transfers such analysis in a fictional or lyrical or dramatic context. The opinion that poetry or literature has to abstain from politics is of course an opinion that is contradicted by almost all great literature.

Ulrike Ernst: *How does the engagement of literature change during the transformation into a democratic society and beyond?*

Peter Horn: I speak about myself because I believe there is no one single answer. My basis is my interest in making the transformation process succeed. But I also reckon with the fact that the people who politically bring about the transformation do not necessarily see all the consequences of their decisions. That means that the function of the writer is still the function of the critical analyst; for this reason the writer is intensely occupied with the concrete. When I write a short story, I don't write about the criminal in general, but I examine a special type, for instance a pickpocket, and depict him. This kind of imagination is an imagination that aims at the concrete. And because it aims at the concrete, it also sees what partly horrible consequences well meant political decisions can have for the life of real people. In that sense, literature becomes critique when it criticises well-meant decisions, which not always think far enough or don't think into the concrete.

Of such decisions there were many. To quote but one example: It is correct that nearly all good teachers are concentrated at white schools, the worse educated at black schools, and the worst educated at black schools in the rural areas. It was OK to take a couple of good teachers and put them into those areas where there are no good teachers. The consequences were a catastrophe. A large number of teachers disagreed and took their pensions and said good-bye. The few idealists who really did it came into the black schools in the townships, and then came AZAPO (Azanian People's Organisation) and nearly killed them, saying we don't want any white teachers here. Right, we have to guarantee a better education, but the ways in which this was envisaged led to a complete breakdown at many schools. The misery that we have had for the last two or three years with the catastrophic Matric results, is closely connected with these decisions. There it is the task of the writer to maybe take a specific teacher and write a short story or a novel and show the picture.

We are thirty, forty years behind the development of the rest of Africa. But there I read Chinua Achebe's *'Things Fall Apart'* and see how he very critically accompanies the transformation process and shows where the mistakes are and where the catastrophes come from.

Ulrike Ernst: *Writers influence their societies not only through their literary texts but also through their non-literary statements. Your short story "A Ritual in the Kloof" (1999) focuses on a critical outsider whom you call an intellec-*

tual.[4] *Under what circumstances would you ascribe the tasks of intellectuals to writers?*

Peter Horn: The context is our media society. When you are a good physician like Barnard and you can transplant hearts, then you are suddenly asked about all sorts of things that have nothing to do with heart transplantation. The same happens to you when you are John Coetzee or André Brink. You are asked about all sorts of things that you don't know anything about at all.

Well, literary specialists believe of course, because they read and write a lot, that they have a knowledge in every field. My own very limited experience as administrator at a university showed me that it is much more difficult to make politics on a small scale than to critically follow up a cause from the outside. That I would tell every intellectual very clearly: you are not a specialist, at the most a specialist of the general.

What intellectuals can do is to keep their ears open and to listen to what is happening in the 'polis' and to interpret its meaning. And on the basis of this ability to listen, they can speak up and intervene. One should be a critic without arrogance, one should not believe that one knows things better than specialists. This specific ability - which one should have as writer - would enable one to be much more aware of the surrounding environment, and to formulate that in a way that it goes somewhere, for instance into the newspapers or onto TV.

Ulrike Ernst: *Could you elaborate on the problem of representation in your writing and the relation between the notion of representation and intellectuals? How do you see yourself in this context?*

Peter Horn: The question is - what does one represent - a political party or a liberation movement? A transition from a liberation movement to a political party is what has clearly taken place during the last five years. The ANC is not a liberation movement any more in the sense as it had been before 1994. This transition from a liberation movement to a political party implies, that as a party it no longer stands for the general. That means that within the alliance there are spheres that the party for political reasons refuses to represent. That means for me that after 1994 I cannot unequivocally identify with a liberation movement. It has anyway never been unequivocal. My positive role is limited to saying the direction that we are going is basically correct, but - there is always the 'but'.

The writer cannot be partisan in the same sense in which the politician can be partisan. The politician cannot and is not allowed to see certain things. That is where writer and politician part ways. If I support the current government, then it is with reservations, with the proviso that I can criticise where I think that critique is necessary. I think that is the function of the intellectual in general, not simply to accept a party line without question, but to make visible the interventions and contradictions.

There is this tension. N.P. van Wyk Louw, the Afrikaans writer, stood in similar relation of tension to the National Party in his days. He called it 'lojale verset'. One could translate that as a 'loyal revolt' against the government.

Ulrike Ernst: *Outside of South Africa the literature of this country has been especially connected with the name of Nadine Gordimer, who won the Nobel Prize for literature in 1991. But inside the country, even within parts of the anti-apartheid movement, the standing of her work and her person is disputed. How do you explain this difference in her reception?*

Peter Horn: I am not sure that within the anti-apartheid movement her work is so highly disputed. It was the white literary establishment that largely ignored her. And when she received the Nobel Prize, the reaction of the South African media was absolutely poor. It was shameful, that one reacted in such a mean way. Inside the anti-apartheid movement, there were of course quarrels about how to represent the reality of South Africa during apartheid and how to represent the struggle against it.

One can, for instance, argue about *'July's People'* and say that it represents an end of the world scenario, which is typical of white ideology - when the blacks reign, everything will be chaos. I think one misinterprets Gordimer there, but those are accusations that were brought against her. Well, about *'Sport of Nature'* one can hold very different opinions. I don't think that inside the anti-apartheid movement one wanted to take away her importance or her place. My experience inside of COSAW was that she was generally accepted, without exception, as a leading voice. One could of course ask whether everything that she had written was acceptable.

The differences between Coetzee and Gordimer, and the challenges from other sides (also from outside of the strictly delimited anti-apartheid movement) were much more severe and more important.

Ulrike Ernst: *Could you elaborate on this dispute with Coetzee?*

Peter Horn: Coetzee has been accused over and over again of being an apolitical writer - which he not is in my view. Coetzee just chose a completely different way. First of all Coetzee is someone who refuses any kind of violence. That goes so far that - if you read his last book *'Disgrace'* - he preoccupies himself intensely with the lives of animals. He is searching for a way other than the way of violence. That does not mean that he is not emphatically against any form of apartheid. I think that he has written literally very interesting pieces.

It was of course clear that in a political situation which grew more and more restricted, especially during the second half of the 1980s, which is the period in which COSAW became prominent as an oppositional writers' organisation, the fact that he did not join COSAW had to lead to a harsh confrontation between him and Gordimer. This was despite all the respect that they otherwise showed to each other.

Then there was the argument about Salman Rushdie: Coetzee could not understand that his invitation was cancelled, while Gordimer insisted that one could not guarantee Rushdie's safety in South Africa. An acrimonious fight ensued.

I believe what it was all about was the method by which apartheid was to be abolished. What offended many people about Coetzee's stance is one thing - and Nadine Gordimer criticises this as well. She quotes exactly this one sentence from a scene in '*Michael K*' where Michael K decides, instead of going with the revolutionaries into the mountains, to continue growing his vegetables. Gordimer said that this would have been the moment where he could have written a real South African novel, where he really would have entered the resistance struggle; but that he does not do. There one can see very clearly the opposite positions of Gordimer and Coetzee.

Ulrike Ernst: *How do you evaluate Gordimer's work after the political changes?*

Peter Horn: It became a bit weaker but she gets a bit older. I find *'My Son's Story'* weak. I think the heights of her work were *'The Conservationist'* and *'Burger's Daughter'*. What came after that was nice novel writing but not of that importance and greatness. In the two earlier novels, she caught the core of the case; and technically those were the best.

Ulrike Ernst: *In your essay "Wendezeit in South African and German Literature" (1997), you discuss the relationship between truth, history writing, memory and art in the transitional literatures of both countries. You single out Christa Wolf's novel 'Medea' for close analysis.[5] Christa Wolf's person and her work, including her non-literary statements, gave rise to heated debate after German unification. How do you evaluate the role and function of Christa Wolf in the process of the German 'Wende'[6] and thereafter?*

Peter Horn: As far as I can see, nobody knows exactly how Christa Wolf acted in this spy affair - whether she was being spied on or whether she spied on others. I believe that in *'Medea'* we can see the best depiction of Christa Wolf's own problems. It is the problem of someone who is initially convinced of a case and subsequently tempted to enter the circles of power, so becoming a member of the 'SED'[7]. In *'Medea'*, she describes her own fall into sin rather openly. I find it interesting that she is able - even though historically alienated - to approach her own problems in this way.

I find these fights terrible, horrible. In Vancouver I saw this terrible debate between Schädlich and Monika Maron. It was a mudslinging match in which all sorts of things came up, from political statements to information on the most private and intimate situations. Monika Maron was Schädlich's wife.

Fortunately I am very friendly with some GDR dissidents, for example Jürgen Fuchs. Through him I know the whole inside story. I find it disgraceful how Christa Wolf was treated after the 'Wende'. She was a very important writer in the German Democratic Republic and not one given to cheering the GDR along with some of the others. I always got the impression that she was very critical of certain deformations of the system. One can read that in nearly all her books, in *'Der geteilte Himmel'*, or in *'Kassandra'* or *'Kindheitsmuster'*. A critique is always there, and it often includes an auto-critique.

Whatever happened then can be termed a blunder, but there I am ready to say, well, OK - amnesty.

Ulrike Ernst: *What importance would you ascribe to Christa Wolf in the transformation process and thereafter?*

Peter Horn: She was practically switched off. The last time she spoke publicly was when the GDR had just emerged from state socialism. That was basically her last political appearance. Then she was sidelined in such a way that she could not participate in this process. The rather embarrassing spy-story *'Was bleibt'* (*'What Remains'*) that she had written, she would have done better not to publish in 1990. I have the feeling that the end of the GDR catapulted her into a situation where she simply does not know what to do. I think that she welcomed the end of this eventually quite degenerated GDR but that she won't see her way into this new, unified Germany. My perception is that she does not know how to react to these new challenges.

Ulrike Ernst: *In the course of our interview, we spoke about the importance of writers in the transformation processes of their countries. If you compare Christa Wolf and Nadine Gordimer under this aspect and in relation to the notion of representation, what parallels and differences would you identify?*

Peter Horn: It is virtually impossible to compare them. The differences are very clear to me. Christa Wolf stands in - even if critically - for a position that is so thoroughly disavowed in the ex-GDR as to discredit and marginalize even what she had written beforehand and even her most exiting and interesting work. It will take some time before her importance for and within GDR literature will once again be understood and appreciated. The sad thing about Christa Wolf's case is that her public efficacy, which had extended even to West Germany - it is astonishing how many people were intensely preoccupied with her work - was practically cut off in 1990. (I tried to arrange a meeting with her, but she was ill. It was clear that she was not inclined to discuss her work with anybody. Of course she did not know me and she did not know that I hold her work in high esteem. But during the time of my sojourn in Germany, she cut herself off completely).

With Nadine Gordimer it is very simple: she is on the side of victors. Not only did she receive the Nobel Prize, but also if you watch the videos of big events, Mandela's presidential inauguration for example, she is always present. She is a figure of the new republic, in the public of this new republic, even if (I did not have the time to read her last essay collection), what she wrote between 1990 and 1994 is not an impressive contribution to this new republic. She is part of this new republic, a public figure, only because of her contribution before 1990. She never hesitated to say very clearly what side she stood on. She never denied that she was on the side of the ANC.

She is now the kind of stately poet or writer that Christa Wolf had been for some time in the GDR. That is precisely the kind of counter-rotating fate that writers are likely to experience in terms of their public-political efficacy as writers. I do not speak here as much about Gordimer's work as about the way in which she puts herself on stage.

The work of these two authors is so different that one can hardly draw parallels because the situations in the GDR and South Africa are very different. One might be inclined to see these two historical events together because they took place at about the same time, but I think that the end of the GDR and the end of apartheid are two very different things.

Ulrike Ernst: *One last question: apart from an official political system of representation, a democratic society needs the critical voice of public intellectuals who represent through their voice and persona those who are misrepresented even in a democracy. If you compare Christa Wolf and Nadine Gordimer in the light of this requirement, where would you locate them?*

Peter Horn: Nadine Gordimer was of course the voice that was not only heard in South Africa but also outside South Africa as the representative of those without voice.

Ulrike Ernst: *What about her role after 1994?*

Peter Horn: In the time after 1994, well, no. Of course not. Now she takes the side of the established government, those people who now hold power. I do not have the impression that she comes out with any very clear criticism or that she takes the side of people - also Whites - who are not exactly preferentially treated by this government, for instance the large number of unemployed people. As far as I know, she has not spoken out for such groups. Not even for someone like Mzwake Mbuli - who is possibly rightfully imprisoned - but who is somebody she was friendly with, or whom at least she often met in COSAW. As far as I know, she has not even visited him in prison. I do not have the feeling that after 1994 she specifically stands in for those who are not represented in the system and for whom the system does not cater. She was critical against the apartheid-regime - yes, very critical. But I do not have the impression that she is particularly critical of the current government, in those instances in which criticism would be necessary.

Ulrike Ernst: *Thank you very much for the interview.*

References

[1] **Ndebele, Njabulo S. 1986.** "The Rediscovery of the Ordinary. Some New Writings in South Africa". In: **Ndebele, Njabulo S. 1991.** Rediscovery of the Ordinary. Essays on South African Literature and Culture: 37-57. See also: **Ndebele, Njabulo S. 1994**[2] (extended edition of 1991). South African Literature and Culture. Rediscovery of the Ordinary. Introduction by Graham Pechey. Manchester/New York.

[2] **Sachs, Albie. 1990 [1989].** "'Preparing Ourselves for Freedom'. ANC In-House Seminar Paper on Culture". In: **de Kok, Ingrid/Press, Karen (eds.). 1990.** Spring is Rebellious. Arguments about Cultural Freedom by Albie Sachs and Respondents: 19-29.

[3] **Horn, Peter. 1999.** "The Greenhouse Effect". In: **Horn, Peter. 1999.** My Voice Is Under Control Now. Cape Town: 155-167.

[4] **Horn, Peter. 1999.** "A Ritual in the Kloof". In: **Horn, Peter. 1999.** My Voice Is Under Control Now. Cape Town: 168-177.

[5] **Horn, Peter. 1997.** "Parallels and Contrasts - Wendezeit in South African and German Literature". In: Literator 18 (3) Nov: 25-40.

[6] 'Wende': German word used to describe the political changes in East Germany after the peaceful 'revolution' on 9 November 1989.

[7] Sozialistische Einheitspartei Deutschlands.

Mandla Langa

Mandla Langa interviewed by Ulrike Ernst
on 27 March 2000 in Johannesburg

"The Arts Start to Play Second Fiddle"

Ulrike Ernst: *Mandla Langa, you have a reputation as a writer, a politician and a cultural and media organiser and representative. Bearing in mind your different perspectives, I would like to ask you the following: parallel to the ending of apartheid a literary discussion evolved which criticised the notion of culture as a weapon in the struggle. In your earlier work, 'Tenderness of Blood'[1], you tell the story of a photographer arrested for his political involvement. In 'A Rainbow on a Paper Sky'[2] you, as a militarily trained Umkhonto we Sizwe member, take an actual incident where ANC guerrillas set up a base in rural Northern Natal to train villagers. But even in these early works you do not stereotype the struggle nor digress into sloganeering, to use Njabulo Ndebele's or Albie Sachs' terms. You have always tried to tell truths, no matter how difficult people might find them. How do you see the development and the importance of literature in the South African society after the end of the old struggle, after apartheid?*

Mandla Langa: I think that if you look at the South African literature for the past years, it has been a literature that has been formed by and large by apartheid. What that meant was that apartheid somehow managed to put forth a template in which writers could function. I have always been aware of this, and I have also always been reading quite a lot from other writers, including other writers who had come out of situations of upheavals, of struggle, the post-World War II writings for instance, the post-Vietnam War writings, the post-Holocaust writings in Europe and other parts of the world.

So I have always been interested, I think, to try and tell stories of people in moments of upheaval, but to tell it in such a way that I would be dealing with the human dramas rather than use the big drama of struggle as a vehicle for telling the story. I think to that extent then a lot of writers trapped themselves or painted themselves into a corner where they got to be identified either as polemicists, or propagandists, or struggle writers. I think that is a very unfortunate set of categories and an unfortunate set of labels.

Coming to today's South Africa, I think that much has happened, a lot of people are beginning to realise that writing or literature has got to survive on its creative merit. So what has happened then, now, if I look at the story that I write, I try to deal with what Njabulo Ndebele himself calls 'the celebration of the ordinary', where everyday people and their everyday lives can be reflected in print without it becoming a big story, a big issue, a big moral canvas, where apartheid, where black and white, where good and evil are explicated. I just believe that writing about the struggle of somebody who is struggling, possibly with poverty, struggling with the issue of child abuse, or struggling with the issue of religion, or a struggle of coming to terms of making sense what happens between two people, between men and women, sometimes between men and men and women and women, mother and child, father and son, and such things. That is what I think a lot of us would be moving towards. There are a number of themes that are beginning to come up. People are more interested now, or are beginning to explore their own relationship with the land, the issue of the environment, the issue of what is happening in Mozambique right now, the floods. I am certain that can start to have an impact on literature, natural calamities, joblessness, how do people deal with all those arenas.

Ulrike Ernst: *The democratic society needs a defined official representational system, but apart from that, it also needs the critical voice of the independent intellectual. With your collection 'The Naked Song and Other Stories', you challenge the emerging new South Africa.[3] (You have another work coming out in April 2000.)[4] What role and task of intellectuals would you ascribe to writers in a society in transformation?*

Mandla Langa: I think that what we found at the time when Albie Sachs said that people must be careful about saying that culture is a weapon of struggle, what he didn't say was what becomes of the role of the writer or the intellectual. I think that one has to be very careful there because sometimes we place too much emphasis, too much importance, on what a writer should be doing. What is it that writers should not be doing? One of the things is that writers should not see themselves as a continuation of a polemical kind of struggle. Writing comes from inspiration, comes from being motivated, being driven by a talent, and being driven by dreams. Although we come from societies that might be writhing in pain, we have to find a way of reflecting that pain without making it detract from our humanness. We are human beings, and we would like to create as much as possible. This is a mission entrusted to about everybody on this world, to try and create a more humane society a more democratic order, a more functional, satisfying environment in which children can grow.

That brings us into the debate that has been raging for a long time: what about a writer who is very good, but who is himself or herself a repressive person? How do we deal with that? I believe that at the end of the day, goodness and the capability of writing somehow, to my mind, are two sides of the same coin. If a writer is very bad, inevitably that will reflect itself in his or her writing. I can quote some examples from both film and literature to a certain extent. I cannot see *'Mein Kampf'* for instance as a successful book, no matter how publicised it might have been. Nor can I see Leni Riefenstahl's work as being examples of artistic activity.

I do think that writers have a role, but they do not have the role that is given to politicians. As a writer, your role is to try and reflect a world as clearly and unashamedly as possible in a way that would make the coming generations or the people that read to feel that there is a need to secure this because it has been evoked very beautifully and very meaningfully. That is the role that writers can play. If I depict a situation in KwaZulu-Natal that is full of beauty and possibly horror, it must make the person who is reading feel that I would like to contribute to this, I would like to make sure that that horror does not succeed, I would like to make sure that that beauty that this writer has written about, is allowed to thrive and be sustained.

Ulrike Ernst: *Will this show in your new book?*

Mandla Langa: It does show in the novel coming, in the sense that I tried to deal with here and there, the best aspects of people. I am always trying to deal with things that celebrate the invincibility of the human spirit.

Ulrike Ernst: *You held various ANC posts abroad during your time in exile. You were the ANC Cultural Representative in the United Kingdom and Western Europe. How would you retrospectively discuss the theory or ideology, the workerist or populist stance as well as the organisation and the structure of the cultural work of the ANC in exile?*

Mandla Langa: We were moving, we were operating specifically on the understanding that we needed as much as possible to publicise the cultural excellence of our people inside as well as outside South Africa. We also moved from the understanding that had been articulated by scholars and ideologues such as Cabral when he wrote in *'The Return to the Source'* and *'Towards a Revolution in Guinea'*, of the role which culture could play to ensure that it becomes an adjunct of the political continuum.

For instance, a graphic example of this is what happened a long, long time ago during the Second World War in what was then known as Stalingrad. This was a city that had a very famous football club, and during the siege of Leningrad, when people were hungry, they had no food, and they were really weak, the people said to themselves: to fight the Nazis we have to go back to all those things that we used to celebrate as a people and of those things that we are known for is football, soccer. So, tired and weak and hungry and starving under siege as they were, they managed to get people who played football and they would collect people who were hungry, who were everything, under siege, to come and watch this. Somehow that whole participation in playing soccer, in being cheered, in invoking and recalling what used to make them great at a particular time, gave people the capacity to resist. This is an analogy I use all the time. If people, if you as a cultural worker, are able to evoke for the people and for yourself the image of what being human is and what it means, you are then able to make sure that people will always struggle, will always fight will always make sure that they are not defeated by anything in their quest, in their attempt to reach that level of humanity that has temporarily been taken away by oppression.

Basically, then, my work at the ANC office was to interact with as many formations in the United Kingdom and Western Europe as possible to give people there an understanding of what was happening in relation to arts and culture in South Africa and elsewhere and also to make them see what role they could play in this big struggle that all of us were fighting: to rid this country of the racist regime. These were the parameters within which I operated. At the same time we would create concerts and create conferences and symposiums where aspects of struggle culture etc. were discussed. It was the time when we had the cultural boycott, and it was explained to people why such a precarious instrument was used because as you well know a boycott cuts both ways. It is a double-edged sword: it cuts the boycotter and the one who is boycotted in equal measure. How do you justify this to the international community? So this was what we wanted to do as much as possible.

Lastly, the whole exercise and the whole impetus were to try and create cultural structures, both internally and externally. It was also to sustain and to ensure that whatever was beginning to come up could find dissemination internally and externally. To support structures, to support activists, to support any new voice, new writers, singers, graphic artists, poets, whatever, to ensure that we would be able to recreate the best there could be about this country.

Ulrike Ernst: *Which cultural structures did you set up? Could you explain this a little bit?*

Mandla Langa: From the time when I was in Botswana, it was a long time ago, we set up a media arts ensemble where we worked together with the nationals of Botswana together with the South African exiles. In the United Kingdom, we supported and set up structures like Zabalaza, which also came up with conferences, came up with conscientising forums which worked together with the people of the country, the people of the UK, or any other part of the world, so long as that at the end of the day it was understood that this is the channel that we are taking, this is the route we are all going, and this is the end result we would like to see. Around the time you found conferences, for instance in 1987 in Amsterdam called Culture in Another South Africa, where you created an interaction between South African artists internally and world artists externally to find a forum for dialogue, discourse and for common strategies and initiatives.

Ulrike Ernst: *Issues connected with the returning of exiles, artists returning to South Africa, are highly underlined in your present writing. I think here for example of "The Resurrection of the River Artists"[5], or the very sensitive "Naked Song"[6]. I was struck by the incident where the psychologist, perturbed by a hungry and voiceless singer who had a nervous breakdown after the return from exile, asks himself, "what have we done for the artists [...] who come and expose the more unpalatable features of our society?"[7] What happened to the cultural politics of the ANC after its legalisation and its return to South Africa between 1990 and 1994?*

Mandla Langa: I think that there are two stages to this. One is, of course, when you are a political person, when you are a political/cultural person and you are also in exile, when you get back in your country, a number of layers begin to slough away or are taken away. When you are in exile, you operate in a certain disciplined set-up. You have a vision of the kind of country that you want to create in the future. When you get into the country, a whole lot of realities seep in, take place. In certain instances, and I think I raised this elsewhere, the disjuncture between the host country of exile and your motherland can easily for many people mean that when they return they are returning to a wholly different land altogether.

The land to which you return could be very strange. When, for instance, the ANC then operated in exile, it was operating as a liberation movement, had policies, some of which I have articulated, in ensuring that culture would act as an adjunct of the political continuum. When people came back into the country, there is number one the issue of the vastness of the task itself, the fact that there are so many, so many other priorities, so a decision, I am certain, has to be taken at some level: to what extent do we put aside resources for the continuation of the cultural struggle? To what extent do we deal with what is happening in KwaZulu-Natal with the joblessness, unemployment? You then start to find a shift in the thrust and in the focus of those who have been involved and the arts, to my mind, start to play second fiddle, start to lose the importance and start to get off the rungs where they had been elsewhere.

A lot of things do not then get done, because people feel that people have got to eat, there has got to be education, and there has got to be this and that. You are contending for very scarce resources. I know lots of writers, for instance, lots of people who when they came back, started saying, I don't think I will continue with this, I have to find a job, I have to earn money, I have to get a house and so on and so forth. All those elements at the end of the day do impact on the cultural output of people.

There is also another story that needs to be told and that is to what extent, if you go back to the original opening remarks I made, where apartheid acts as a creative crucible for people when that goes away, in most cases other people start to find that they are without that crutch, without that wherewithal, without that wellspring that used to feed their creativity. So we find that they say, what am I going to write about now? What will I paint?

Ulrike Ernst: *This was the period between 1990 and 1994. What is your opinion of the cultural discourse and the cultural policy of the ANC after its accession to power with the first free elections in 1994?*

Mandla Langa: I think you can judge the seriousness of a liberation movement, of a political party in government, outside government, by the seriousness it accords number one to the cultural workers, number two the cultural industry itself. You can judge to what extent does it give resources to that. I think we are one of the few countries in the world that can boast a Department and a Ministry of Arts and Culture. It doesn't happen in many countries, even in some of the most advanced Western societies you still do find culture and the arts at least being parcelled off and given to foundations etc., but not to become something that the state will invest a budget and resources for ensuring that there is some kind of progress there. In South Africa we do have that. We are very fortunate. The policies that were informing the ANC then by and large do find themselves reflected in how this country treats or tries to treat its artists.

It is not satisfactory, we have many more hungry artists now, we have many more unpublished writers, we have many more singers who are on the bread line, but at least, at the end of the day there is a recognition now and then you do find in some of the events that take place, where for instance, I think on 30th March 2000, with the South African music awards, there will be recognition of the stalwarts in music: Hugh Masekela, Jonas Gwangwa, Caiphus Semenya, and a host of others. A while back the former president of the Republic, Nelson Mandela, gave artists some recognition for their work: Miriam Makeba and others. I think people do understand one thing that perhaps without the arts we would not have become the kind of human beings that we became and we could have become very patriotic monsters when there was this ascension to power. We would have become very unthinking, uncritical, unreflecting surfaces of a political reality.

This has gone a long way not only in humanising us but also in making us understand that what happens in this struggle happens not to make us hate other people but to make us understand them. To understand what makes them tick, so that the worst thing that can come to human beings is to become a mirror image of the monsters that were oppressing them. The arts have a very big role in reminding us that this is the route to take, this is the role that we have to play, not only for ourselves but also for the coming generation. I think it is very important.

Ulrike Ernst: *In the preparation of the transfer of the presidency from Nelson Mandela to Thabo Mbeki there was a shift from the 'Reconstruction and Development Plan' to the implementation of the 'Growth, Employment and Redistribution Programme'; the political and economic aims have been changing. What do you think: does it manifest itself in the official cultural politics?*

Mandla Langa: Going back to the Department of Arts and Culture itself, you have, for instance, cultural industries' growth strategies, where there is a beginning of recognition of the fiscal role that the arts can play in an organised kind of circumstance. But you also look at the kind of energy that is beginning to emerge very slowly in some field that I am very familiar with, in the broadcasting sector. For instance, in the IBA, the Independent Broadcasting Authority, in 1995 we set up a triple inquiry, into local content. So the broadcaster has to produce a certain percentage of indigenous local content. To that extent the artists and musicians who are now very busy trying to come up with the kind of output that is of such a standard that it can find its way into the broadcaster. There is energy there which marks a definite shift from the kind of involvement in the arts of the past, where people just said, I am involved in the arts, without even thinking of the managerial aspects of the arts, without even thinking what is the administrative aspect, to what extent can this make a contribution to the fiscus?

We used to believe in a romantic notion of artists starving, the artist is this and that, you've got the saxophone that is put together with wire and things, you draw pictures of people starving, scraggly dogs trying to upturn garbage cans. We cannot legislate against that, but you also have to say to yourself in the development of society, to what extent are you creating a circumstance where the artist can become a curator, the moving spirit behind his or her product, rather than all the time it has to come from some white foundation, as has been happening throughout history. To what extent can this be turned around? I think the impulse that is obtaining at the moment, that is coming from the administration of President Thabo Mbeki, is that whereas in the past we might have been moving from the perspective that we are oppressed, to what extent are we really considerably in a realistic manner going to assume and take the reigns of control and run with that? We stumble; if we fail, it is still part of the process.

To move away from the psychological bent or inclination we still have to have a paternalistic kind of set-up that is going to help us reach a certain goal. I think the time of Nelson Mandela was of course the time of reconciliation, and reconciliation unfortunately comes with a price. You pay for reconciliation, especially if that reconciliation is a one-sided street: the blacks were reconciling, the whites were not reciprocating that. All the time it was our people bending over backwards, forgiving, and going to shake hands with the wives of former dictators. As a lead in this new administration nobody is going to be doing that because it is somehow sanctioned from the highest councils of our country.

Ulrike Ernst: *You have been very intensively involved in the work of the Congress of South African Writers, whose last chairperson you have been. Now one does not hear a lot about the Congress any more. How do you perceive the importance in the development of the Congress and in the changes of the literary scene?*

Mandla Langa: What has happened to the Congress of South African Writers is again a merger of the development in this country. Now development is a terrible word, it usually seems to mean to a lot of people that things are going well. But development can also mean that a thing developed badly for a specific structure. COSAW is one of those. At the time when COSAW was created, it was part and parcel of the mobilising energy, to try to get as many people as possible to become writers, to be able to articulate the vision of the libratory process.

With the changeover to a democratic process or circumstance, some of that energy was blunted and a lot of the people found it easier and possibly much more experienced to do work elsewhere, in other arenas. There was a haemorrhaging of very good personnel, and at the end of the time the organisation becomes a pale image of its former self. But it does not mean that organisations do not then adapt to the changing world. With COSAW, one of the more tireless workers, Raks Sekoha, got COSAW to become part and parcel of the Southern African Writers' Forum and also to link in with the writers' organisations of other parts of Africa. So the original mission has not changed. It is just that the energy that was there before has dissipated, some of the people who were the driving force have found other priorities, and at the end of the day the organisation as it was either had to change or it had to destroy itself. To this extent the spirit of COSAW still lives on. I am sure whenever all of us have the time, can make the time, we do still continue to participate in writers' workshops to ensure that, again going back to the younger generation, you can impart something that can inspire and give tools to younger people - how to write, how to deal with the written word, how to deal with text, how to get creative material from around us, from the radio, from television, from the newspaper, from stories that are being told by the older generation, etc.

Ulrike Ernst: *Which other organisations have had an impact on the cultural discourse in the country?*

Mandla Langa: The South African story, I keep on saying, is the story also of the region, it is the story of Southern Africa, the story of the whole African continent. There has been a lot of interaction with cultural workers, writers, from all over the world. We have had people here and still do now and then, like Wole Soyinka for instance, the Nobel laureate from Nigeria. When Ken Saro-Wiwa was hanged, was killed by the Abacha regime, we had a cultural conference here which I think was one of the last glorious things that COSAW did in 1995, where we pledged solidarity with what is going on in Nigeria. We had other writers from the US on that, quite a lot of people, quite a lot of influences. But we are also looking at what other countries, what other formations are doing in other countries to ensure the continuation of the possibility of safeguarding the cultural treasury of this country. So be it countries in Africa, in Western Europe, in the United States, in Asia, wherever, we have participated in those colloquia there, conferences, and also invited people as much as possible to allow this kind of exchange that we think should, can and must be encouraged as much as possible.

A lot of people who had been outside the country, who had been in exile, who came back, writers and scholars, have also tried as much as possible to impart whatever it is, whatever little that they might have learned or gleaned elsewhere inside South Africa to make sure that people share everything, they even share poverty and resources.

Ulrike Ernst: *And inside the country, which impact do you give for example to the National Arts Coalition?*

Mandla Langa: We are in discussions, we are in, I can call it, a dynamic contact, we share, exchange views as much as possible. Some of the people who are in COSAW are part of that, people like Andries Oliphant, with whom we do engage now and then in areas of need. At the moment, for instance, I am certain, I can think that that is what is happening, and there is the issue of the African Renaissance. I am certain that people who are part and parcel of the NAC also are part and parcel of the energy that brings about creativity in the African Renaissance.

Ulrike Ernst: *Outside of South Africa, the literature of this country is largely connected with the name of Nobel Prize winner Nadine Gordimer. However, it seems that at home her work and her person are often not so well received. How do you explain this difference in the reception?*

Mandla Langa: I think that South Africa to a large extent does recognise Nadine Gordimer. I think that we need to face this: there might be some people, there might even be formations, who would feel uncomfortable or unhappy with the kind of prominence she has reached or has attained. She is white and I think that this country is still very racialised. But that is a very sometimes childish view which seeks to punish or disparage a personality on areas where she should not be disparaged, which are not of her own making.

Nadine Gordimer did not create apartheid. She is not the one who set up publishing houses. She might have benefited from the fact that she is white when the publishers cast around in their heads and said, we want to promote a book, a writer. So, which writer are we going to do? And because they would feel more comfortable with her, being white, being like them, they have a disinclination to reach out into all sorts of corners of this country, to get the kind of text that can also be promoted. But we must not make the mistake of blaming the wrong person. It would be like blaming me - let me just think of a place - in the middle of Antarctica for the snow being white just because I am the contrast.

What still needs to be done in South Africa, I believe there still is a great need for the economics of publishing to be re-examined, for the price of books to be looked into, for the literacy to be spearheaded and to be almost force-fed upon the people of this country, because without a broad reading base you will not get people who will buy your books. We also need to look at things quite clearly. I do not know to what extent Gordimer earns money as a writer in South Africa. People in most cases have to be published outside first before they can make an impact on this country. Same thing with theatre - I am talking from experience. Mbongeni Ngema has to have his plays and theatre and musicals manifested in Germany before they then come back to South Africa after having won awards elsewhere. We are dealing with a very dicey, critical scenario that needs to be put on the table honestly, for people to say, OK fine, let's look at this. Because in looking at it we are looking at ourselves. That is how I would deal with that question of Nadine Gordimer.

We cannot also account for the appetites of the Western reading public. They have been used to hearing this one voice from Southern Africa. People are creatures of habit. They will keep on going to what is familiar. People are very conservative. They do not like taking risks. They do not like dabbling and experimenting with the unknown. That is to my mind one of the defects of our societies.

Ulrike Ernst: *Now I would like to turn to a slightly different area of questions. At the beginning of March 2000 we met at a literary panel discussion in Pretoria in Afrikaans-speaking surroundings. Anglophone and Francophone writers had gathered after the end of the Time of the Writer Festival in Durban. The questions were posed in English and French and translated to the audience and the writers. Then a young man posed a question to you in Zulu. Even though it was apparent that he was proficient in English he insisted on having your answer in Zulu. You answered in English. For your fiction writing you use the English lan-*

guage, which is not your mother tongue. How do you locate the terrain of languages as part of cultural and literary politics in South Africa?

Mandla Langa: The thing I said when the question was asked was that people must use the kind of language that they feel they can use, that they feel comfortable in. There are many English-speaking people in this country and elsewhere where I studied who do not know how to use the English language. Who read my works and say, but how did you come to express things like this? Where did you learn all this? I look at Nabokov who was not a native English speaker, who wrote *'Lolita'*. I look at Joseph Conrad who was Polish, who wrote *'Heart of Darkness'*. There is a host of people. One gets to the point where you get asked the question, because implied in that question is, why don't you write in your mother tongue?

The issue here, I think, is not so much the language in which you write, but to what extent are you able to carry the pain, the anxieties, the lifestyle, the culture, the whole cultural expressiveness of those people about whom you write, in whatever vehicle that you use. For instance, a long time ago I was in Hungary in Budapest. We went to the Soviet Union, as it was then, and we travelled with a writer, a Colombian who was very close to Gabriel Garcia Marquez. What was good about him was that he knew Russian too. So, we are somewhere in Moldavia and he is looking at the Moldavian translation of *'A Hundred Years of Solitude'* and sees that they have censored the book very badly. What had happened was that there was a moment of epiphany, of illumination, of revelation where someone who comes from another culture, another language, but who has an insight into the other language, whether an adopted or a language a person feels comfortable in using and was able to ascertain that something wrong was happening.

I think it is to what extent you are able to, I always put it this way: to what extent you are able to reflect love using a language - and if you are not, then you shouldn't be using it. It is sometimes artificial when people say, I will use Zulu or Xhosa or whatever just because they feel there is a certain pressure. Then it comes out very artificial. I know this from my own engagement all over this country. There are things, of course, that I can write only in Zulu, which can never be written in English, and there are things that I can write only in English, that can never be written in Zulu, or that can never be expressed with as much emotional intensity in either language. You've got to recognise that.

People then cite the example used when Ngugi wa Thiong'o said that he is no longer going to be writing in English and the issue I have with that is that in this quest of writing, if you write, you also write to be read. You are not writing for a specific thing to be put in a vault in the privacy of your bedroom. You write so that people can have access to this and unfortunately given the circumstance of languages in this country, and elsewhere, unless that work in Zulu has been translated it will be read by a very small minority in this country. Ngugi can write in Kikuyu but he knows he is Ngugi and his work will automatically be translated by somebody into English.

Ulrike Ernst: *Closely connected to the question of language is that of tradition. Already with the appearance of the collection 'Black Mamba Rising', a discussion emerged about the correct picture of history and the appropriate use of African tradition in literature. How would you assess the ways in which African tradition is represented in the South African arts?*

Mandla Langa: I think that we have to go back again to what sustained us as young people when we grew up here. The poetry of Dhlomo, the poetry of Mxai, the evocations and the literature and the short stories and the novels of Nyembezi and so and so forth. We look at the stories of AC Jordan, Pallo Jordan's father, and all the praise songs of all the royalty, be it Xhosa, Zulu, Tswana, whatever. All that carried in it something that can only die when a person goes to the grave, in that I can remember all the things that I learnt, that I read, that were imparted to me as a young person from when I was small up till today, which speak of the tradition, speak of the grandeur, speak of the incredible dignity of people, sometimes even the worst travails.

I would think that there are people, who regard themselves as traditionalists or purists. I think all power to them, really. I do believe that tradition and creativity will only survive for as long as they give value to the lives of the people. Tradition and creativity that reduces the possibility for people to celebrate themselves, will inevitably come to a lot of problems. I will give you an example. Right now, the activists in Africa, and of course the activists world-wide, are beginning to question, and the noise and the clamour is becoming deafening, to question the issue of genital mutilation of women. That is a cultural construction, but to what extent is it standing in the way to make women full human beings and citizens? Other religions, for instance, place women into a secondary role. To what extent are they not, those religions, finding constant barrage of protest and resistance, not from somebody outside but from within, within themselves. To me this seems to suggest a possibility for those religions and those cultural practices of either adapting to the reality, or seriously being undermined. Once they become undermined, they become repudiated, and once they become repudiated, inevitably they are on the way to not surviving, to being destroyed.

We need to be very careful about how we deal with the issue of tradition. There are things of course that will sustain us: the language will sustain us, the storytelling possibilities that go all the way to all those thousands of years in the past. But once we make a fetish of all that then we are getting into a hell of a problematic situation.

Ulrike Ernst: *In connection with these considerations, I would like to ask you a final question. You were following the hearing of the Human Rights Commission regarding racism in the media in your capacity as the chairperson of the Independent Broadcasting Authority. How is the question of racism handled in your opinion? What bearing would it have on writing in the future?*

Mandla Langa: I think racism is a sickness, and I think that inevitably people are always trying to find ways, antidotes, to that sickness. Sometimes, as in this country, that sickness reached epidemic proportions. To a certain extent, writing and reflecting perhaps on some of these issues will hold the key for people to understand why certain things are not just anti-human but they are also ridiculous and they also reduce the one who is a racist and take them away from the royal fellowship of humanity.

It is only when people start to understand, I mean, James Baldwin has got this thing of saying that if you don't know my name, then you certainly don't know your own; if you reduce my humanity, that process of reducing another's humanity is actually eroding your own humanity. If I go out and I beat up somebody, I beat up a woman, who is weaker, in doing that I might be doing physical harm to her, but at the end of the day, what kind of spiritual wilderness am I in really to do a thing like that?

The writer then, in society, in dealing with issues like this, without being again propagandistic or polemical, can start to shape the way forward, to lay down the agenda and help in getting people to understand the most important thing, and that is their value as human beings. It is only when you understand how valuable you are or your humanity is that you regard as sacred another person's humanity. The biggest irony, is that these years there have been a whole series of discoveries at the Sterkfontein caves of what can be said to be the origin of humankind. It is ironic that this is being discovered in South Africa - a country that was at some stage for the whole world a symbol of the worst aspect of humankind. Perhaps this is one way or this is one aspect where we can start to have a lot of faith that these are steps that break the cycle or that fulfil the cycle, that it is also here in South Africa where there once was the most unbelievable racism, which was made sacred and made sacrosanct in the statute books, and that it is one country that is also going to be very crucial and contribute a lot towards the eradication of racism here and world-wide. I believe so.

References

[1] **Langa, Mandla. 1987.** Tenderness of Blood. Zimbabwe.

[2] **Langa, Mandla. 1989.** A Rainbow on a Paper Sky. London.

[3] **Langa, Mandla. 1996.** The Naked Song and Other Stories. Cape Town & Johannesburg.

[4] **Langa, Mandla. 2000.** The Memory of Stones. Cape Town & Johannesburg.

[5] **Langa, Mandla. 1996.** "The Resurrection of the River Artist". In: **Langa, Mandla. 1996.** The Naked Song and Other Stories. Cape Town & Johannesburg: 115-147.

[6] **Langa, Mandla. 1996.** "The Naked Song". In: **Langa, Mandla. 1996.** The Naked Song and Other Stories. Cape Town & Johannesburg: 67-91.

[7] **Langa, Mandla. 1996.** "The Naked Song". In: **Langa, Mandla. 1996.** The Naked Song and Other Stories. Cape Town & Johannesburg: 90.

Stephen Gray

Stephen Gray interviewed by Ulrike Ernst
on 28 March 2000 in Johannesburg

"History is Invented the Morning After"

Ulrike Ernst: *Already before the end of the apartheid era, Njabulo Ndebele spoke out against the limitations of so-called 'protest literature'. When Albie Sachs (1989/90) criticised the idea of 'culture as a weapon', a huge controversial debate as recorded in 'Spring is Rebellious' broke out.[1] Professor Stephen Gray, you are a leading literary scholar, critic and writer - how do you see the development and the importance of literature in South African society after the end of apartheid?*

Stephen Gray: I personally welcomed the Albie Sachs debate. It became a huge media event and discussion point, and it penetrated into circles where people who had not said anything for their entire lives began to speak for the first time. It was an historical watershed for people who, if they were on the left called themselves 'cultural workers', or if they were on the right, called themselves 'traditional artists'. In a way it wasn't just a debate about the issues that Albie Sachs mentioned; it was a debate about the fact that Albie Sachs might become part of the next government and be our cultural organiser. It was taking positions in order to ensure a future that was as little changed as possible by most of the conservative people; on the other hand it was a rallying call and a proclamation of what was to come for the future leaders. But even as I talk, I realise that is too simple. There had been many smaller debates like that before, going back at least to conferences in the early 70s where, in my world, the world of English departments, this kind of cultural politics had been active and not just in a journalistic way; in a deeply confrontational and merciless way. Sachs just brought it to a head. His timing was perfect. What people seemed to forget was that Sachs himself was making a critique of facile and unconvincing struggle literature; if one goes back and looks at his paper now, you almost wonder why it created such a storm of reactions and responses. As you see, it spawned two whole books of responses, but there were many more in the press at the time.

Now you want to ask me do I think that Sachs was important? I personally think it was because we could see that, amongst the future leaders would be intellectuals who were apparently prepared to be critical. Just in one stroke, it meant for people inside South Africa that the ANC was going to be a matter of intelligent government in which discourse would be about living issues of cultural policy.

Ulrike Ernst: *How do you see literature and its stand in South African society developing?*

Stephen Gray: I suppose all of us who were trembling on the edge with anticipation, before the election, dreamed that at last the terrible conditions under which we all worked would be relieved. And it was a dream that there would be an African Renaissance, or that any other type of renaissance one had treasured would come true overnight; which of course it didn't and hasn't. Now, six years later, one sort of fights a kind of post-electoral 'tristesse' in a way, a sort of sadness about how the arts haven't developed. The arts used to be very polarised in South Africa: There was the exiled community that had lived in exile for twenty, thirty, forty years sometimes and created an alternative South African culture, which was so complete that it had the dynamics and the communications of a discrete cultural system of its own, living in a Diaspora across the world. Then you had within South Africa very divided pro-liberation arts, which everybody became towards the end, except maybe one or two die-hard unregenerates. Up to 1994, I think everybody was in favour of getting rid of the old order as quickly as possible. But talking about the disappointment, one thought that there would just be a national outbreak of celebration in the arts. In fact, there has been silence.

Ulrike Ernst: *Maybe we can structure this a bit. What is your opinion of the cultural-political discourse and the cultural policy of the ANC after its unbanning and its accession to power?*

Stephen Gray: You mean infrastructural aspects, like for the first time having a minister who is responsible for culture?

Ulrike Ernst: *... even if you talk about the time after 1990 until 1994 when the ANC with its cultural politics came back to South Africa.*

Stephen Gray: Well, for the first time it looked as though the arts were not working against the government. For once. That we would have a government that would sponsor the arts and that we would all be playing on the same team, to use those silly American expressions. It would be the same ball game for everybody. With relief, one greeted the end of things like the censorship system. Like the discrimination that was in place for decades *vis-à-vis* languages, you know: that Afrikaans was prioritised, that English was put in the second position, and so on. One just looked forward to more free space in which to work.

Ulrike Ernst: *Do you remember how it was for instance when the National Arts Coalition was formed because some artists said that they wanted or needed independence from the ANC?*

Stephen Gray: No, I was never a participant in that. I don't know the details of that. Do you want to get *my* position? My position is that I am an independent scholar and I am independent of everything. I speak from my own freelance non-organisational base, and that is the only power I have, and that is my integrity. So I was never a member of any organisation pro or anti the ANC, or of the previous government, and I never will be. I wasn't even a member of the PEN, which started as a rebel group in Johannesburg. Because I am a non-joiner.

Ulrike Ernst: *Can you elaborate your position - you stated your point, but why do you act like this?*

Stephen Gray: Well, because I think that the arts are an independent cultural institution that should not allow itself to be co-opted by a political institution. We experienced that coercion in the past to such a serious degree that the arts couldn't have any integrity, so anyone advocating that that should happen again would in my view compromise the arts once again.

Ulrike Ernst: *However, in the changes of the literary scene of the country, cultural and literary organisations are involved. In your short story "Business as Unusual" in 'Human Interest' you have ironically acknowledged "[t]he depleted but oh-so-resilient Congress of South African Writers".[2] So, how do you see the importance of the development of such organisations like COSAW, PEN, or the National Arts Coalition in the new South Africa, even though you are not a member?*

Stephen Gray: I was not a member of COSAW, but I did have a big involvement with COSAW. And COSAW has died because of the non-renewal of donor funds. But it has also died because of what I feel is corrupt management.

Ulrike Ernst: *Could you give an example?*

Stephen Gray: Well, yes. Why isn't it flourishing today? You can't even get an answer on the phone. What happened to all the money? Something went wrong there because it is not being correctly audited, and it is now working against writers and against their interests. Because there is a place for what COSAW stood for and it is not functioning properly.

I am not a member of COSAW. But you didn't become a member of COSAW. You just were, if you were a South African writer, you were automatically under the COSAW umbrella.

Ulrike Ernst: *And how do you see the story of PEN in South Africa?*

Stephen Gray: That was a very interesting debate. But that was mid-'70s to early '80s. Do you want me to talk about that too?

Ulrike Ernst: *If it is important for the understanding of COSAW.*

Stephen Gray: No, because they are not really comparable. But what was interesting about the PEN debate was that there was a South African, pretty well ineffective, all-white PEN which functioned in the Cape, following the old international PEN organisation and its rules, but in a very lax way. PEN in Cape Town would occasionally make a stand for a writer in prison, but only one stand for one writer, not a continuing stand for all writers. It was very exclusive and elitist, but that is what PEN is anyway, in the world at large.

Then this rival PEN started in Jo'burg, where all the normal entry qualifications for PEN, which knocked out most developing or younger writers, or beginner writers let's say, were waived. To be a member of PEN, previously you had to have one book published by an acknowledged publisher. But for a beginner with one short story half written there was no representation, so this PEN in Johannesburg moved into that space to try and create a writers' group that could stand up for writers' rights and have an educational component too, hence organised workshops and so on. Which I am very much in favour of, obviously. But it eventually crumbled because it was not run competently. It elicited funds because of this rather glamorous policy, but it was totally impractical.

What it did was in fact sink many young careers that were trying to develop. COSAW has done that as well. It has sunk the writers that it represented. So, if you look at it from the point of view of the flourishing of our cultural life, both organisations have been profoundly counter-productive. Even destructive. So I welcomed their disappearance, and I'm afraid we all have to remain in an atomised, individual state, unrepresented.

Ulrike Ernst: *Now I would like to move to a more theoretical level. In your essay "An Author's Agenda: Revisioning Past and Present for a Future South Africa" you are searching for the role of the writer and the form and content of a post-protest literature.*[3] *To your own question, what is a writer's task? What are the politics of putting pen to paper? May I add the question as to the intellectual's tasks in a society in transformation? What happens in the process of the establishment of a democracy and thereafter?*

Stephen Gray: Well, there was a date on that opinion. It was meant to be a position paper for a panel discussion, where there were due to be, I think, four or five of us. We were asked to represent different viewpoints. Serote was to come and give the opening, which he never did, but his speech was eventually published alongside.

I was trying to define in more detail some superficial attitudes to literary politics because I felt at the time the term was used in an unsubtle fashion. My theme was that my main thinking occurs in my own poetry. At about that time I was deciding that everything was political and that the spectrum of personal through to public was something that I wanted to interrogate for myself. I don't want to use the word interrogate, I hate that. That I wanted to examine for myself. That is why I asked the question about the relation between the writer, the intellectual and the politician.

Ulrike Ernst: *Could you elaborate a little bit on this question of when does a writer become an intellectual?*

Stephen Gray: It is not common to talk of intellectuals in the South African tradition that we have inherited from the British colonial way. Firstly, the British hated intellectuals and did everything they could to starve them, beat them, kill them, torture them, you know, turn them into dust and blow them into the wind. Britain has always had, especially in the colonies, a profound fear, a phobia of any intellectual activity at all, because that might become too probing of government procedures. That old Anglo-Saxon way of starve the poet and electrocute the intellectual is something we have inherited in South Africa. It has come through our churches, it has come through our literature, it has come through government speeches, it was General Smuts, it was Dr Verwoerd, and it was everybody up to the last minute of 1994.

But I was beginning to realise that the old sort of Russian Revolution concept of the intellectual, someone like Ari Sitas for example, who could be a spokesperson without being an artist necessarily, was a category that I would like to explore in my own life, as I struck out for my own personal independence. So I suppose I have become a freelance academic, but in Europe you would call me a public intellectual.

Now I saw that was a rather dangerous position, and I admired Albie Sachs for being one, if you want to connect it up with the Sachs debate.

Ulrike Ernst: *It struck me as very interesting how you, from your earlier novels onwards to 'Born of Man'[4] or in 'Drakenstein'[5], review older genres. I was intrigued to see how you are not uncritically using forms that conventionally carry ruling patriarchal, fascist, heterosexual or the like messages, as you say. Could you elaborate on the problem of representation in your writing? How do your texts work?*

Stephen Gray: I have had a publishing career stretching now for twenty-five years, so there have been different phases at different times. But in general, although at first I was doing it instinctively, I am now doing it more as a planned tactic. I realise that old genres should be revisited and renovated, and that there was no escaping them. But I am a post-modernist unavoidably, and that is what we do: we collage and reassemble. It is a technique hardly unique to me, by any means.

Why do I revisit old genres? Because I like to take readers down a familiar route but give them a different experience. I don't see any other way, as a tactician, to work. And I must tell you, to my own profound horror, a book like *'Born of Man'*, which I think is completely innovative, which revisits the epistolary novel tradition of the 18th century (it is where the English language novel started, but also in German: Goethe) and rewriting it with revised gender perspectives and a revised class view, I thought people would be devastated by it. But it has totally disappeared without trace, and the other novel which I wrote, which uses traditional form without any experiments, without any jokes, without any sort of reworking, *'Time of Our Darkness'*[6], which is an absolutely orthodox, realist, first-person novel became a best-seller. And I would like it to have been the other way around, because I thought *'Born of Man'* was more adventurous. And also more true to what I wished to do. But people seem to like the old forms. They understand the old forms, even though in *'Time of Our Darkness'* I was trying to subvert them. But one can't shrug off one's inheritance; one can only devise ways to use it against itself, in order to release fresh meanings and fresh thinking.

Ulrike Ernst: *In your non-fiction writing you draw upon Raymond Williams' model of cultural change being three-phased: residual, dominant and emergent.*[7] *In your fiction, you challenge the fixed categories of race, class and gender which determine human attitudes in South Africa. How do you think these categories need to be reworked?*

Stephen Gray: Gosh. Do I really do that? (Laughs) Do I really say all that? Hmm. It is not something that stays static, Ulrike, it is skirmishing with day-to-day issues and changing one's footwork at every moment in order to guard one's independence and stand up for the right to be creative. No matter what. So I regard myself as that old outsider figure still today. A lot of the old enemies that we've had haven't exactly disappeared, but are hardly one's major preoccupations any more. And a lot of new ones one still has to identify. I think people are a bit timid about identifying them now. I think a lot of people have been bought out to silence, I must say it is my feeling. But I do sit down and find a few things to write about. Because the freelance and outsider figure must remain outside. But we are talking about some things of the 70s and 80s in my career.

My new book, *'Gabriel's Exhibition'*[8], I think is very challenging for the late 90s. Most of it was written at the time of the '94 elections and just afterwards, and I think that those events leaned on me powerfully and released a lot in me too. Gave me new freedoms to try new things. Absolutely. One can only be excited and grateful.

Ulrike Ernst: *In "An Author's Agenda", you carefully distinguish yourself from Nadine Gordimer's "self-evident truths"[9] and Njabulo Ndebele's dialectic between politics and art as in his "Redefining Relevance".[10] Outside South Africa, the literature of this country is especially connected with its Nobel Prize winner Nadine Gordimer. Inside the country, her achievements as a writer and a political figure have been the subject of heated controversy. How do you see the role of her work, form and content, and her role as a public person including her non-literary statements in the time of transformation?*

Stephen Gray: She has had a long and very articulated career. I don't agree with her current endorsement of ANC politics, and I certainly don't agree with her endorsement of what their cultural policy has turned out to be. And I think that in a sense she has sold herself out. She should have stayed an independent writer. So I partly mistrust her writing now, because I think there is an element of serving masters other than herself.

In a way, she is also conducting debates that are not of great interest or force within South Africa, but of course terribly important overseas. She is more intellectually challenging than she is often taken to be.

Ulrike Ernst: *Would you advocate social realism?*

Stephen Gray: No, God help us, surely that is over. It is not a social realist period in literature at all. That idea that the relationship between language and its society is a one-to-one, unproblematic one surely we cannot maintain any longer. And that is where much dialogue about South African culture is so naïve, because its symbolic content is not evaluated. I ask you not to look at the European-type novel as typical of South African culture. What Gordimer does is something very eccentric on the fringes. What JM Coetzee does is almost not South African at all; it is an exercise conducted in the powerful intellectual forums of Europe and America.

What really happens in South Africa is in the Market Theatre. It is in contact with audiences. It is a kind of communicative mode, which is so subtle and intelligent that most critics don't even know how to assess it. But the public gets it every time. What happens in South African culture is poetry. And poetry is difficult to decode. One has to learn to be clever. And it is something not for foreigners. It is for our own audience and our own listeners. When I do a poetry reading, I am reading for my people and not for Europeans or Americans. Because I am working in a different area of South African life, where literacy itself is not common, and English is certainly not part of the general discourse.

We have to look a bit at the class structure of South African cultural life. Well, it is down there, at the grassroots. Ask Ari Sitas, see the kind of projects that they do. Our culture does not really happen in the pages of a book.

If you want me to give my most desperate cry of distress about what has happened post-1994, it is that the one moment when South African cultural life and its work and its teachers and its future students arrived at a situation where they now all could freely have access to literacy, at that very moment literacy was pulled out of reach by prices that are so exaggerated, that literature has become even more expensive than before. Who can buy a book any more? Even I, an ex-university professor, cannot afford to buy books. How can I now keep up with that literary culture which is diminishing and vanishing as we speak?

So, don't give me the novel as the measure of South African culture. And I don't think the novel is where you find the big debates.

Ulrike Ernst: *But which pieces would you like to mention? What is 'truly' South African?*

Stephen Gray: Look at theatre. It is that which has been our major art form. For many years. And when you go back to the Albie Sachs paper, it was theatre that he was criticising. Saying that some of it was crude and unwieldy and not well rehearsed, or had the right sentiments but wasn't skilful enough. Drama, drama is where South African life has really happened.

Ulrike Ernst: *Recently we had two very different pieces in the Market Theatre. One was 'Love, Crime and Johannesburg', and the other one was 'The Zulu'. What would you say about them?*

Stephen Gray: I was actually thinking of leading up to 1994, that is where I am sort of fixated at the moment (laughs) while you talk to me. Because you really want to know about the inference of the Albie Sachs debate. What about productions like '*Woza, Albert!*' when they first happened? It had a devastating impact. What about productions like '*Sizwe Banzi is Dead*' I think they are both masterpieces. And they both served to change the way South Africans thought about all kinds of issues. Mostly identity issues. Relationships between the individual and society. Plus implicitly they kept saying: small people can have a big voice.

That is the tradition out of which I come. They were also nicely collaborative works, you know, South Africans getting together to make a statement that they could all work in a democratic fashion and that their art could represent all

South Africans' cultural wishes. That is the South African cultural life I love, and which I have always felt at home in.

Ulrike Ernst: *And what do you make of the last two pieces?*

Stephen Gray: I was a little disappointed ... *'Love, Crime and Johannesburg'* by Malcolm Purkey [and Carol Steinberg] (1999) had its heart in the right place but wasn't strong enough. It was very good to see the issues aired, but they threw it all away, I thought. That is my personal opinion. Since I am now writing drama criticism for the Mail & Guardian newspaper, I will have to get sharper on those particular things, but I didn't want to review them. Because I didn't want to be too critical of old friends.

I did review *'The Zulu'*. I thought it was a wretched show. It was just about everything we don't want now. It was full of a kind of crude ethnic pride, it was not compassionate; it was flagrantly offensive in terms of human rights issues, and it praised killing and stupidity; and I loathed it. And I'm very distressed that it is running forever, because to me it is spreading poison. However, they do have the right to do that. And I have the right to say I don't like it!

Ulrike Ernst: *Why do you think it has such a huge audience?*

Stephen Gray: It is not so huge. It is not pulling in big crowds. It is just running forever because there is nothing else on. Because the theatre scene in general has died.

Ulrike Ernst: *I would like to conclude with a question related to the field in which you originally gained your reputation: you cleared the ground for further literary study with your 'Southern African Literature'.*[11] *Now, Michael Chapman published his 'Southern African Literatures'*[12] *at the time of the discussions of the colloquium of the Centre for the Study of South African Literatures and Languages. This comparative literary history raised controversial intellectual and emotional reactions regarding language issues, ethnicity and gender, representation, marginalisation and also the question of empowerment or disempowerment of different interest groups. How would you perceive issues of history, language and tradition in relation to contemporary South African literature?*

Stephen Gray: When I started doing the PhD study which became *'Southern African Literature: An Introduction'* - may I remind you: it was actually in 1969, so it's a third of a century ago - I was advised not to undertake it because there was said to be no interest in South African literature worthy of PhD standard. So you see what I have been working for in the interim. To say not only that the culture is worthy of study, but one has a duty to study it, in order for there to be an intellectual discourse at all.

But it goes a little bit back to that Raymond Williams model of the three phases of any culture. I, for many years, functioned on this simple slogan that 'you cannot understand your present until you understand your past'. That has recently become rather a commonplace in South African life. But a particular sub-interest of mine is the historical novel of Walter Scott, and also your German philosophers like Herder, and the life of Hölderlin, Goethe and so on, and this developing dialogue about the organisation of nationalism. I think unless one has a sense of the appropriate history, one won't have a sense of contemporary affairs.

But during apartheid, that was an intellectual crime. Remember the circumstances under which we lived. We were all encouraged to be forgetful, because if you were forgetful, you couldn't be in opposition. And forgetting meant forgetting everything. Forgetting human values, it meant forgetting everything except the most basic skeleton of a historical outline that was phoney and false, that was forced into South African children year after year after year. Where history didn't become ... wasn't history. It was just nationalist myth. Herder style, right? To say 'have a memory' was a radical act.

History became the most important discourse during the middle and late apartheid years, particularly through something like the History Workshop at Wits, where I think all the major ideas of the intellectual life were launched and exposed and pushed and propagandised. And ultimately perhaps that forum saved some integrity for our very stunted intellectual life. So history was a much more powerful cutting-edge discourse than literature ever was. Because the literary writers weren't using that mix of ideological weapons, except in theatre I think. So to have said 'remember' was to say, find a way to escape your diminished conditions.

Ulrike Ernst: *And what should one now remember about history, or how should tradition be represented in the arts?*

Stephen Gray: Well, that is the big debate of the moment, and I don't think it has settled down into many positions. Apart from obviously trying to redress old imbalances, which of course I am committed to and in favour of. I think history is invented the morning after by various skilful dialecticians, and it is interesting to see the new mythology which is developing, which I think has as little grasp on the realities of South African life today as it ever had before.

Ulrike Ernst: *Thank you very much.*

References

[1] de Kok, Ingrid/Press, Karen (eds.). 1990. Spring is Rebellious. Arguments about Cultural Freedom by Albie Sachs and Respondents. Cape Town.

[2] **Gray, Stephen. 1993.** Human Interest and other Pieces. Johannesburg: 91.

[3] Gray, Stephen. 1991. "An Author's Agenda. Revisioning Past and Present for a Future South Africa". In: Petersen, Kirsten Holst/Rutherford, Anna (Eds.). 1991. On Shifting Sands. New Art and Literature from South Africa. London et al: 23-31.

[4] **Gray, Stephen. 1989.** Born of Man. Johannesburg.

[5] **Gray, Stephen. 1994.** Drakenstein. A Novel. Johannesburg.

[6] **Gray, Stephen. 1988.** Time of Our Darkness. Johannesburg.

[7] Gray, Stephen. 1991. "An Author's Agenda. Revisioning Past and Present for a Future South Africa". In: **Petersen, Kirsten Holst/Rutherford, Anna (eds.). 1991.** On Shifting Sands. New Art and Literature from South Africa. London et al: 27.

[8] **Gray, Stephen. 1998.** Gabriel's Exhibition. Belville.

[9] Gray, Stephen. 1991. "An Author's Agenda. Revisioning Past and Present for a Future South Africa". In: **Petersen, Kirsten Holst/Rutherford, Anna (eds.). 1991.** On Shifting Sands. New Art and Literature from South Africa. London et al: 24.

[10] **Ndebele, Njabulo S. 1989.** "Redefining Relevance". In: Pretexts 1(1). Cape Town: 40-51.

[11] **Gray, Stephen. 1979.** Southern African Literature. An Introduction. Cape Town.

[12] **Chapman, Michael. 1996.** Southern African Literatures. London/New York.

Michael Chapman

Michael Chapman interviewed by Ulrike Ernst
on 5 April 2000 in Durban

"There is No Essential Africanness"

Ulrike Ernst: *Professor Michael Chapman, you are a leading literary scholar and critic, and you have always been involved in the discussion concerning the relationship between literature and politics. When you suggested in "The Liberated Zone: the Possibilities of Imaginative Expression in a State of Emergency" (1988) that given the political circumstances, "the more 'skilfully artistic' responses in the mid-1980s of, for example, Gordimer, Fugard and Coetzee, seem marginal to what is most crucial in our state of emergency", i.e. struggle literature,[1] Stephen Watson suggested that you should resign your professorship and fight actively in the struggle.[2] When Albie Sachs criticised the idea of 'culture as a weapon', a controversial debate ensued, in which you were involved.*

What happened to the debates about art and culture and to the cultural politics of the ANC after its legalisation in 1990?

Michael Chapman: The article to which you refer was written as a provocation. It was a deliberately rhetorical piece but posed an important question: what is the responsibility of art - or the artist - in conditions of gross inhumanity? The question was not new; Brecht asked it. The anti-poetry of the 1940s asked it: can the poetic imagination compete with the images of the death camp!

Today, I don't think that the ANC has a cultural policy. It has been, perhaps necessarily, caught up in the globalisation debate, and certainly if you're in the world of culture, you don't get a great deal from the government in the way of funding, and so on. But, why should writers or playwrights have imagined that the government would bail them out? (To me the collapse of the European film industry is because it never had to be very competitive and commercial.)

But let me return to the debate about art and politics. What provoked *"The Liberated Zone"* in the mid-1980s was my sense that many writers and critics were avoiding the referential difficulties of the State of Emergency by invoking - spuriously, I think - a case for imaginative transformation, an international postmodern style. In fact, I was not alone in questioning the relationship of political obtrusiveness and imaginative reply: André Brink asked at the time whether novelists had lost their way; whether the truth was being captured more compellingly in the stories of the emergency as reported in the alternative press (the

Weekly Mail, now *Mail and Guardian*, and *New Nation*, now defunct). Similarly, JM Coetzee in his *Jerusalem Prize Acceptance Speech* asked whether the imagination could deal with what at the time seemed a political overload.

Culture and politics are not divisible. So I don't agree that South Africa has achieved some sort of liberation and now artists can be artists once again. But that was the immediate, fairly predictable reaction of a large segment of the art world in this country after 1990. They embraced Albie Sachs's politically understandable but fatuous comment that again we could all be human beings. I know where he was coming from. He had to counter the demonisation of the ANC: that behind MK were actual human beings. That is correct but, unfortunately, his comments gave many writers and artists an excuse to try to consign the expression of the emergency to the dustbin of history. But if you trace the history of South African literature back to its beginning, you will see that it has always been a literature of the public event, a literature of necessity.

It is interesting ... I was commissioned in 1987, by Longman Publishing in London, to contribute to their Literature in English series on southern African literature. The title then was going to be *Southern African Literature in English*. Longman has this series of books, most of them of course British and American. But there is a section at the end called 'Other', in which at that time there was *Canadian Literature in English* and *Indian Literature in English*. The other 'Others' hadn't yet appeared. When I took on this topic, Southern African Literature in English, I realised that a past paradigm had collapsed. In fact, the corollary article to *"The Liberated Zone"* is *"Towards a Theory of Reconstruction"*. I had actually used the word before it became fashionable. When, at a conference, someone asked me whose theory this was, I said it was mine. Whose theory it was! I suppose every theory must emanate from a Frenchman at the Sorbonne, or otherwise it doesn't count.

But, it seemed to me then that it was necessary to develop the idea that the literature, the culture, of this country had and has always been driven by an overwhelming political imperative. The time had come to anticipate the future, not get bogged down in small settler-community disputes, which is how the literature tended to be understood. So you had an Afrikaans literature and an English South African literature, and a Zulu literature, and a Xhosa literature, and so on. I said to Longman that I couldn't write a book called *'Southern African Literature in English'*. You had to find a theory of translation and cultural transfer to open, to crack, the language barriers. But Longman wouldn't accept this at the time because it violated the terms of the series. So I was fortunate that history took over. I mean the unbannings of 1990; South Africa's return to the world as a single, multicultural society. Longman relented on the 'in English' requirement, and the book appeared as *Southern African Literatures*.

The book viewed the southern African region as sharing a confrontational history. It looked at a 'story' that crossed language divisions. For example, South African literature in English bears the marks of settlers having encountered the Xhosa on the so-called frontier. Similarly, Xhosa literature took the forms it did because of conflict with a British settler presence. Mandela's personality is an amalgamation of many strands: Xhosa tradition, British constitutionalism, Marxism, Christianity, Africanism, Gandhi-inspired passive resistance. Perhaps - if the ANC had a cultural policy - it would explore the question: is South Africa, Africa, or the West? It is probably, in 2000, both; it is probably neither. My point is that in a society like South Africa we've got to find new identities. We need to interrogate the past while charting a way forward. Retreating into language division, or irony or scepticism - a kind of postmodern splitting of any narrative - is inadequate to the challenges ahead. So - a long reply to your question.

Ulrike Ernst: *The political and economic aims in South Africa have been changing towards a neo-liberal market economy which also seems to influence cultural politics. What is your opinion of the cultural discourse and the cultural policy of the ANC after its accession to power with the first free elections in 1994 and thereafter?*

Michael Chapman: Well, it seems one part talks in new market terms. My field is English literature, but I am the Dean of Human Sciences, and there is no real encouragement for the humanities. There is an attempt to divert money towards science and technology in the mistaken belief, I think, that somehow science and technology can rescue our economy. Now, that is a bit short-sighted. The ANC and its various organs seem to have forgotten first of all that mathematics is so badly taught and so neglected that there is no quick fix for a new generation. But secondly, that science and technology cannot be removed from a cultural context. Decisions such as, do you mine on the North Coast or don't you? are not simply economic or technical or scientific decisions; they've got to do with people's livelihood: with communities destroyed or communities needing work. So these debates are complex.

I think that, unfortunately, debates about the interrelationship of human sciences and natural sciences have not reflected the complexity. We have a fairly technicist idea of the new world order against a kind of symbolic discourse about an African Renaissance. The comments that are coming out of both camps at the moment to me really do not have the level of complexity or insight that we need to move forward into a new kind of South Africa, one which has to find its locality at the same time as its role in the world.

Ulrike Ernst: *Which cultural and literary organisations have had an impact on the cultural discourse in the country after 1990, and how have they been affected by the broader economic, social and political transformation, for example* *the Congress of South African Writers or the National Arts Initiative which then became the National Arts Coalition?*

Michael Chapman: I don't think they have influence any more; in fact I'm not even certain they exist. I don't think that the Congress of South African Writers exists. If it does, it doesn't exist in any way that has a compelling voice. And the National Arts Coalition - again, if it exists, it exists in a few people's minds, but nowhere else. There are many 'arts and culture' organisations in this country, but I don't think there is any coherent movement, and why should there be? In most societies there is no coherent arts movement. Arts movements of the past were linked to political movements, and the political movements have splintered into the difficulties of now. I suppose it is a bit like Fanon's comment about moving from the phase of nationalism to the phase of economic imperatives.

Ulrike Ernst: *Now I would like to turn to literature and writers. In 1996, you published your comparative 'Southern African Literatures' in which you underline the dynamic relationship between literary and political history. How do you see the development and importance of literature and critic in South African society after apartheid?*

Michael Chapman: I completed the book in about 1993, and what I tried to do was to take a post-apartheid perspective. I think that the challenges remain. In fact, I wasn't concerned with what writers should write. I don't believe that writers have the sole genius. Philosophers, writers or critics – all can offer valuable insights. My view is that of a critic. The challenge is again of what consequence does the voice, the expression, the word, have in a social milieu. Whether writers choose to opt out or not is not really my main concern, it's theirs. My main concern, as a critic, is how I make sense of the expression. Criticism is a social activity. If it's not, I think it's a trivial pursuit. Watson's comment about my becoming an activist sets up a false dichotomy. Any critic should, in a sense, be active in the shaping of a social vision.

I am currently compiling an anthology of poetry. In 1981, I compiled an anthology, *'A Century of South African Poetry'*,[5] and I have nearly finished the manuscript of one called *'The New Century of South African Poetry'*. It is not an update of the previous book; it has had to be a completely new book. One of the new realisations is the way in which poetry, or let's say any culture, involves the whole society. The earlier anthology focused on poetry written in English; the current anthology makes full use of translated poems. It also seeks an oral past, even if that is symbolic. It seeks something that we can regard - in the expression of the San or Bushmen - as a common heritage.

I don't think we are ready to move into a world of high art which says, here is a book of the best poems that have been written. I actually did an exercise. I tried that, and to me it robbed our poetry of all sorts of things. So I've deliberately put in, tried to put in, lyrics from songs of oral expression - the expression at a Xhosa beer drink, for example. That is part of our poetry. We are not a society of high art. We are an uneven society: the expression emerges from many aspects of life. This needs to be respected by people who believe they occupy a world of literary culture.

Ulrike Ernst: *In non-democratic political systems terms like 'resistance culture' and 'protest literature' have been coined. In the cultural struggle of South Africa, the notions of 'worker culture' and 'popular culture' emerged. What happened to these cultural ideas, notions or species? How would you theoretically discuss the political importance of literature in a democracy?*

Michael Chapman: Well, I don't think we have a democracy in the Western sense. We are not a fully functioning society. We are a society of huge disparities. A great many people are completely marginalized, illiterate. One of the interesting things about a society like ours - one might say the same about Brazil and many other parts of the world - is that the pre-modern, modern and the postmodern actually co-exist. Hence, the culture of these different conditions also co-exist. This is a challenge for the critic because you've got to understand that there is no essential Africanness. We are talking about different forms of pre-modern and modern understandings. So folk expression is alive today alongside the postmodernism of JM Coetzee.

There will still be concepts today like 'workers' culture', but they don't have the totality that they did in the '80s because the society has become more complicated. 'Workers' culture', if it ever existed, was probably a sociological invention of our university sociology departments. If anything is in disarray in this country today it is sociology. I don't think it knows where it's going. Anthropology is close behind it.

What remain are expressive forms that were rooted in popular tradition, if I may use the term in its sense of actual people's lives rather than as a Marxist category. People still have to leave rural areas to go to the city. They still play Zulu guitar music about the laments of migrants who move from one place to another. Those voices are still part of modern South Africa.

Ulrike Ernst: *How do you see the relationship between critical theory and literary practice?*

Michael Chapman: I think that in a society like ours, theory should not predate practice. I think the practice should allow you to look at things and then try to make sense of them at more abstract levels. I don't think the other way round is helpful; it will lead us back into another round of neo-colonialism, which is in fact fairly widespread among intellectuals. They have simply replaced Leavis with Foucault or with Derrida. But unless you can make use of these insights in your own particular contexts, you are not going to get very far.

Ulrike Ernst: *'Southern African Literatures' raised controversial intellectual and emotional reactions regarding language issues, ethnicity and gender, representation, marginalisation and the question of empowerment or disempowerment of different interest groups.*[6] *But already with 'Black Mamba Rising'*[7]*, a huge discussion emerged about the correct picture of history and the appropriate use of African tradition in literature.*

Bearing these discussions in mind, how would you perceive issues of history, language and tradition in relation to contemporary South African literature?

Michael Chapman: The controversies about the book here are partly about its displacing Afrikanerdom as the central narrative.... that was partly the intention. But the other debates about how I dared write about Afrikaans literature or Zulu literature, I think, are a sad reflection of how much of the apartheid mentality many had absorbed. The fact that you can cross language barriers destroys the romantic notion that somehow language is the essence of one's soul. I think that is a dangerous thing for us to believe in a country like ours. I would not want African tradition to freeze into some monolithic thing which, as I say, I don't think ever existed. In any case, we know very little about so-called African tradition before the colonial period.

Even our knowledge of San or Khoi-Khoi traditions comes to us via mid-19th century people's memories. These San were by then already colonial subjects who were recorded by colonial linguists and missionaries. While it is important to look back, we must always understand that we are looking back at a historical construct, not at anything that comes from the source. I think that all of our traditions here should be historicized because otherwise there is the danger of essentialist thinking.

African critics such as H.I.E. Dhlomo never said that there was a static tradition. Dhlomo always said that tradition lives - a good phrase to keep in mind. Tradition lives. Our praise poems are not frozen in Shaka's time, but continued to be adapted to the demands, say, of the trade union movement. Praises occurred when Mandela was released and will continue to evolve in the culture.

I think it is important to keep in mind that we are an evolving culture that is influenced by many sources. Not only Africa and the West, but in Durban we have a large South African Indian population, and today we have the Internet to add to our understanding of where we are and what we are.

Ulrike Ernst: *At the turn of the millennium, the notion of the African Renaissance has at times been used in misleading ways. How do you understand its concept?*

Michael Chapman: It can mean anything you want it to mean, I suppose, but I think there is obviously a need for Africa to find itself as an active and an equal partner in a conversation with the world, rather than being viewed as a basket case, which is mostly how the West views it. At that symbolic level it can focus the mind, as long as you realise it is a symbolic thing, not a reality. The reality would be to get down to economics, forms of expression, the complexity of living in the global world today, the need to understand your locality, etc.

Remember the European Renaissance was not only about great art works, but about power struggles and Machiavellian intrigue. We have it here. We have the Congo, we have Zimbabwe, and we presumably have ourselves. So one shouldn't see the African Renaissance as more than a necessary way of trying to focus our minds on the challenges of our locality in the 21st century.

Ulrike Ernst: *A democratic society needs a defined official representational system, but apart from that it also needs the critical voice of the independent intellectual who independently speaks his or her mind. What role and task would you ascribe to writers and critics as intellectuals in a developing democracy? How do you see yourself in this context?*

Michael Chapman: I think in the past we had an oppositional voice because it was quite clear as to what you were opposing. Today it is difficult to define what it is that you are criticising. A danger, though, is silence. Many intellectuals who were activists in the struggle have become silent. They feel they can't criticise the new government for its mistakes. Others, who are basically conservative at heart, have mounted all sorts of criticisms. Like the Democratic Party or Alliance at the moment. It has no viable alternative vision, so all it can do is hammer away at the crime rate. I think it is difficult to be a creative critic today because it might mean that you've got to express opinions that could be hostile to the ANC. But I would think that criticism has to reflect the complexity of the transition. The transition is something that is ongoing. It throws up its own kinds of bogeys, but it has opened up possibilities. To strike a balance between a positive vision and sniping is not easy. But I think the movement towards a more humane society, one of greater openness where people have a chance to fulfil their lives, is an ideal worth dedication. This should temper one's negative response without blunting critical accuracy.

Ulrike Ernst: *Outside of South Africa, the literature of this country is largely connected with the name of Nobel Prize winner Nadine Gordimer. Inside the country, her achievements as a writer and a political figure has been the subject* of heated controversy. In fact, in "The Liberated Zone" you "wonder whether Gordimer should not for the time being have remained silent" because the then recent work struck you as "self-indulgent".[8] How do you explain this difference in her reception? How do you see her work today?

Michael Chapman: Nadine Gordimer is enormously important. She was the conscience in the world of literature and culture against apartheid. But like many writers, like many of us, she did perhaps lose her way in the '80s. I think particularly of her novel *A Sport of Nature*. I don't think it quite knew what it was trying to achieve. Deconstruction has taught us to make meaning out of anything. But Gordimer's novel that was written towards the end of apartheid, *None to Accompany Me*, is a more powerful story, but powerful in a very uncomfortable way. The character Vera Stark, I think, has strong autobiographical sympathies with Gordimer herself. And to some extent Vera Stark more or less says, look, leave me alone. I've done my bit, just leave me alone; let me be what I am, which is not a particularly nice person.

The interesting thing is that when you revisit Gordimer's novels such tensions were always evident. There has always been a tension in her work, between what it is to be a political witness and what it is to be a person, a writer, who somehow transcends the political milieu. What we should do is return to many of our writers and re-read them in the light of South Africa today. Gordimer's big theme might be the difficulty of having to be a political writer when she wanted to be a writer about human beings.

Ulrike Ernst: *In your essay "South Africa in the Global Neighbourhood", you elaborate on how "since the unbannings of 1990 - the identity of both white and black people has been assaulted by an array of new local and global discourses, programmes, modes of thought, accents and subjectivities. [Hence] [w]hereas pre-global times were characterized by oppositions, global times are about proliferations; instead of unitary systems we have diverse modalities and rapid mobilities." On the other hand you discuss how "the empire not only writes back to the metropole, but displaces [its] ... very categories".[9]*

How do you think categories like race, class and gender need to be reworked?

Michael Chapman: I think that they need perhaps to be seen in the multifaceted ways in which they operate. We can't use the word 'race', for example, outside the set of contexts that informs its meanings. Similarly, gender and class. When conditions change we shouldn't believe that we no longer need the categories, because we are still a society where race will dictate certain actions, as will class or gender. But we need to avoid the binary idea that there is simply a white group and a black group. In fact, such dichotomies collapsed soon after the negotiations began. Some of the worst violence characterised IFP - ANC rivalries. These rivalries were about tradition and modernity, scarce resources, patronage, people jockeying for political power, and the use of symbols - Shaka for example. We need to be circumspect about terms: they must be analysed with greater nuance.

Ulrike Ernst: *What bearing does the globalisation have on methods of literary or cultural analysis?*

Michael Chapman: A country like this is always vulnerable to the latest import from London, New York, or Paris. We remain a kind of colony in the world order. Universities have been notorious in imitating Oxbridge. When many intellectuals hear terms like the African Renaissance, they wish to flee to Harvard. But the West has never been our saviour, even though most of us are westernised in different and valuable ways .

We have to keep abreast of the globalisation debates, otherwise we are in danger of becoming parochial and imagining that we exist outside of the world. But in keeping abreast of debates, we need to apply the issues to our particular context. Take current debates on identities, for example. In Western societies that believe they are homogeneous it might be 'risk-taking' to champion split identities, hybridity, etc. In South Africa, apartheid sought to divide people. A need for greater homogeneity in a very heterogeneous society might not, therefore, be a hankering after a pre-postmodern condition, but a yearning to overcome past tactics of divide and rule. My point is: we need to analyse 'import theory', accept what is appropriate, but offer also our own return. In a conversation between the margins - us - and the West, what do we offer that might be illuminating? Most of Europe now lives in various pockets of First World and Third World - migrant workers, etc. I doubt that Europe wants to hear anything that we might want to say, but perhaps it could learn something.

Ulrike Ernst: *Where do you think South African literature is turning to?*

Michael Chapman: At the moment, I don't know. I think it is one of these periods of bits and pieces. I'm not certain what its role could be in a new society, one that has moved from a closed Calvinist one to one where anything goes. Many young people, white and black, for example, are not particularly interested in literature. They have been brought up on a diet of television and computer games, and numbers for literature courses at universities are seriously diminished. The new generation seeks a world that will give them jobs; they enrol for accountancy, law and engineering. White, black, Indian, they have similar ambitions. A secure, well-paid career.

It is not as though literature study has not evolved with the times. Since the mid-1980s literature at South African universities has mingled popular culture, magazines, and the 'great works'. But the drift away by students has continued. We have begun a media and communication degree. This has proved attractive to students. I think they all believe that they are going to end up as presenters on TV, or journalists in exotic parts of the world, I don't know. But media and communication, internet studies - these are the attractions in the humanities.

Ulrike Ernst: *What are the most interesting books for you at the moment?*

Michael Chapman: I have been trying desperately to complete the poetry anthology that I mentioned earlier on. I've had to re-read South African poetry, including poetry of the last ten years, poetry which I tended to neglect because I was trying to finish the book *'Southern African Literatures'*. Poetry is an academic interest which I would like to bring alive to a wider audience.

Other than that, I've read Coetzee's *'Disgrace'*. I found it a compelling book, but one that raises difficult questions as to how an aesthetic experience links to a set of moral values. His vision - as I have suggested - is basically conservative; it has difficulty in dealing with the 'new' South Africa. It is a problem that interests me as a critic. Another book I read recently was not a South African book, but a German book by Bernhard Schlink, *'The Reader'*, written forty years after the Holocaust. It made me think what a post-apartheid novel could be once we have attained sufficient distance from our recent past.

I am suggesting, I suppose, that an important aspect of our literary culture will be comparative studies. Not comparative in the sense of comparing the themes of two books, but in understanding that our traditions have been influenced by many other traditions: from England, Holland, crucially from Africa. Its magical realism goes back to folk tales, for example. We need to understand literature in that larger, comparative sense. When literary circles speak of magical realism they tend to think of modern South American novelists. As in South America, so in South Africa, or Africa, magical realism takes us back to oral tradition, to folktale. Our challenge is comparison in this larger perspective. I return to my, perhaps, rhetorical question: is South Africa, Africa, or the West?

References

[1] **Chapman, Michael. 1992 [1988].** "Writing in a State of Emergency". In: **Chapman, Michael/Gardner, Colin/Mphahlele, Es'kia (eds.). 1992.** Perspectives on South African English Literature. Johannesburg: 525.

[2] **Watson, Stephen. 1989.** "Letter". In: Southern African Review of Books. 4-5: 22-23.

[3] **Chapman, Michael. 1989.** "The Critic in a State of Emergency. Towards a Theory of Reconstruction". In: Theoria (74).

[4] **Chapman, Michael. 1988.** "The Liberated Zone. The Possibilities of Imaginative Expression in a State of Emergency", in: **Chapman, Michael/Gardener, Colin/Mphahlele, Es'kia (eds.). 1992.** Perspectives on South African English Literature. Johannesburg: 514-542.

[5] See also **Chapman, Michael (ed.). 1982.** Soweto Poetry. Johannesburg.

[6] **van Vuren, Helize. 1997.** Review Article. JLS/TLW. 6-7 1997: 190-209.

[7] **Sitas, Ari (ed.) 1986.** Black Mamba Rising. South African Worker Poets in Struggle. Alfred Qabula, Mi S'Dumo Hlatshwayo, Nise Malange. Durban.

[8] **Chapman, Michael. 1988.** "The Liberated Zone. The Possibilities of Imaginative Expression in a State of Emergency". In: **Chapman, Michael/Gardener, Colin/Mphahlele, Es'kia (eds.). 1992.** Perspectives on South African English Literature. Johannesburg: 514-542.

[9] **Chapman, Michael. 1997.** "South Africa in the Global Neighbourhood". In: Critical Arts. 11 (1-2): 17-27.

Ari Sitas

**Ari Sitas interviewed by Ulrike Ernst
on 4 April 2000 in Durban**

"Art Should Nation Build and the Idea Cracked"

Ulrike Ernst: *Even before the end of the apartheid era, Njabulo Ndebele spoke out against the limitations of so-called protest literature. When Albie Sachs criticised the idea of 'culture as a weapon' a huge controversial debate emerged in which you were involved as well. What happened to the cultural politics of the ANC after its legalisation between 1990 and 1994? How did the ANC in its early transformation from an anti-apartheid to a post-apartheid movement manage the narrow path between control and facilitation in terms of cultural policy management?*

Ari Sitas: I think a lot of the cultural ideas that were discussed in the 1980s primarily have been turned into policy documents, have been turned into forms of legislation that were supposed to address inequality. But at the same time given the fiscal policy of the state, very few resources had been put in those directions and therefore a lot of the cultural initiative could not be funded or sustained.

More important for me is the issue of what happened to creative people in this transition, and how do they manage to continue being creative in this context. If you look at specifically, let us think of four movements: the writers' movement, COSAW, the Labour Movement's cultural groups, then the authors or producers who were in their own right sympathisers or were doing so-called progressive work and fourthly the broader kind of the production of art and culture amongst ordinary communities, not politically linked.

The first group, writers. Many of the writers who were leading writers became bureaucrats. They became administrators. They found a lot of opportunities in this transition and at the same time the writing went for a walk. It is not as expressive as it used to be. It is not as sharp or critical as it used to be, and a lot of them have been boring about equity and distribution of resources and issues like that with a lot of energy coming out.

Secondly, in the trade union and the cultural movements, what happened is that even before the transition a lot of the activity was crushed with the violence in KwaZulu-Natal. More and more people were killed or injured, percentage-wise, who were leading people in cultural organisations than let's say shop stewards in this province. Because of the nature of the conflict and the war in the townships and the peri-urban areas, any public gathering was being attacked, so a lot of that activity and those spaces died even before the transition. The few people who managed to continue found that they had no access now to any of the new opportunities that were now coming through. For example, TV opened up its channels, but unless you had resources to produce plays, you don't get on TV. Local performances had become showcases so you became a window dressing for a lot of activity. Not saying that creativity has died, there are a lot of creative people out there, but instead of a release of energies, there was a retraction of them. So if you take individual authors and performers, they were particularly successful in being noticed internationally; during the anti-apartheid struggle any voice from South Africa was heard internationally. Some of them have made wonderful careers out of that. But at the same time, although a lot of individual authors are continuing, many of the more collective ensembles are finding it very difficult to survive at the moment, given the resources. So, theatre is dying. I am sure that you have noticed it in Johannesburg. It is a serious crisis there.

Finally, in terms of the broader kind of creativity at the grassroots and in the countryside or the urban areas now there is funding, provided you are in tourism. So a lot of resources exist, provided you link your activity to tourism and to become I suppose here in this province a 'postcard Zulu' or dance for tourists in order to get your bread and butter. A lot of the creativity has been packaged into being nice to people who pay. So we are experiencing a lot of difficulties. The other thing that happened is that the opening up of apartheid and the importance of TV, radio and so on what we had is the packaging of a lot of identity stuff that comes from the United States primarily, from the African American community, that is much cheaper than any local production. And that is invading everything, which has marginalized a lot of people. The only counter move at the moment in this province are initiatives for instance from the African Renaissance Trust, which gives a voice to indigenous kind of self-expression and its platforms are filled with a lot talent, a lot of energy. Wonderful new dance groups are emerging, and singing groups and music groups.

Less so literature. Now some of the new voices, especially in poetry, are beginning to emerge that have a critical edge to them. There are people like Lesego Rampholokeng who is, well, Lesego is Lesego. He is going to speak out his mind no matter what, no matter who and in whatever context. And as you can see, the rap influence is quite dominant there. There are younger people in Johannesburg and in Durban and I am sure in Cape Town who are beginning to be critical of what they are seeing around them. Some have got a very fascinating usage of English, which has been broken through all kinds of patois that they are mixing. They are very critical of the status claims of the new middle class. Very critical of the promise of delivery and nothing happens. Very critical of the people's kind of new mental models and how they carry out their lives. So there is some discord in poetry.

If you take theatre, what has emerged is the grand musical, people like Mbongeni Ngema has turned what was a very grassroots, urban black working class experience that defined his earlier plays up to *'Sarafina'*. The dance manoeuvres that he engineered. Now it is turning into a musical, and it is popular and lots of people go and see it, but it is a musical. You say, ja, you've seen an interesting show, but it is not challenging in any way. But you do get some groups that are beginning to deal with very serious issues. So, I don't know.

Going back to the debate that Albie Sachs started, that was very useful. It generated a lot of self-criticism. I think there is a naïveté there, as if people can abstract themselves from what they are in order to do something else, which somebody sees as valid. I think artists, writers, for good or bad had to deal with what they were facing at that moment, and a lot of it was crass, a lot of it was wonderful. You have to understand the context through which that creativity was coming forward. We have had some wonderful examples of creative work during the 1980s, and some appalling ones, so be it. I think the point was, how do we transform conditions for creativity to come out in the post-apartheid period. For that we haven't managed exactly. What exists is due to a lot of self-activity on the ground. Whether the KwaZulu-Natal Arts Council or the Durban Arts that have resources, how they distribute those will be quite crucial in terms of how sustainable all of this activity is. This is broadly speaking what I think happened in the last four years.

Ulrike Ernst: *And if you talk about the official discourse and the cultural policy of the ANC, do you see a change after the ANC's accession to power with the first free elections in 1994? From 1990 to 1994 and then if you set a marker there - do you see a difference afterwards?*

Ari Sitas: There is an obvious difference that the main discourse in the earlier days was art as mobilisation of consciousness and of expression, celebrating people's ability to resist and so on. After 1994, it is about nation-building. Art should nation build and bring people together in the rainbow nation, and the idea cracked. It wasn't enough. Most artists were very cynical about that ideas, black or white, the rainbow didn't work as an artistic form of expression. Then the idea of reconciliation and forgiveness were powerful in the Truth and Reconciliation Commission that created work on the side, but again that was not enough to mobilise creativity fully. Now there is the emphasis on the African Renaissance that has got some echo on the ground, but it also has its problems. All of them are ideas of nation-building and creating a new identity. I think that is the main shift.

On the practical level, it is basically the provision of funding for the arts and culture, which has been negotiated and given over to Inkatha at the moment. And that has its own little contradictions in its own right. I think the official ANC discourse at the moment is for arts and culture to help nation build. And unfortunately it can't.

Ulrike Ernst: *Which cultural and literary organisations have had an impact on the cultural discourse in the country after 1990, and how have they been affected by the broader economic, social and political transformation?*

Ari Sitas: The most active were for instance the Congress of South African Writers, and here in this province, the Natal Culture Congress that negotiated the transition to the new policy for the arts here. The other organisations were much weaker. You have to understand that from the mid-1980s to 1994 there was an alternative political economy based on donor funding, which came in to support anti-apartheid. These organisations could sustain a lot of structures out of that kind of funding. The minute the transition happened, a lot of that went out of the window, and COSAW has a little office now in Johannesburg; the Natal Culture Congress has dissolved. So a lot of arts organisations have experienced incredible strains. Now it is free for all, and that is where people are! The most energetic is Sancofa, the Centre for the African Renaissance, which is based in the University of Durban-Westville. It has a very strong rural agenda, and it is mobilising a lot of cultural groups all over the province.

Ulrike Ernst: *Sometimes the concept of African Renaissance is used in misleading ways. How does this group define the term African Renaissance and what does this concept mean to you?*

Ari Sitas: I think the leading figure here in Sancofa is Professor Pitika Ntuli, who is a fine artist and also poet. To crudify - his position would be a kind of strategic essentialism. In other words, decentring white dominance and discourse by asserting strategically an Africanness and forcing things to redefine themselves instead of belonging to Africa. But his, unlike the Jo'burg crowd, is a more inclusive Africanism. It is not genetic, and it is not colour based. But the definition has to be African. That's his position. His slogan is, if I can remember it, is 'to fly backwards towards the past in order to rediscover the lost future that was there'. That's it basically. And his own work is very competent in terms of art and sculptures and things like that. So, that would be his agenda.

The African Renaissance initiative in the province is led by an ANC minister, Sbu Ndebele, who is the chair of the ANC. He is trying to argue that you can't go just to the past but you have to understand the history of the last hundred years and what is valuable in terms of traditions that developed in this province, from Gandhianism to Luthuli's time to the Shembe church. Again more inclusive. But there are African fundamentalists around as well that are very, very specific about indigenous Africans as opposed to all the other foreigners. They are forming a strong pressure group. So the African Renaissance idea here is contested, but because of that the Luthuli - Ndebele alliance it seems to be more inclusive than what is happening in Gauteng.

A lot of students and a lot of other people find it quite empowering. If you go to any kind of grassroots area you will find I suppose three or four groups being active. One would be neo-Gandhians, who are out there to self-help and organising communities. You find a lot of the church, social justice and economic justice groups, especially around the Catholic church being very active at the grassroots. You find communists being active, and you find African Renaissance people active. But it is not a party, a particular party, that is active, but it is these kind of currents that are active at the moment. So there is some turbulence, but there is also significant support for the ANC in the province, and Inkatha support at the same time. If you drew a line at the Tugela, to the north of the Tugela is Inkatha territory, to the south of the Tugela is ANC territory.

Ulrike Ernst: *Now I would like to turn to the trade union's cultural work. It is firstly a more historical question. Before the formation of COSATU in 1985, the then biggest Federation of South African Trade Unions, FOSATU, had taken a workerist stance. For FOSATU, culture was a contribution to the preparation of workers' power. Cultural work was sought to enhance the formation and education of the working class.*

How, in retrospect, did the more populist stance of COSATU develop and change a) the ideological content, and b) the structure of the cultural work of the trade unions?

Ari Sitas: When you look at three things here: first is that the same leadership that was in FOSATU was also the leadership in COSATU; that is here, in KwaZulu-Natal. We are talking about the same people moving across. Secondly, FOSATU at its end, just before COSATU was formed, was nationally 75 000 people. In three years, COSATU Natal was 120 000 people. Just in this province. There was an enormous mobilisation of people that happened in those two to three years. FOSATU was small. Thirdly, FOSATU was as guilty as COSATU was of instrumentalism in terms of the leadership. The minute you opened up a platform for creative people from the working class, unpredictable things happened. You couldn't in a sense straitjacket it, to push a line, in any way it was an enormous platform for cultural expression everywhere.

There is no doubt that then the issues of nation, race, identity and so on were there on the cultural platforms of FOSATU as much as they were in COSATU. There is no way that you can understand Qabula or Hlatshwayo or anybody else in a narrow idea of trade union and/or a simple class politics. Look at the poetry: it talked about other things as well. So there was always tension in FOSATU.

I think the workerist-populist debate is basically a debate that missed the point at that time. It was positioning in terms of strategic power at that moment. But there is no doubt that by the mid-1980s, the struggles in South Africa were very complex. You couldn't wipe out the community side. What was the critique here? It was the critique of the non-democratic representation in the United Democratic Front, not the need for the United Democratic Front to exist. That is why after the violence started here, the United Democratic Front and COSATU came together to form what was then the MDM, the Mass Democratic Movement. And you already had in place forms of community participation linked to the trade unions since the early 1980s.

So for me the debate that was articulated by FOSATU intellectuals basically went something like this: you cannot participate in these broader community struggles because it will dilute the class power of organised workers on the shop floor and the democratic culture that exists on the shop floor. Then you would dilute the line. But the line could hold as long as struggles were situated on the shop floor. But struggles were not about the shop floor alone, so it became a broader issue immediately. Then how that translated into politics of resistance became out of the hands of FOSATU people, they couldn't control what their own workers were bringing onto the agenda in the union meetings. So you find I suppose 'wopulists' as opposed to workerists and populists. There have been dangers there, because there were very strong nationalists who saw union as a platform for mobilisation for nationalist issues. So there was serious, serious tension. But to say that race is not important in South Africa, or was not important in South Africa, or cultural domination was not important or that national oppression of the majority of people was not important would have taken a big leap of the imagination to do so. I understand the situation as being much more fluid than it appears in the *'South African Labour Bulletin'*, where intellectuals of the various movements are debating. It was a fascinating debate, but it died. So, what do we do with it?

There are serious differences in COSATU at the moment about policy and politics and priorities, and there are serious tensions between unions, within unions, between unions and the ANC and between the kind of much more working class politics at the moment and a national middle class politics. Those kinds of debates continue.

Ulrike Ernst: *In your various speeches and articles during the late 1980s, you seemed to suggest that there was something exceptional about conditions in Natal, about the working class in Natal, that it was divided between rural and urban, traditional and modern, ethnic, tribal and working class consciousness,* *royalist and democratically minded, Inkatha and ANC. These divisions were played out not only within a divided working class, but also often in the identity of one and the same person.*

Why were the cultural projects within the trade union movements particularly well developed in Natal?

Ari Sitas: I can think of three reasons. The first was that starting from a very specific history of the Dunlop factory, and the success of that first play and the emergence there of people on that factory floor that were committed to taking culture seriously and make it a union function was important as well. Secondly, as unions became more confident and mass-based, the fact that a lot of the shop stewards from Dunlop became leading shop stewards both in FOSATU and COSATU in the province and brought cultural activity with them as a good thing. And then what happened was emulation: as factories saw what others were doing, they started doing their own thing. Thirdly, it was organised as the Durban Workers' Cultural Local or the Pietermaritzburg Local and so on. Locals. Of course, activity was to get this energy going. In doing that, a lot of the oral forms and a lot of the poetry traditions, especially in recently proletarianised youngsters burst onto those platforms, and because there is a linguistic homogeneity here, communication was easy. And once people saw that those things and all those oral traditions were OK, we can do this, we can do that, a lot happened.

What Johannesburg did was much more than say, introduce culture because it is a good thing in a kind of an instrumental way. A lot of activity happened there as well, but it didn't have those organised clusters of people who were doing the work, here. That is the only difference. Those people were very successful in getting people to do things. And were very careful to put projects and project money to support activities that consolidated those efforts. Like Nise Malange was pulled out of the trade unions to work for Culture and Working Life, to facilitate and support. Hlatshwayo left Dunlop to do the same. A lot of resources went into this.

And then all of a sudden, when COSATU was formed, then they realised that culture was important, and Hlatshwayo was appointed as the national co-ordinator. But the minute it comes from the top, and given the movement was growing so big, it is very difficult to co-ordinate if there haven't been embryonic structures in place, like in the Western Cape and the Eastern Cape and in Johannesburg. So that is why it was different.

I suppose it tapped into some incredible oral talent, which immediately brought recognition, and they enjoyed that recognition and on they went, they went and went on doing their things. So that was the difference about this experience.

Ulrike Ernst: *And content-wise? Was cultural work in the unions of Natal an important means to bridge the gaps between rural - urban, tribal - working class, and traditional - modern?*

Ari Sitas: It could within certain principles. If you look at a lot of the plays, for example, major moral battles were being fought out there about women, about family, about kinship, and about countryside and the city. But for example, if you look at Qabula's work, there is a romanticisation of the countryside as the place of community versus the city and the factory that are hell. So there is that, the back home as a migrant, that is very important. You take a textile woman activist who did plays around migrancy. She shows the countryside as an alcohol soaked destitute pit, from which women escaped to find paradise in jobs in the city, but then find out that that is also a mess. So you are having the same movement from a woman's and a man's perspective that is quite different. Then you have plays about the morality of just breaking away from tradition, coming into the cities and ignoring your kinship structures and what happens to you there.

So that country-city thing was very active as content in the plays. The values were about organisation, co-operation, working together but always in and through these dilemmas about tradition and its collapse; what does modernity mean; is this new world of industry and how you cope with it. It dealt with it. It bridged a lot of that gap. And if you think about it, migrancy and movement between country and the city is very dominant in KwaZulu-Natal. So it did.

Ulrike Ernst: *Have the changing political conditions changed the impetus for workers' cultural projects?*

Ari Sitas: Yes. A lot. Now from being on a kind of national agenda of resistance and being an aspect of what liberation culture is all about, and after the transition and the collapse of the movements and the reconfiguration of movements, you have a fragmentation of empathy now. For education purposes you have workers' things for workers, you have women's issues for women, you have youth things for youth, gay for gay, religious for religious. You have a fragmentation of that audience, or the public, in interest groups at this stage. A lot of the creativity in the trade unions now is much more focused on narrower issues that are relating to your specific campaigns or specific thing of the moment, or the factory floor. You also have employers using what is called 'industrial theatre' in order to get their workers to be more productive. They learnt from the 'bad' people and now they are putting it to good use. So they are coming with using culture on the shop floor quite effectively they say - I would like to see it, how effective it can be. Then there are festive occasions, around Christmas, at the end of the year, or May Day, when there is a lot of cultural activity in the trade unions, when Factories close down. So, it is there, but it doesn't have the status or the energy the old movements had. It is understandable, sociologically, why this is happening. We will see what happens. Nise wants us to reorganise.

(Laughs)

Ulrike Ernst: *In the preparation of the transfer of the presidency of Nelson Mandela to Thabo Mbeki, or with the shift from the 'Reconstruction and Development Plan' to the implementation of the 'Growth, Employment and Redistribution Programme', the political and economic aims have been changing towards a market economy. Which perspectives does this open or reopen for the cultural work of the trade unions in South Africa?*

Ari Sitas: There is no doubt that all the unions are against GEAR. There is no doubt that a lot of marches and protests about privatisation and downsizing and chopping labour to become competitive are there, and by implication a lot of the creative effort of workers is going towards those campaigns. So before long, you will start seeing very significant cultural 'products' criticising GEAR. This fiscal policy and monetary controls and chopping the budgets in terms of government and trying to be competitive has an impact on social services and on what the government has for creative work. So it is impacting at a second level.

It is hard times for trade unions at the moment, and protests are increasing. I have been reading quite a few poems that are very, very critical about GEAR and downsizing and what is happening in factories. It is there.

Ulrike Ernst: *Let us turn to literature and writers. You were starting at the beginning with it, now let's talk about it again. When you were asked to comment your statement on the Sachs debate, 'A Philistine's Response'[1], you said you were hoping that "with the debate one would be heading towards an aesthetic pluralism because no aesthetic norm can claim truth value and through that push others out. It was a mistake that Soviet artists made. We should be arguing for a variety, multiplicity within common projects within common directions".[2] How do you see the development and importance of literature in South African society after the end of the struggle?*

Ari Sitas: The end of the struggle? (Laughs)

Ulrike Ernst: *After apartheid.*

Ari Sitas: I still believe in that idea. I believe in it more strongly now than I did then. If we look at the 1900s to 1930 with the triumph of socialist realism and so on, there was a combination of an idea of science and theory and truth and one correct way of doing things. These were supposed to be understood by party intellectuals, which would then be the correct way of doing things. If you go to the

99

Soviet artists of 1910s, 1920s and so on, there was a lot of energy, a lot of competition and so on, but each one of them was so vehemently against each other because they held to that dialectical truth that they represented, whether it was Mayakovski's crowd, or Gorki's friends, or the constructivists, the futurists, the whatever school and so on. Everybody believed that they were right because of some scientific thing or another. That created a discourse that was exclusive. Once Stalin concentrated things and all of a sudden the socialist realists were canonised as opposed to these 'aesthetic madmen'. Then it became one way. I think that was absolutely wrong, philosophically wrong but totally understandable sociologically. There is no way you could push for uniformity. In fact, provided you have a broader ideological conception of something around - a civic virtue, a kind of democracy that is about socio-economic equality, that encourages participation, that fights the gender battles, that understands that the environment has to be preserved and so on. Beyond that you can't legislate. You cannot say what artists can or shouldn't do. Your work as people in leadership should be creating the conditions for more and more and more self-expression within those limits.

We went in COSAW through some of these debates over the Salman Rushdie issue. We came out very strongly against the idea that you either have to ban and/or discipline and/or attack artists. It is the right of communities to protest, but artists should be protected to express what they have to express. In a complex society like South Africa, diversity and hybrid things that happen are strength. I believe in that.

What is happening at the moment in terms of literature? Firstly, the old authors, and I won't name any, but predominantly white, quite progressive, experimental in form, are finding it more and more difficult to connect with this new society, and they are creating an exile about themselves in a sense of not being able to own any of this that is happening. There is a kind of a bitter distance there. Secondly, we have the younger generation of predominantly African writers who are very much into describing the failure of what has happened. Thirdly, you have increasingly women writers, saying you are all talking a lot of 'shit' and come to our perspective to understand what it really means to be a South African. Broadly speaking, that is what is happening.

There is also a great exploration that has happened elsewhere about roots, rootedness, identity, who am I, where am I, do I belong, where do I belong, and an attempt to come to terms with the past. I haven't read much, in terms of formal literature of late that I really said, wow! It seems we haven't got there yet. Yes, wonderful individual writers, but we're not there.

Ulrike Ernst: *During the cultural struggle, the notion of the cultural workers or even 'worker izimbongis' emerged, which you strongly supported.[3] How do you* *think the change of the political system in South Africa has affected the positions of cultural practitioners?*

Ari Sitas: If you talk about 'izimbongis' themselves, from a critical platform that both affirmed and criticised, many of them have become ceremonial people who go to mass rallies to praise the new leadership. A lot of it has become a positivity about celebrating new rulers. But many of the others still keep a lot of the critical edge. I don't know whether you have seen some of Qabula's latest stuff, from two, three years ago. He is very critical about what happened.

The idea of somebody who was a cultural activist or cultural worker was something that was very much with us in the 1980s. There were a lot of people who were actively organising people to be creative. That has been affected. At the moment you have appointed people, through all kinds of democratic structures, who are cultural administrators as opposed to the old idea. A lot of them are the same people, but when you are a cultural administrator, you have to follow a whole range of democratic processes, accountable processes, financial discipline and so on. You have to keep within budgets, so you have a different kind of creature in place. I am not saying it is necessarily bad, because we mustn't throw the little savings that we have from our labour away, madly. But it is a different function that is emerging there.

The cultural worker has died in the last four years. He doesn't exist. But the 'imbongi' craft continues. It continues wherever people gather. But it doesn't have the movement characteristics of the older one. It is being encouraged through African Renaissance initiatives. There is a pressure for it to become again canonical - praise the king, the chiefs, the leaders, the dogs, the cell phones, the BMWs! (Laughs) A lot of it has become rather superficial.

Ulrike Ernst: *Now I would like to turn to literary theory. In your critic on Sachs, you noted his lack of theoretical dispute on the notion of protest or revolutionary cultural expression. How would you theoretically discuss the importance of literature? How does the role of literature change with social transformation? What is its role in a democratic South Africa?*

Ari Sitas: If you look at literature, broadly speaking, the post-theoretical level is that literature as an autonomous field of activity originated in Europe after enormous struggles by writers and intellectuals to establish that sphere of autonomy and therefore also the aesthetic sphere. And as something that happened, that was exemplary, and it was won by people like Baudelaire, Flaubert and so on, and the idea of a society being 'civilised' had to correspond with its also having this autonomous sphere. Initially, the bourgeoisie in Europe was a bit 'pissed off' and didn't like what happened, but then adopted it as part of its marker of civility. So that you have to understand in its transmission to the colonies. In the colonies, for the aesthetic elites of the European metropolis, the colonists were a bunch of backward 'idiots' that didn't have any sense of culture, and so they were worse than the 'natives', because at least the natives had the stuff, the colonists had the military marching bands and nothing, which created a counter pressure from colonial authorities to also show how civilised they were and have culture and art and literature. But they were borrowing from the most conservative and discredited schools in order for the local population of colonists to appreciate their mother culture. You see it in French colonies, you see it in English and the German colonies and Portuguese and Spanish ones, where it is not Baudelaire, Rimbaud and the others that are exported, but certain people that are about the importance of the metropolis and that becomes the autonomous sphere. Therefore the natives have to have their separate (quoting Mamdani) and/or they can enter the cultural portals of civilisation by imitating what is happening there in what those elites think is important.

So you have a lot of African and other writers trying to enter the school of the 'civilised' and write like Keats or Blake in South Africa, but expressing an African sentiment, and their whole effort is about the patronage of the civilised so-called colonial elites. And that gets fragmented later by African nationalism - they say enough of this patronage, let's reconfirm our traditions and so on and so forth. And ideas of a national literature begin to emerge and education and literature become very important to the various national movements. By the 1940s, the link between literature and the national movement for liberation is quite close. Then it goes through further mutations. Historically, in this country, if we look at the literature that was primarily written and performed by African people, it was quite linked to the idea of national independence. It goes all the way down to Wally Serote and other people. It has a Black Consciousness moment, then you have a Mass Democratic and Union and other moments. So it always was, in a sense it had to play a social enlightening role. That was in a sense its animus, what energised people.

By the 1980s - if you can imagine a borderline, and you have three positions on the one side and three positions on the other. You have writers, and the borderline is between people who can't be involved with what is happening out there, and the other side of the borderline is people who are involved with what is happening out there, the mass movement. So the three positions are as follows: the one is that my craft and my art cannot be in a sense polluted by all that; in fact the value of it is to be distant from that. The second position is, listen, my class, my colour, my social position make it difficult for me to be out there. I will be as honest as I can as an independent and distant person. The third one is, I was there. I saw the ugliness; I am independent. On the other side you have people who argue, no, no it is a question of commitment being down there. And the second position would be my class, my race, traps me there and I am being as honest as I can. And the third is, I was on the other side but now I realised, now

I am moving to this side. It is geographical positions we are talking about, fighting each other. You can have about thirty debates, mathematically, six times five, and it was those debates that were happening about the role of literature.

What we're all realising, which affects our theoretical position, is that the new world order of neo-liberalism and mercerisation is beginning to cut at the foundations of creativity, especially in the 'Third World'. You increasingly are beginning to see the semi-autonomous forms of schooling in certain traditions, whether it is the 'imbongi' or sitar playing in India, those are being undermined by the market, by world music, by a whole range of interests that are moving in and making culture and arts a very serious business. You are witnessing the book die globally and other media taking over. You are witnessing the concentration of publishing companies in fewer hands and the usage of some artists, some writers, almost like pop celebrities. But if you ask Bertelsmann, it used to be literature and books now it is 80% pop and the new sounds of the world. But the authors they have, they treat them as celebrities.

We are having very difficult times for people who write at the moment. The markets are shrinking. If you are clever, you move towards the Web and the new technologies, otherwise you are not heard. In South Africa what has happened in a long-winded way, is that our publishing industry has more or less died. There are very few places where we can publish poetry these days, very few places that can do novels. It has shrunk. A lot of the independent publishers have collapsed and it is very difficult for the written word. For the oral word it is a bit easier, but the oral world is very particular, very specific, very context specific. Its nationalisation is more difficult. You get an 'imbongi' from here and take him to Northern Cape, and everybody says it is an interesting piece of exotica. It is not happening.

I think if you look at literature it is in crisis, but the various positions about its role, are still busy arguing with each other. There is no victor in this.

Ulrike Ernst: *A democratic society needs a defined official system of representation, but apart from that it also needs the critical voice of the independent intellectual who through his or her commitment in person represents those who are misrepresented or silenced. What role and tasks of intellectuals would you ascribe to writers in a society in transformation? How do you see yourself in this context?*

Ari Sitas: How do I see myself in this context? I don't think I ever wrote to bring into voice those who were silent. They were supposed to be silent but were very loud and very assertive in the 1970s and 1980s about who they thought they were. And that was in a sense for me one of the most wonderful experiences, to learn a lot from people and what they were saying. I never assumed or tried to assume the role of a speaker for other people. But that doesn't mean I never spoke for certain principles. I think those principles continue. Formal democracy and representation have produced major changes in this country and none of us would want to go back. There is nothing romantic about the '70s or the '80s. You get nostalgic sometimes because of the forms of solidarity and meaning you got out of those, but that was 20%; 80% was violence, was pressure, was people cracking up, and was not something we need to go back to ever. But it was a prod for creativity, yes, it was. A lot of those moral questions at the moment remain and those questions one has to deal with. As a person who wrote poetry for instance, poetry was for me late at night; during the day doing a whole range of things, at night reflecting on it and reflecting a critical voice around issues.

I don't see the role of an independent critical intellectual dying in the country. In fact, it is a heavier burden now because half of your heart is with the transition, and you want it to continue and make real what's in the constitution, what's in the legislation, but 50% of your heart is somewhere else, where you hear voices that are very, very dissatisfied with what is happening. And you have to be as honest as you can from your perspective, your own biography and the pressures around you and just express yourself in the best way you can. And you should be encouraged and protected to do so, however discomfiting it might be. On that then I see the role. But like a character out of magical realism, we might be occupying an imaginary platform with nobody listening, nobody taking it seriously, and like Don Quichote or like some characters in Zulu myths and folk tales you have to continue to be wily about what you do and try and bring it to people in whatever form you can. The struggle of the pen and of dance continues, because life continues in all its contradictions. I don't see easy solutions to many of our problems.

Ulrike Ernst: *With 'Black Mamba Rising', which you introduced and edited, a discussion emerged about the correct picture of history and the appropriate use of African tradition in literature.[4] How would you assess the ways in which African tradition is or should be represented in the South African arts?*

Ari Sitas: Firstly, there can't be any more anything but African traditions. Even whiteness as a category will disappear quite soon, defined as a category against others. You will have whites grouping together, but that old colonial, apartheid idea of whiteness is going. And it is going to be about African traditions. I refuse to accept that Africa was an anthropological clump that was Africa and tradition - two clumps that come to us from the past. In fact, what is more exciting is the variety of what is called Zulu and Zuluness as opposed to its uniformity. I see African traditions and their contestation and learning from each other being very important. And people who are purists, who say, look at these workers, they are not doing the 'izimbongi' form right. Because they are using it instrumentally for other purposes of what its role was. That is a fundamental reactionary type of argument. You could say that there was one pass that was correct, or one spiritual inheritance that was correct, and everybody has to be manifestations of that. And I don't buy that in any way.

What was exciting for me about what Qabula and Hlatshwayo were doing, is that they were in a sense innovating the tradition and introducing all kinds of dialectical contradictions in the imagery itself that were very revolutionary in the form. And because those things were reconcilable in their lives and they had to find conflicting metaphors to capture within the 'izimbongi' form. So that was for me very exciting, and a lot of people have learnt out of that.

Now there could be other transformations of that tradition. The idea that African societies are static or not evolving in dynamic ways, I don't buy. I thought the *'Black Mamba Rising'* was a very humble undertaking that was supposed to be for trade unions, and it was produced with the simple purpose of communicating to other people, workers, and so on something that is happening here done cheaply and affordably, which was elevated to a debate about national culture, tradition, class politics, who licenses workers to be poets and whether they got poetry certificates from the poetry elite and so on. It went out of their world, a lot of this debate. They are smart enough, they understood what was happening, but that was not the intention, it was the historic moment that did this to *'Black Mamba Rising'*. Had we been conscious of what its impact would be, it would have been a different type of publication. It was wonderful that it happened and it had a lot of energy.

Ulrike Ernst: *Part of the question of tradition is that of languages and identity. Different Nguni languages were promoted to serve the colonisers' ruling order. I was intrigued to see how you as a sociologist mentioned the influence of the mission schools on the aesthetic development in South Africa. In your essay "The Logic of Fragmentation and Reconstruction" you warned of "neo-traditional Africanism" which is a repressive re-emergence of a version of ethnicity in the footsteps of the 'Customary'.[5] How do you locate, let me ask you vis à vis Mahmood Mamdani's 'Citizen and Subject'[6], the terrain of languages and tribal politics as part of cultural and literary discourse in the new South Africa?*

Ari Sitas: Wow! Mamdani's. I very specifically used the word 'neo-traditionalism' which is not traditionalism, but it is an attempt to say, there are these values and norms that make us African and distinguish us from Europeans and whites and in our institutional battles in the state bureaucracy and the corporate sector, we have to assert our Africanness, which is given by a lot of popular sociology or anthropology. But it is brought forward by modernising people. So you will find the most neo-traditionalists amongst urban petit bourgeoisie becoming bourgeoisie at the moment. Not the chiefs. But now, because the customary is important, part of your values, you have to refer here in KwaZulu-Natal to the king. Of course he is a symbol of our cultural survival, and therefore he is the manifestation of what is customary and has been held in prison by colonialism. Therefore pain, unlike the whites, who are loose here, we link up with those kind of customary institutions. Of course it creates problems immediately around gender and the role of women. A lot of women who are professionals now are neo-traditionalists but are trying to define something else about what they mean and forward come only motherhood and kinship and earth mother in the old traditions. It is something very modern.

I think Mamdani's dichotomy is too static to capture the rural in the urban and the urban in the rural and what is happening. But where I buy his argument is that there was a defining ideology of the native as other, as non-employee, as couldn't be in the urban areas, as this, as having to be tribal and ruled through indirect rule and so on. All those things were there. But I don't think he understands the power of modernism or modernity in South Africa whether it's church related, whether it's secularisation, whether it's national movements that emerged in the country and migrant worker organisations in the country. I think he is missing the point there. It was an important corrective to literature that was forgetting the customary in Africa, an important corrective to modernist ideologues in the cities that hypothesised the working class without understanding its material bases, both in the countryside and in the city, but beyond that he has to nuance his arguments.

Ulrike Ernst: *Maybe in the end I could just ask you: how do you think that the notions of class, race and gender should be handled in the new South Africa? And what impact would that have on writing in the future?*

Ari Sitas: Whew, how could it be handled? You are calling for a management course! (Laughs) Handling! You see, you can't 'handle' those conflicts. You know there are institutions that are trying to mediate those conflicts. But those conflicts are real, and they manifest themselves in various forms, and until and unless you have gender equality, not in principle, but indeed, those struggles will be there. Until we have socio-economic redistribution and equality and a better life for the majority the class questions will be quite sharp, and racial questions will intensify on the shop floors of the country with empowerment programmes and with the issue of competence: blacks can't do this, whites can't do that, Indians for this, and so on because apartheid linked performance so much to colour. So that is going to continue until there comes a point where that is not necessary any more.

So, in terms of reflecting on these issues, be sure that those will be crucial issues in the future, and no gloss can hide them so easily. So at that level those conflicts exist but within a new empowering environment of very progressive legislation in which the reality of women's rights exist in the constitution and the legislation could be translated into reality on everyday bases. It is not happening at the moment. Those struggles will continue, carried out by women, not writers, or woman writers.

Ulrike Ernst: *Thank you very much for the interview.*

References

[1] **Sitas, Ari. 1990.** "The Sachs Debate: a Philistine's Response". In: **de Kok, Ingrid/ Press, Karen (eds.). 1990.** Spring is Rebellious. Arguments about Cultural Freedom by Albie Sachs and Respondents. Cape Town: 91-98.

[2] **Sitas, Ari. 1991.** "Interview Ari Sitas". In: **Brown, Duncan/van Dyk, Bruno (eds.). 1991.** South African Writing in Transition. Pietermaritzburg: 65-72.

[3] **Sitas Ari. 1989.** "The Publication and Reception of Worker's Literature. An Interview by Bruno van Dyk and Duncan Brown". In: **Meintjes, Frank/Hlatshwayo, Mi et al. (eds.). 1989.** Worker Culture. Special Issue of Staffrider 8 (3/4). Johannesburg: 61-68.

[4] **Sitas, Ari (ed.). 1986.** Black Mamba Rising. South African Worker Poets in Struggle. Alfred Qabula, Mi S'Dumo Hlatshwayo, Nise Malange. Durban.

[5] **Sitas Ari. 1998.** "South Africa in the 1990s. The Logic of Fragmentation and Reconstruction". In: Transformation 36: 37-50.

[6] **Mamdani, Mahmood. 1996.** Citizen and Subject. Contemporary Africa and the Legacy of Late Colonialism. Cape Town.

Nise Malange

Nise Malange interviewed by Ulrike Ernst
on 5 April 2000 in Durban

"To Understand the Gumboot Dance"

Ulrike Ernst: *Nise Malange, you have a reputation as a writer, cultural organiser and trade union activist. Your name has been closely connected with the work of the Culture and Working Life Project in Durban. May I ask you at the beginning to speak about your own background in terms of culture?*

Nise Malange: I think it comes from where I grew up, and I think it is common in South African people that we grew with our culture being playing, singing, being dancing, being handicrafts. It is part and parcel of our growing up as African people. We had no resources, so the resources that we had all the time were what we knew. But if I am more specific in terms of me as Nise Malange, it has been the home environment. I come from a home of beautiful singers - my parents, my aunts, of whom all have died, but I always have these voices, that are healing voices, and I try keep holding on to them so that they don't disappear.

My uncle was a trade unionist who introduced me to the trade union movement at a very early age. I think most of my skills, even technical skills, come from him, because I had to type without going to typing school, type pamphlets for him, to distribute during the Fattis and Monis Strike in the Cape, and I got involved in that strike. At a very tender age I got involved in the Red Meat Boycott, and with my uncle we used to go out and collect food parcels for migrant workers. We had always people coming from the Cape. We learnt a lot of rural skills, how people in rural communities survived. We learnt different languages that they speak and that are spoken in the township.

To add on that, I went to study in a rural community. I spent most of my teenage life in the Eastern Cape in the rural villages where I went to school, where participating in culture was one of the things that entertained people in the community. Today, kids talk about going to multi-cultural schools or multi-racial schools, but our age group, our generation talked about boarding a train for three days to go to school and spending your whole life there and going home during holidays, the two big holidays, summer and winter holidays. Most of the time you were part of that community. If it is time to harvest, you have to be there to do your part in harvesting. If it is time to cultivate the land, you have to be there, and take your part in cultivating the land. If it is the time where boys are going for initiation, we have to whitewash the houses and repaint them. You have to participate because it was a communal thing. So I've learnt to live with communities, I've learnt communal skills; I've learnt to relate to different people regardless of their status. I feel great that I had that background, and I was able to apply it in my adult life.

Ulrike Ernst: *Since you have an insight into the cultural politics of the ANC, of COSATU and know the development of literature in South Africa, I would like to structure our interview accordingly. In 1990 when you were asked about your opinion of Albie Sachs' paper "Preparing Ourselves for Freedom"[1], for the collection 'South African Writing in Transition', you welcomed the rethinking of the notion of the use of 'culture as a weapon'. You did not interpret Sachs' ANC in-house paper as degrading of the contributions of the cultural workers. Its point, you seemed to you suggest, lay in the fact that it raised the issue of criticism in solidarity.[2]*

Furthermore, you stated the problems cultural workers had experienced with the Mass Democratic Movement after its unbanning, for example in the preparation for the Mandela Natal peace rally on 25th February 1990. At that occasion you said: "All the cultural workers were censored", in the sense that people that did not entirely conform to the aim of the rally were ruled out. Therefore you felt that the Sachs paper was overdue.[3]

However, according to a statement in the Weekly Mail in 1993, you still seemed to have difficulties with the role of the ANC's Department of Arts and Culture. You said: "Since 1990 we have experienced self-censorship. There has been a fear: if you become critical of the ANC you might be marginalized, you might be eliminated."[4] You argued: "As a parent I know there are stages when it is difficult to let go. But now we are saying to our parents: Let it go... Let us see for ourselves what future policies we want."[5]

Did the cultural parents let go? What happened to the cultural politics of the ANC after its legalisation between 1990 and 1994?

Nise Malange: You did your research very well! I was quite shocked at some stage! (Laughs) I like to remain independent as an artist and as a 'leader', and as a role model of people. The situation hasn't changed much. I think we've kind of let things go as what the liberation movement wanted. We have kept quiet in terms of issues of cultural expression and the right to express yourself. I think we are struggling with what is our right as people, as the civil society. We have not been in a position to really assert ourselves as artists. We try to romanticise it through for example poetry - I remember in one case where I was asked to recite or to prepare some poetry in COSATU's launch of DITSELA, their worker education organisation. I did a poem which people were really comfortable with because it was dealing with love and affection, but relating to an organisation. But when I started going back, reading some stuff by other workers and my own old poems, to say to the workers, don't forget where we come from. By reading those poems, I realised that people didn't really want to associate with the past.

On another occasion I was asked during the COSATU presentation in the Truth and Reconciliation Commission to do a poem, to really show what workers have undergone in terms of oppression. I titled my poem "The Blood, the Tears and Oppression", which is taken from BTR, which is the kind of stuff that we used to use against union bashers. The BTR some called struggle. But none of the people could really see what I was trying to do. There were very few that came to me and responded to the kind of history and the bashing and the repression that workers and women and migrant workers had to go through in this country.

That really showed me that people want the truth, but at the same time they don't want the truth. Peace is very fragile and we've been in the forefront of peace. I mean we were there first, especially as writers in this province, to work with everyone on peace projects. And we had a collection of poetry, a peace poetry collection that we did, in 1994, and had a lot of readings.

What I am saying is that the minute that you become much more vocal and critical on the issues, using especially poetry, that is when people start looking at you twice and questioning you about your loyalty. There is confusion in terms of being critical. I mean, I am not a political fanatic, I am not a religious fanatic, and I am not a fanatic of any sorts. I am really grounded. What I believe in I believe in. That is the problem, that you find people would use you for their own benefits. And I refuse to be used for those reasons.

There are no changes. What has happened is that kind of self-censorship - if you look at poetry today, you try to pick up what are the issues that the young poets are writing about. You are not in a position to get the kind of vibrant discussions we had in the past. We had an international poetry festival here, and one last year or two years ago I hosted one evening where Stephen Gray read a poem about our politicians with their BMWs and all sorts of things in a very humorous way. And I responded when he finished by using Mandela's words, where Mandela scolded somebody not doing what he wanted. I used the very same words saying that to him, you are not supposed to be doing what you are doing here. Like where artists are scolded like children by people up on top and situations like that. Then people try to put humour, and sometimes that humour gets missing in terms of the content of that. What I am saying is that we don't have that kind of vibrant debates. We have a stream of work that is coming out that gets attacked.

On the other level, parliament people like Wally Serote writing poetry are also critical of what is happening inside but if, as an ordinary artist, you would do that and go out and recite that kind of poetry, then you would be received more or less the same way like inciting the public. So now you have to look at platforms where you could do the kind of critical poetry. All the time we get called to do praising, poetry for the President. Because now we no longer are doing these things that we have done in the past, where we just composed a poem about our President because we wanted to. People come and ask for them: can you write this poem, this kind of poetry. It's in competition for our President. In the past we never had to go through that. It was coming from within us. They didn't have to prescribe what we can do and what we cannot do. A number of poems that came about our leaders, they were non-stop.

I think what our politicians should ask themselves: what happened to that culture that was praising and encouraging and educating our communities? Why is it not there? It is still there, but people are cautious, they might not be scared, but cautious, of what if I do this. That is the kind of caution that happens all the time. So the freedom that we fight for is for artists, and it's seriously not really there. The level of discussions that we had and the level of participation are no longer there. Now that we kind of pull back is because of what happened, which has really created this kind of silence that we have at the moment in terms of grassroots community literature.

Ulrike Ernst: *We started to talk about the early period of 1990 to 1994, and I think you were jumping already to the time after the accession to power of the ANC. Would you see a difference, or what is your opinion of the cultural discourse and the cultural policy of the ANC after its accession to power with the first free elections in 1994?*

Nise Malange: Before the accession, the ANC tried to push the kind of policies that were supporting the ANC, which was a problem because it was taking people's independence away, and they tried and tried and tried, and that never succeeded, and that is why the ANC Cultural Desk vanished. But then when you need a policy on certain issues, it is different. One day I even thought, hey, I am now the Provincial Arts and Culture Council here; that is a government structure that will have funding to create policy and vision for the arts in the province. I was thinking, hey, in terms of culture, the ANC maybe saw the problems that the desk created and decided that they were not going to be responsible for this because there was too much fire there and gave it to the IFP. For all these years we never had policies in terms of how funds should be distributed, or what should happen in terms of cultural programmes. We haven't been in a position to say as artists, this is what we want to happen. It is still in the hands of the politicians.

We are struggling at the moment, for 'arm's-length funding', because that is what we have been asking for. Then we can decide what we want to do in terms of culture. We are administrators; we know how to deal with funds. They don't want to give that decision to us because they know that that freedom would induce certain cultural expressions, that would come with freedom of expression, and that would educate people. When people are educated, we know what happens. The masses are educated through culture. Whatever form, it could be music, or it could be anything. When you provide those platforms, that is when people get educated. That is when people get motivated also in terms of writing and expressing their views. That is not happening because there is nothing there to facilitate it.

The past has created some problems. Those problems will take a lot of time. People talk about the redress. The redress is one particular thing. Redress the imbalances in terms of resources. But in terms of content, it will take time for people to be at the kind of position that we are at as people in this country in relation to literature and in relation to theatre and other forms where there are words to explain things. It will really take some time to say to the government, stop and listen to the people. It will take time to say, stop corruption but give money to people. It will take time for us to say, as poets, there is so much poverty but you are driving your BMWs and earn big salaries, and you cry for more money, and people are starving. It will take time for us to say stop and look at the kind of houses that you give to people. This poetry we need so that the kind of little toilets that they are saying were houses for people are stopped before they mushroom like the forum houses. I have always said that you can't stop the revolution when it starts. In our culture they always say that where the water has stopped, if there was flooding once, the floods would come again. So there is a Zulu phrase, which is used for that: 'Where the water has stopped before, it will go back there and stop in the same place'.

Those are the kind of things that have been happening because pre-'94 and after '94 there is a gap. Artists have become hobos. A popular artist like Alfred Qabula is sitting at home with a stroke. No one remembers him. He was the person that really hoisted the flag of the ANC through his praise singing that revived the culture, and made sure that culture has not died out but that it was being used - for a lot of the time, without recognition by the regime at that time - to consolidate the movement to make sure that the messages went out and he educated a lot of illiterate workers who listened to praise poetry. The cries that you hear, even now like with Mahlatini, who died a pauper and a lot of artists that are dying, are getting pauper's funerals. That is the sign that there is nothing that has happened since 1990 up to the present time to redress the cultural imbalances. But at the same time there is nothing that facilitates those debates because of the politics of Arts and Culture today. The kind of earlier promotion is gone, if you look at the Freedom Day and a number of other things, you don't see the grassroots poets. You don't see the grassroots musician because they are trying to avoid the presence of the people that are going to say things that educate the community. COSATU itself celebrated the ten years of COSATU, but the groups that were there were not the worker groups that made COSATU to be where it is today. They have forgotten about all those people because they know they were going to be critical.

So anything that is critical has to be sidelined. All the artists that are trying to be relevant to people are sidelined. They will never be invited anywhere. That is the situation at the moment: if you are critical, they sideline you. That is why we have all these commercial events rather than worker events or ANC or liberation events. They are doing it in a nice way that you don't see it. So if they can't really do anything to say to people, don't buy his music, then they have got to buy you in and say compose music for us, come play with me, you know? And that is what they are doing as part of discouraging the musicians and poets. And I think the dampening thing is that poet Mzwakhe Mbuli. We'll never know the truth, which is what I always say to people, we will never know the truth about Mzwakhe. We'll have all what we have, doubts, but that silenced the whole movement. For people were saying, hm, Mzwakhe used to be popular and look what happened to him. They can do whatever they want to do in order to put you in the right place, and the right place for him is 14 years in jail. That scared a lot of people, a lot of poets particularly, out of their wits. Like I said, we'll never know the truth about him. But for us that was one thing that says, look and watch and listen to what you say.

Ulrike Ernst: *You have been the vice-president of the Congress of South African Writers. Which cultural and literary organisations have had an impact on the cultural discourse in the country after 1990, and how have they been affected by the broader economic, social and political transformations?*

Nise Malange: COSAW played a very, very important role in shaping literature in this country and I think Southern Africa generally. It also played a big role in promoting writers and poets that were not known, who went in exile thirty years ago and kept an African writer's perspective. We took up their campaigns, for instance, for our president, Njabulo Ndebele, when he was not allowed, in 1990, to come and work in the country. We did also raise a number of issues, like with Ken Saro-Wiwa. It is another thing I would like to be part of the picketing and everything against the Americans and Abu Jamal's issue of hanging. But these are certain things that now you can't do because of your status and your role and how the political talk shapes up our lives as writers and artists.

COSAW played a big role in developing literature and shaping literature in this country. Firstly, with young upcoming writers, trying to break the whole problem we had with publishing in this country because when we first published '*Black Mamba Rising*', it was a big thing. Secondly, to demystify the whole issue that writing was only for the elite and the educated one. COSAW picked up the pieces because we were the first within Culture and Working Life to come up with literature, worker literature. And COSAW facilitators, because we already had people now, aspiring writers.

I can give you a number of young writers who are now coming up because it motivated them. I was vice-president and responsible for projects. I used to travel all around the country, running writing workshops, which is still one of the roles that I play. I do writing workshops; I have published already two to three publications with the youth, youth writings, with some of the things that we never saw in this country. I facilitated a writing workshop with IFP and ANC youth to express their views on the violence.

Most of us still carry on with that work that COSAW created. In one of the townships we've got a library. People that were training COSAW run writing workshops once a month. They are getting a lot of books, and we host a lot of writers in that community. We try to bring literature to the people. I think that role that COSAW played has created an environment where even now in schools there are writing workshops that people facilitate, although in terms of publishing there is a gap. COSAW used to have books published. That is gone now. So people don't have that avenue where they could publish.

The role that we played at the time was in making people aware. We also played a role in terms of policies that helped to shape. For instance the whole censorship laws that we have developed and the literature policy - the book publishing people now are looking into those things. They know that they've got resource people that they can call, and they can contribute one way or another in terms of development. The language is one of the things that we dealt with a lot: a language policy and the development of languages. So all the things that we have exposed people to now people are able to participate in. Because if we had never played that role, people who would be making these laws would be people only who have been on the receiving end, the elites, but now our own people are able to participate fully. Because the elites know if the people say we are talking about the development of language, they know what they are talking about. They know that we are talking about books being published in our own languages and being marketed, and they know that we know about censorship and copyrights. What needs to happen is a step forward for people now to start respecting other people's works. It will start with our institution because we had a culture here of no respect of academic work. When I talk of academic work or intellectual work I am not only referring to institutions, I am referring to all the other people on the grassroots level that produce works. They should be respected in their own right.

So I speak proudly of COSAW, regardless of what has happened in the present situation. Because what has happened was that we said new and young people should now take over because they are the government of tomorrow. We would follow them. But I think we missed the boat somewhere. That is when problems started. I still say that I am very proud of what we developed in this country in terms of literature. Now the government, through NAC, the National Arts Council, through the provincial Arts and Culture Council here, and through other para-state structures tries to take up where COSAW left. They try to make this country to be a country where all participate, in the development of literature, in discussions and debates, and to stop all these conferences being just a kind of elitist conference. The 'time of the writer' still has to happen there. Make it as vibrant as it used to be. And I think people would participate because they know that we did this and they have to pick it up and take it forward.

So I could say that with COSAW we really did a lot of good work, and you could go anywhere, you could still see the remnants of COSAW's structures. To give an illustration: I had a friend who was dying of cancer, and we did a lot of writing workshops with him, and I was sitting and reading one of Ken Saro-Wiwa's statements before he died, saying: "Life for us artists, we shape it. We either go forward or fall but everyone who follows us would learn a lot of things from us because we always leave a legacy behind". He kept on saying, "Take all my poems, take all my short stories". He has written a book *'The Stories That Fill'*, and I want them distributed everywhere because I know that they would help one or two people somewhere. And it is his dying wish that I should do that for him.

So we have all these undying connections as writers in this country. We think of each other. We have forged solidarity. The solidarity that we forged no one will ever be able to break it. Whether we are vocal or not vocal. But whatever links we have one day when those links go out again, that would be another revolution of its own. Because it would be something that we have kept, something that we still want to see working in this country.

Ulrike Ernst: *Now I would like to turn to the trade unions' cultural work. Firstly, a historical question: Before the formation of COSATU in 1985, the then biggest Federation of South African Trade Unions (FOSATU) had taken a workerist stance. For FOSATU, culture was a contribution to the preparation for workers' power. Cultural work was thought to enhance the formation and education of the working class. How, in retrospect, did the more populist stance of COSATU develop and change a) the ideological content, and b) the structure of the cultural work of the trade unions?*

Nise Malange: FOSATU was seen as a white union. They had some differing politics and struggles there like unions have to register and people were against registration. We worked on that to educate workers why it was important to register as a trade union movement, why non-racialism was important in order to gain the kind of momentum we gained later and also that not all the white people in the country were racist and oppressors. We are the people that really kept that culture of non-racialism within COSATU. The UDF and other organisations came and upheld the light but we did that under very, very difficult conditions. We came from segmentations of trade unions where you had a Coloured union, an Indian union, a White union and an African union.

With FOSATU, we had resources. We had the FOSATU newspaper, and I think that is where primarily the whole worker culture formed itself. We were looking at various forms of educating the shop floor because we realised that a number of people there on the shop floor didn't know what was happening. People were coming from the 1970 strike, which was big, but then with all the changes and the development that was taking place, they were up there, but the people on the floor didn't know.

FOSATU facilitated the workers' cultural development. We had groups that were developing ideas around repression, or around exploitation of workers. And those plays had platforms. We would perform at rallies, at education conferences. There was much more education that was happening to inform the shop floor, which was what I really enjoyed those days. We were dealing with issues of migrations and how women were impacted, or we educated men that were leaving their women at home.

We facilitated all those things where our own experiences and ideas were then put in, in the content of the poetry and the plays and even paintings. By the time of COSATU or the merger all the events we had - all these regional talks that were happening, union to union, federation to federation - were on top level, on shop steward level. So our role in FOSATU as FOSATU workers' cultural movement was to educate the shop floor. Whatever was discussed at the top, we took it down, through praise poetry, through music. The campaigns; Mayekiso will campaign if you listen to the music that was composed at that time - release Mayekiso; otherwise you might get into trouble. All those things were happening. That was also when the system, the police started targeting cultural workers, because they knew then that something was happening there, people were getting excited and were going out doing things.

At the time of COSATU's launch, already all the information had flown down to the workers, and there was this big worker participation. We had COSATU locals now, and COSATU locals were used to be composed of shop steward and cultural workers locals. And the youth. And the women. And all these people would come together, and when there were conferences you would see the merging of all these people coming together. There were always platforms for workers. Issues were debated, and I think the knowledge and the skills that the cultural workers had helped a lot because they were also conflict resolution skills. Another time those were not very specific skills that were known and that there were organisations like trade unions today that train people in conflict resolution. But those were the skills that we possessed as cultural workers and that we used. Most of the workers were used by management to bridge the gap between management and the workers because of a number of strikes and misunderstandings that were happening, due to language, due to cultural differences. So we played amazing different roles: from education to literacy education. Our own people that we trained played those roles then as educators. Most of them are personnel officers today. We have always been proactive in terms of culture.

Then Cultural and Working Life, was formed. And then COSATU started its own cultural desk. COSATU was becoming envious and ambitious of what workers were possessing and thought that they would be able to mould that. Because we had now visual artists that were coming out, we had recorded musicians out of workers, or we had theatre groups that were travelling all over South Africa and abroad. And those things were coming from workers; we had books published by workers. It was becoming an industry on its own. COSATU had a project for unemployed workers who were involved in culture. So whoever was unemployed, if you had a skill, you were able to fall under the cultural structure. COSATU never ran short of shop stewards; you always had people who were already trained - who had writing skills, who had conflict resolution skills, who had management skills and who had all the qualities of a leader. Because we were developing leaders and we were making people to be able to question things. We were bringing up intellectuals, people who were able to review books. And this whole wealth of people COSATU took over. What happened thereafter? They dumped them.

Fortunately, at that time, Cultural and Working Life was there to pick up the pieces. And it also made Cultural and Working Life to shape itself in terms of the needs of the workers. Workers wanted more concrete skills. They wanted more programmes where they could get certificates and where they were able to apply for a job and say I've got these management skills, I want to be promoted in my job. That is what we did as Cultural and Working Life. We did whatever COSATU's cultural forum couldn't do. What we were planning to do more was to take up the campaigns.

We had a cultural rights campaign where we were looking at management and said, develop the canteens: give all these workers who have the skills a place where they can sit and write, paint, they can have a cultural event during lunch time, they can watch the programmes that they developed themselves. We were coming up with several ideas that in other countries had been practised. But then because of the turning points in our politics, we had to close shops. That was a very difficult time for all of us worker artists. But again we left people that we can now call upon and say, come, we want to develop a play, and these people would come.

We are looking at reviving work; we want to have a workers' theatre co-op now where we respond to worker issues. One worry is the AIDS problem and the fact that COSATU hasn't been able to address this properly. When we are going to form that co-op, the first play that we do is to address the whole AIDS issue and how it affects workers.

I hope I have answered your question. The FOSATU-COSATU phase was a beautiful phase and especially when Cultural and Working Life got in. The last phase, that was not really facilitated properly. That was the peak then, where workers were saying, we want to learn hard skills now so that we can compete on an intellectual level as workers. If we qualify to go to technikon through arts and culture, we would like to do that. We were already talking to some other institutions to develop a diploma course for our workers. If a worker paints, he must know the history of art, must know all the other intellectual aspects of the area that he does, even if just on a literacy level. We needed to do that. But the politics were too high for cultural workers.

We were left behind because there was no place for us. But grassroots and worker culture was the only one that people could and can hear. When I finished a poem, workers were coming to me and said, hey comrade, these are things that we have forgotten. Jay Naidoo came and said, hey, you know, we never even raised the issue of women. How these women were affected by what was happening on the shop floor, but you did it in your poetry. We never raised this, we never raised that, but these are the things that you have raised.

So that is the role which in a way COSATU still acknowledges, by calling upon us to do one or two things for them every time. COSATU itself finds things always out very late. That is why we are saying that we want to revive and have a co-op because we see the gap. We see the role that worker theatre and worker literature can play in developing and educating people in this country today about a number of issues. Workers have participated in community projects where they stop crime as workers. If you can turn the clock back now and say, these were the things that we did, these were the achievements, this is how we did them, and this is how we can still do them today. We can build this country much better.

Ulrike Ernst: *In your answer, you were already alluding to my next question. In various articles during the late '80s, it was suggested - for example by Ari Sitas - that there was something exceptional about conditions in Natal, about the working class in Natal that was divided between urban and rural, traditional and modern, ethnic, tribal and working class consciousness, royalist and democratically minded, Inkatha and ANC. These divisions were played out not only within a divided working class, but also often in the 'identity' of one and the same person. Was cultural work in the unions in Natal an important means* *to bridge the gaps? Why were the cultural projects within the trade union movement particularly well developed in Natal?*

Nise Malange: I think cultural work bridged the gaps a lot. I quote one worker who said: "When I am involved with culture within COSATU I can play my Zuluness. I can be a Zulu, and that is enjoyed by everyone". The one thing that united workers was the music, the dance, or the praise poetry. Even people outside of COSATU were influenced, when they saw that praise singing and traditional gear were accepted, that you could go on the stage and start your Zulu chanting, that it was acceptable because it was part of your culture. In FOSATU, you had people who were members of FOSATU as well as members of Inkatha because they saw Inkatha as their cultural traditional organisation that fulfilled them as Zulu people. With the launch of COSATU, people were already prepared. Besides that, the acknowledgement of Shaka and of people's need to celebrate Shaka Day was a cultural achievement. Although, there were all the political problems that we had with IFP and the trade union UWUSA, people knew that COSATU fought for their rights and COSATU still allowed people to practise their culture. And people still had that dual membership.

I had cases when I was in the trade union, where a worker broke his leg because he was dancing. He was excited by something, by some kind of achievement and he started dancing and he threw himself on the floor and broke a leg. And they said that they won't pay, workman's compensation won't pay, that this person was not on duty. That was a very technical thing. If I was a culturally naïve person, I wouldn't have been able to defend that worker and say, Zulus use that for work. That is why you have the 'Gumboot Dance' that is why you have all these traditional things. Workers, when they do work as a team, they do it in unison through either humming certain music or through some kind of rhythmical dance and that is how they get motivated. Like a white man would listen to an orchestral whatever, the same thing as those people; they get their motivation, and they get to produce more. And if a worker was excited and did that, you need to pay for that.

We have had a Zulu journal where we have looked deep into the past and at the present situation and have compared how things have developed and where things are going to take us in terms of democracy and understanding democracy. We have discussed the role of culture. People simply no longer go with bare feet to work, they wear pants, and they have modified some of the things that they have had like their very traditional Zulu pants and say that is why you have those things, because of the time.

I have worked with IFP because they understand that culture is part of educating people. It is not something that you give a person a knobkerrie and say go and kill. But culture is something that we can live on; we can be creative and do things. As for me, the provincial Arts Council is full of IFP people, but they themselves acknowledge and respect the skills and the experience that I have in terms of the development of culture and what needs to be done for the future.

We have always been aware of the divisions: the urban and rural we have debated them, and they are still there. We have a lot of informal settlements because one finds that social and economic positions won't allow people all the time to be in a rural community. Natal is nice in a way that rural communities are able to come to town. We have here the BAT Centre, women who bring their crafts, every day coming here. They used to be scared of coming to town, but now town is where they can sell their craft. And their craft is appreciated. So there is a good relationship between urban and rural through arts and crafts.

In terms of tribalism: people are learning. The Provincial Arts and Culture is supposed to be a Zulu programme, but I am heading it as a Xhosa woman, and I am respected for my knowledge. So I could say that that is also an achievement, that I am acknowledged as a person who brings a very diverse experience to the Zulu people. They always joke and say that, hey, we don't know how we come across with a Xhosa woman like you.

In terms of class, that is the debate that is taking on. COSATU doesn't want to deal with it. We have always said that we are scared of the class differences, of people being classified. I think that is why COSATU had a big debate on what working class was. But on a broader level the whole class issue hasn't been discussed properly, because now, with all our new black elite, in the government and everywhere, including some of the workers, like the shop stewards who are now driving big Mercedes Benz, want to be part of the working class as well as the upper class. The tensions that are there are tremendous. I seriously don't know how the whole class issue is going to be resolved in this country. I also have serious problems with the whole class thing. There is now a terminology of 'them' and 'us'. 'Them' is all those with Mercedes and Volvo and 'us' are more NGO and grassroots people. And within the NGO sector, we have people that are aspiring to be in that class as well, who want big salaries and big cars and want to live in big mansions. Success is measured now not on skills and knowledge; success in this country is measured now on what you drive. I do not drive any car at the moment. I say that I am a working class woman, I am a socialist, and I will remain that way. In order for me to link up with the workers, I go to the taxis and the trains so that I can see things. I have much more information than them. I live in the township. Everyone has run away from the township, not because of crime, it's a class and a status thing that I live in a suburb.

So we are struggling with the class issue, and it is going far. The next revolution in this country will be a class revolution, I tell you. It is creating problems, and elite people don't want to come down to the ordinary people, and that is what they hate. Again, those are the things that we have talked about in the past and it is gone.

Ulrike Ernst: *You are just bringing us to the next question. The preparation of the transfer of the presidency from Nelson R. Mandela to Thabo Mbeki, or with the shift from the 'Reconstruction and Development Plan' to the implementation of the 'Growth, Employment and Redistribution Programme' the political and economic aims have been changing towards a (neo-liberal) market economy. Which perspectives does this open or re-open for the cultural work of the trade unions in South Africa? Does one go back to the call for people's culture, or worker culture as elaborated in the 'Staffrider' special issue of 1998 where a comment reads: "Worker culture has filled a vacuum in popular struggle by sharply probing the reality of workers' experiences at the cutting edge of capitalist exploitation"?*[6]

Nise Malange: We have always been concerned about the shop floor, because that is working class. We have always differentiated between the top leadership, the shop stewards there, because they were the ones that had access to management, that had access to the top of the pyramid, and the bottom of the pyramid are the workers. So, as the dissenting voices we were always concerned about the bottom of the pyramid because that is where the decisions should be coming from.

But now the pyramid has taken over. The decisions come from top, and they never get to the bottom, the working class. Workers see this, but they don't even know that half of the shares are owned by COSATU or by their own unions. That is why you have disputes in the Eastern Cape now, where workers dismiss shop stewards and union officials. That is, for me, power to the workers. If they are able to say, we don't want the shop steward, we don't want these officials, union, back off! Back off, because you are not doing what we have asked you to do. That is what this country needs to do today. It is to choose their own leadership in terms of the worker leadership, and make those people accountable to them, not all these masses to be accountable to the top of the pyramid. That has to stop. That is the only way that is going to make sure that the worker movement addresses the issues of the workers. It talks about the bread and butter issues, it talks about the redress, and it gets involved in terms of privatisation of the assets of the state. The assets of the state, they don't go to the few. That is what is happening: If I am in the union leadership, that is a guaranteed ticket to the next election to go to the parliament, to go to the corporate sector as one of the non-executive directors or director, that is a ticket to this and a ticket to that. If these people are aware of that, then they will stop it.

To re-democratise the workers, the shop floor would definitely do that, the masses are going to do that. Sooner than you expect it, because they are already starting. If PE does it, in Natal, Toyota did it here. Workers have got to take control in this country in order to make sure that things like GEAR don't just go without any consultation. But we are told that the government sometimes doesn't have to consult anybody.

You sweat and produce, but you are told that sometimes we can't consult you on issues. We can't have the kind of free trade zone without having to say something, because it is what we have here. It is what Americans were fighting for; it is what the Mexicans were fighting for. But for us it just comes in because our government thinks we owe the world something. We know that the world has played a big role in terms of our own liberation. But now the world can't seriously dictate on us. Perhaps our leadership uses the world to dictate on us. There are several things that are happening and the workers are not happy about it, but they keep quiet because they want to give democracy a chance. And when they had enough, as the Capetonians said, when we are 'gatvol', we fool them. We pick up. For me that is what is going to happen. And when that happens, hell knows what will happen to a lot of people in this country. It is going so fast. Workers protested against GEAR. In a way it didn't come on the big scale, as it was supposed to be pushed down the workers' throats.

The role that culture has played was to make sure that GEAR, all these things that were coming up, were interpreted and explained in a language that workers understand and to help them to voice themselves through workshops. A person would say this and I would pick it up in my poem, we will pick it up in music, we will pick it up in theatre. There is a gap that we have. There is no one who interprets. You go now to the trade union office, and you find newsletters, newspapers packed up to there. No worker is reading, because they are either in English, or even if they are in Zulu it is difficult, because no one takes those newspapers to workers. Very few have access to those things.

So the flow of information, the flow of education doesn't go to the shop floor. The minute it does, hell knows what would happen. It is a pity that it will be late because more than say sixty, seventy, eighty percent of industries will have been privatised. Most of the companies now have shares and people own shares, so you don't have much say. The employer would say, "Your shop stewards own shares", or "Your union owns shares, so you can't afford to have this increase". By the time they understand what it means to be a shareholder in the company, it will be too late.

What we are doing? We are playing in the pyramid, the dissenting voices around there. But those dissenting voices are not there any more. That is a pity. We couldn't do anything because the European Union said, "We give money to COSATU now because COSATU plays a more political role. Cultural and Working Life, go and apply to COSATU!" And COSATU has its own priorities about that money. And somebody else said, "Oh, no", because we are related to workers, "we can't really give you money because you are giving information to workers, and it is not good for business." So we went and talked to many others. They answered, "Yes, your role is important but knock somewhere else."

Out in the street they say to me, "Comrade, you are a traitor, and you sold us out!" And I said, "Comrades, my children need food and I need a house to stay. You want to see me in the street, being a hobo with two children. Would you like to see that?" They say, "No comrade". I said, "That is the reason, because I was earning a salary, and I was doing all this work. All those that were giving us money said no thank you, we cannot do it any more. That is why I have to go somewhere else to get money. That is why I have little time with you to do these things now. Because the situation has changed. When I started, I was employed by the union. The union will never employ me now to educate you against them, because that is how they see it now. They see us against them."

We are seen as much more controversial. "Why do you talk to these people? You are not supposed to be talking to them; you are supposed to be talking to us on top here. So if you are friends with us at the top, we can do things for you, but we have to tell you what to do for those people down there." You know - *"Them and Us"*. That is one poem that I have written. About them and us and the dissenting voices. I do all those poems; I put them down, and I would go and read them somewhere where it is relevant to do that. We have our little groupings now where your poetry can be appreciated, and that is what is happening. I go to where I am appreciated. If I am not, I don't bother myself.

Ulrike Ernst: *Let us turn more to literature and writers. How do you see the development and importance of literature in the South African society after apartheid? What are the new themes; which writers are important to you?*

Nise Malange: In the past, elections were our concern, the Truth and Reconciliation Commission, the healing of the nation, the reconstruction and development, giving hope to people. Or anti-racism, anti-tribalism and ethnic conflict, and the importance of nation-building. We need really to address this as writers in this country.

We have been a fragmented nation. A nation that has had to endure a whole life experience and each time you think about it, then you say proudly that real South Africans are a forgiving nation. We keep on praising ourselves, but I see all the problems that we have, the high rate of AIDS and HIV. I see ourselves being able to educate through literature. Educate people about their rights and what it means to have a right. That you need to be responsible as well. Develop a culture of human rights perhaps with the help of literature. We would be able to respect the laws of this country because we come from a culture that never respected any law. We were lawbreakers because all the laws were made against us. In educating people, taking people from that culture, literature would play a very important role. To say that the laws and regulations are made for us to guide us and to put us in order. The high rate of rape and incest and abuse of children in this country would stop when you educate people. Men put the blame on transformation and transition and the fear of losing the power, because women are taking over. We could be able to get people into that transition. We haven't had anything, to really work with people and make them feel comfortable during this transition.

In terms of integration of schools we need something that says to people, if you want to know about my culture, this is who I am and what I am. Through my poetry, through my music, through something that will not intimidate you but something that you will appreciate and take home. Listen to the lyrics and say I think I believe in this, I think I like it this way. It is true, like the dancing and the crafts and everything that we do that we would be able to do. Through new books, children's books that could be used in schools through beautiful poetry that we can create and that would form part of transition and transformation of schools. It is not something that dictates what people should do. People would have choices. It is true coming up and saying, you have got a choice now. And make use of that choice responsibly.

The beauty that we are missing is to say to people, be responsible for your country. Make South Africa and become patriotic. We've never been patriotic; we've never felt we owned the country and have been part of it because of apartheid. People can't just turn overnight because the conditions still don't show that. In terms of infrastructure conditions, the high rate of unemployment, the sicknesses and disease.

But we can make people relate to the country. The theatre that we are doing is participation theatre, is saying "I want this, what do you want?" and the other person "I want this". And it makes that you can go and take a rhythm and whoever didn't understand would understand the rhythm and would come with a positive gesture. We had workshops where we do group poems. Those group poems you can take in the street and ask for a line from a person and create this chain poem, where people say this is what I like. Or this is what I want my country to be. And then people feel they are contributing towards the betterment of this country. That is the thing that we are missing at the moment. This is the kind of literature that we as writers want to do. It is still about entertaining, it is about educating people, it is about developing our country, it is about saying we are all responsible, let's be patriotic. Not only sports should do that. I think literature plays a very, very big role. The lyrics, those words, are really important. We can still change people who listen to poetry, read books, and watch television dramas. We writers can start thinking about how to address all these issues, for example the issue of corruption in this country by government officials. On the other hand, there is so much love that we see. There is so much beauty. There are so many beautiful stories, that we can come up with that would really bring us together as a nation.

Some artists are struggling in such a way that they would rather take the safety zone, the old traditions, the Shaka, the Dingane, the Dinizulus because it is a safer zone that everyone wants to identify with. If we talk about the royal family; we've got King Zwelithini, what is beautiful about him? Because he is a living legend.

One other role - we have to encourage Thabo to do the right thing. If he comes with a speech that builds the nation, let us capitalise on that speech and make it a speech that will haunt him. When he promises I will do the right thing for the people of this country, let us make him do that through our poetry, through our music, through the literature that we write.

I do creative writing programmes with children of multi-cultural communities. We want them to create for themselves the kind of utopia, rainbow nation, they want to see. But again educate them about the history and say this is what happened. Make sure that it never happens again you need to know, because if you don't know, you might repeat it. Either through black dictatorship or through another dictatorship. I see my role with the youth, and do it in a humorous way so that they learn and come back and ask innocently "Auntie Nise, did it really happen?" I say, "It happened my Baby, it really happened." "And why? But you are not so wounded spiritually." And I say, "I am a very positive person. I want you to be positive as well." Because I have older role models that are very positive who have gone through hell in this country, but they are positive. I pick up from them and I take it down to these young ones. I am not damaged in any way, I am not a person who is hating, I am not a racist (I am not praising myself!), and I am not a sexist. I am a vibrant person, and I like to work with people, and that is what I do with my creative writing programme. I want to learn from the young ones. Their thoughts are not tainted with blood, with anger, with frustration. I watch them dancing here. We see both black and white kids, really dancing to the rhythm of Africa and I would just say wow! I wish I had had that opportunity! If I work with them I get motivated. I see the future through their stories, through their poems, through their love letters. They like to write about love. They like to write love letters, the cross-cultural relations. At those ages they would like to know what we think as the old ones because they know that we have problems with that. My whole world now, I would like to see it through the eyes of the children.

Ulrike Ernst: *When you, Hlatshwayo and Qabula published the collection 'Black Mamba Rising' a discussion emerged about the correct picture of history* *and the appropriate use of African tradition in literature.*[7] *How would you assess the ways in which African tradition is or should be represented in the South African arts?*

Nise Malange: I think those days, it was more than that, and it was the fact that for the first time workers have produced literature up to a particular standard. In the past - we still carry that baggage - white anthropologists and sociologists and everyone else thought that they had to write about us because we didn't have the skills. So we didn't write anything about ourselves. They interpreted whatever we said in their own way. And then we came out and said, stop, we can do it ourselves.

Our tradition has not changed, but I think the tradition in this country now, it is shaping itself up. It has been modernised, in every form. We have now white praise poets and white people are claiming their place in our society and say 'I am a white praise poet and I am a South African poet'. And we embrace those people because they have a right to say that. No one owns any tradition in this country. We invented things and people become part of that. There are white people that were born on the farms in the rural areas that the first thing that they learned was the African tradition. Maybe in a white home, but in an African environment. So they've got a right to own that. We have poets like Chris Mann, who is also a praise poet; he has even assumed an African name, Zithulele, 'the one that keeps quiet'.

'Black Mamba Rising' was just a catalyst. It was putting worker literature and grassroots writers in the right place and was saying that we would be able to discuss things in our own right. That is what is happening even with praise poets as illiterate as Mahlini Okantanzi. They are able to defend their style, their content and the fact that they know they are spontaneous. No one can say, but in your last poem you did this in *'Izibongo zi ka Shaka'* the praise of King Shaka, and now you are saying this. We had poets mixing the Shakas and Gorbatchevs and all the struggles worldwide. People started looking at the tradition in a much broader way because the praise poetry tradition was seen as a very traditional and a sacred thing. But they took that away from there, because you don't own this. The style and everything else you can create it yourself. The praise poetry or the praise singing belongs to all South Africans. I think that is where other styles came out, like the dub poetry, like Mzwakhe Mbuli and a lot of other dub poets. And rap poets like Lesego Rampholokeng. They all came and said, we are now the new generation, we are coming up with our own styles, like it is happening with music. You have the Kwaito music with the young generation and they try to put all the different styles together.

Culture has to develop. The way we dress, the way we talk, the language that we use, the literature that we write, the paintings that we do, everything that we do, is influenced by the times. The times are changing. Our poetry was written by hand, but they use computers now. They come up with little nice things in metre and the like. Some of the poetry is accompanied by music. The traditions and the cultures are not static.

Ulrike Ernst: *Part of the question of tradition is that of language and of identity. Different Nguni languages were in the past promoted to serve the colonisers' ruling order. How do you locate the terrain of languages and tribal politics as part of cultural and literary politics in the new South Africa?*

Nise Malange: Some politicians push their ideologies now more and more. They can see people are unifying at the grassroots level. People have recognised the fact that we are all Nguni people, the Xhosas, the Zulus, the Swazis and whoever, and we are one nation and one big tribe. Politically those tensions are really high. I wouldn't like to go into that. When you look at political leadership: the second president is Xhosa, we have to have a Zulu deputy president whether we like it or not. So they try to compromise to win but it is not really happening. The tensions that are there are too high, and there is no one to neutralise them. But when you look at the people on a community level or a grassroots level, they have gone beyond the whole tribal, and that is why violence has subsided.

The window-dressing is really happening and is creating a lot of problems and a lot of tensions. I don't see us becoming a nation that is 100% embracing all this, because how also we are geographically created, the KwaZulu-Natal, the Cape being the Xhosa. Even though our king has decided to take as a fifth wife a Xhosa woman to make sure that we are one nation, and a lot of daughters of King Zwelithini, they go and marry Xhosa men. Amongst the Xhosa people, there are always fights between the small tribes. We've got the Sothos, the Vendas, and everyone is trying to assert himself at the moment. The Vendas are also coming up and claiming things. These claims are coming in different ways, and I think part of the transition would be to deal with that. The only way that would ever capture the beauty of all these cultures, the dance and music, and the poetry, would be through coming up with very good cultural structures and platforms.

Ulrike Ernst: *May I add on that issue a more personal question in connection with your experience? Ari Sitas writes about you that as a youth, you were mocked by your own people for not being either a 'real Coloured' or a 'real Xhosa'. How do you discuss such topics today?*

Nise Malange: Whatever experiences one has gone through, they don't have a place. People that still have those grudges are people like us, the older ones. They don't have a bearing on our children. My daughter doesn't even know, she is light in complexion like me, the father is Pedi, he is light in complexion, but the other inheritance ...; we always say in South Africa that no-one can say that he or she is a pure kind of group. I can't say I am purely Xhosa or my children. I always tell them that you are Coloured, because your father is Pedi, and I am Xhosa. So we are a mix, and we are a beautiful mix.

The baggage that we are carrying really doesn't have a place. It will be us that we carry that and influence our children to make those choices, but our children are just not prepared to take our baggage and to take it with them. They want to build this country together because they are in the same school now, they are in the same communities, they dress the same way, they have earrings here and earrings there and everything else and that's cool for them. Let our children work and relate that way. Let them build this country the way they would like to see it and as parents and older people let's look at this country through their eyes and let's give it a chance. They've got the right; they've got the choice.

Ulrike Ernst: *In your essay 'Woman Workers and the Struggle for Cultural Transformations', you protest that in South Africa "the broad issues raised with the rise of the women's liberation movement internationally have not taken root among the rank and file of progressive organisations" and clash with "traditional patriarchal attitudes".[8] How will these old categories of race, class and gender have a bearing on writing in the future?*

Nise Malange: They don't have a place in the future. They don't have a place in the future because we are now - I don't want to use the word 'rainbow nation' - but I think we are a nation that says I would accept you, I would accept if you would decide to go into a cross-cultural relationship or marriage. I would still respect you if you remain with your own grouping; it is your own right. So the minute that we understand each other's rights and choices, which I think is the culture that is developing in South Africa, is the respect for whoever's choice and the right of that person to do that. The laws of the country now allow those kinds of things to happen.

I was struggling with the whole patriarchal kind of stance within the unions, primarily in KwaZulu-Natal, where there was this complex problem of the place of women. We were talking about triple oppression, which was much more a gender thing. Culturally, women in the unions, especially African women, were not participating fully. Their place was not seen as in leadership positions. They were OK with white women being general secretaries; black women were always seen on the administration level.

One of the things that one also experienced was that the workers would never talk to a woman about their problems. So the whole Zulu tradition was one big problem that we have had within the union. Something that I raised when I first came to Natal was the ethnic problem between Xhosas and Zulus. One of the things that I had always said to people was this ethnic problem will one-day blow into big trouble. And people never wanted to listen to that. When we had the violence between Xhosas and the Zulus, I then repeated that we need to discuss these things.

I think what I can say in terms of all that experience, and I think as women in this country, we have taken our place. We had all these discussions, and I assert myself, you are labelled as a feminist. I don't know when was the last time I heard the word 'feminist'. Because feminism divided us in this country as women, black and white. It really divided us because people saw it as a Western thing, but when you look at it now it was never a Western thing; it was a woman's thing, worldwide. We are asserting ourselves; we are taking up key positions - I am the director now of this BAT Centre; I am the chairperson of the Provincial Council the majority of which are very traditional Zulu men, and I can make men stop and listen to me without intimidating them, they realise that.

That is why we also have so much pressure in terms of crime, in terms of rape. Because men now can see that there is nothing that they can do to really put us down. No words, no sexual harassment, nothing. The only thing that can put us down is when you get raped. But we are uniting against rape of women in this country as well, and we are saying that it has to stop. If it needs that, we'll make it stop, and we'll do it as women across culture and colour line. Those are really the struggles that we are facing as women. Seriously, what is happening is just terrible. I really see that it has nothing to do with transformation; it is the power that they had and lost. The rights are protecting both men and women. We just have to find a way as women now to say, stop doing this to us, and make sure that the justice system, the policing protects us as women before we get out of hand and protect ourselves. So we have to be constantly saying that you give all these avenues to men, the *'Domestic Violence Act'* protects us according to the law, but the justice system, the magistrates and police still have to come up to that.

Ulrike Ernst: *Let me ask you a last question: Outside of South Africa, the literature of this country is largely connected with the name of Nobel Prize winner Nadine Gordimer. Inside the country, her achievements as a writer and a political figure have been the subject of heated controversy. In the above-mentioned essay, you claim "women representatives who have the political consciousness, information and the awareness of the power of writing must come forward and set an example."*[9]

How do you explain firstly the difference in the reception of the work of Nadine Gordimer, and secondly, is she such an example for you?

Nise Malange: I have to be honest. Nadine Gordimer has been one of the COSAW members, and I've served with her. She was also one of the vice-presidents. We are both Scorpions; I am 19 November, she is 20 November, but other than that I have nothing in common with Nadine, and to be honest, I have never even read Nadine's books.

I think we as South Africans, especially activists and organisations and individuals, we've really created monsters, somehow we created certain people that represented us. I think that time it was good that we had a person like her. But, Nadine goes to New York, has family there, she sits there and has leisure time to write as a full-time writer. None of us will never find that opportunity and would never have that even in our next life. We are struggling artists who will struggle until we go to the grave. Even if we try to make laws that there should be grants for artists to write full time, we will never get there. All the opportunities we'll ever have is to go to Germany, to Stuttgart, for six months to be able to write a novel, or go to America for three months, to Iowa, to be able to write. We have always found time in between either house chores or school work or work, where you find time to sit and write, but we never had, what I can't even call a privilege. We can't blame people like Nadine for what they have, for the wealth that they have. It is a very sore point for a lot of us, and we are struggling with that.

I have never counted my success in literature through the number of books that I publish. I count my success through the number of other young writers that have published. I have been able to publish them through my own Barefoot Publication route that I have chosen to take. Or through helping them through to get them published. I am now the advisor of Kwela Books in Cape Town, where I have managed to get a lot of other young writers to be published and helped them to distribute and launch and sell themselves. That is how I see myself as a successful writer. All my concern is to sit down with young writers, talk about their writing, help them. Or workers, I have manuscripts of workers that are in Zulu; they want to have them translated into other languages and get a little bit of that published. That is my concern. That is how I see the development of literature and the development of writing. I have three manuscripts that have never been published. Every publisher wants them, but I said no, wait until I have achieved at least five young writers to be published, then I would give my work. I am also willing to have all their other stuff and have a collection with them, so that they can use my name to get their writing sold. I always look at those strategies and I respect a person who would do that.

I am not saying that what they have is wrong; it is right for them to have what they have; it is right for me to have what I have. I don't want to be compared with people. I don't compare myself with anyone. I like Nadine as a person, but I don't like when someone is made a goddess, because I don't believe in idols. I believe in me, and I believe in the Creator. And we have done that, we have made gods of people in this country, and we have made them tokens. Nadine has been a token in literature. She has published widely, but she has been a token. I remember one debate we had, which was part of the department of Arts and Culture of the ANC desk, where we were talking about the development of literature and development of writers, and I don't know what she said, but one writer was very, very annoyed. He said, "You know, I don't know what happened to you, Nadine Gordimer, maybe you just woke up one day and looked at yourself in the mirror and saw yourself being black, and you had lost all the skills and the wealth! Because the way you talk is as if you neither have money, nor skills. You talk as if when you are sitting at home you don't take calls at particular times. You are not accessible to people. You will never go and help people because you've got commitments; you've got agencies that are waiting for your manuscript to be completed; you are going to New York to do this and that, and please don't come and tell us that you are part of us, because you never, and you never will be part of us."

We will never be friends because the distribution of wealth and skills in this country. Wealth and skills, those two, work together. If I've got the skills, then I can acquire wealth and the other way around. But as I said to you, I am a socialist, and I don't care about wealth. I care about bread and butter issues: my children's education and food and paying my rent, and that's all I care for, and be able to take you out for a drink once in a while. Any big things, they are not part of me; they are not in my veins. In ten years when you come back here I will be fifty. I haven't acquired anything, and I am not prepared to acquire anything. My real satisfaction comes with the programmes that I run, making other people happy, and making those people feel that they are part of the community, and that they are contributing something. Make them feel that they can achieve something in their lifetime. That is for me what I go for. That is a spiritual achievement.

Ulrike Ernst: *Nise Malange, thank you very much for the refreshing interview.*

References

[1] **Sachs, Albie. 1990 [1989].** "'Preparing Ourselves for Freedom'. ANC In-House Seminar Paper on Culture". In: **de Kok, Ingrid/Press, Karen (eds.). 1990.** Spring is Rebellious. Arguments about Cultural Freedom by Albie Sachs and Respondents: 19-29.

[2] **Malange, Nise. 1991.** "Interview Nise Malange". In: **Brown, Duncan/van Dyk, Bruno (eds.) 1991.** Exchanges. South African Writing in Transition. Durban: 41-45.

[3] **Malange, Nise. 1991.** "Interview Nise Malange". In: **Brown, Duncan/ van Dyk, Bruno (eds.) 1991.** Exchanges. South African Writing in Transition. Durban: 41.

[4] Malange, Nise quoted in: **Gevisser, Marc. 1993.** "Cultural Parents 'must learn to let go'". In: Mail & Guardian 1-7 Oct: 45.

[5] Malange, Nise quoted in: **Gevisser, Marc. 1993.** "Cultural Parents 'must learn to let go'". In: Mail & Guardian 1-7 Oct: 43. 45.

[6] **Meintjes, Frank/ Hlatshwayo, Mi et al. (eds.). 1989.** Worker Culture. Special Issue of Staffrider 8 (3/4). Johannesburg: 4.

[7] **Sitas, Ari (ed.). 1986.** Black Mamba Rising. South African Worker Poets in Struggle. Alfred Qabula, Mi S'Dumo Hlatshwayo, Nise Malange. Durban.

[8] **Malange, Nise. 1989.** "Women Workers and the Struggle for Cultural Transformation". In: **Meintjes, Frank/ Hlatshwayo, Mi et al. (eds.). 1989.** Worker Culture. Special Issue of Staffrider 8 (3/4). Johannesburg: 76-80. 77. 79.

[9] **Malange, Nise. 1989.** "Women Workers and the Struggle for Cultural Transformation". In: **Meintjes, Frank/ Hlatshwayo, Mi et al. (eds.). 1989.** Worker Culture. Special Issue of Staffrider 8 (3/4). Johannesburg: 80.

Nadine Gordimer

**Nadine Gordimer interviewed by Ulrike Ernst
on 24 April 2000 in Johannesburg**

"Writers Need Readers"

Ulrike Ernst: *Nadine Gordimer, you have gained a world-wide reputation with your ever growing, voluminous corpus of novels and stories which, having been a distinguished contribution to the anti-apartheid struggle in South Africa, earned you the Nobel Prize for literature in 1991. Throughout that time you have also shown a wide range of interests and engagements in your non-fiction work, with essays such as in the early 'Black Interpreters'[1], 'The Essential Gesture'[2] or 'Writing and Being'[3]. In 1999, you published a new collection of essays, 'Living in Hope and History'[4], and added the documentary film 'The Wall in the Mind'[5].*

When you compared your fiction and non-fiction output, you seemed to suggest that you valued the first higher than the latter when you state in the essay 'Living in the Interregnum', "Nothing I say here will be as true as my fiction"[6], or more recently, "The best there is in us as writers is in our books"[7].

What importance do you ascribe to your non-fiction work in the time of transition of the South African society?

Nadine Gordimer: Well, first of all, there is no 'seems to' about it - there is no question: the non-fiction work that I have done, this comes out of often a sense of indignation, of outrage about things that were happening, and it is my reaction as a citizen, as a South African and as a human being, rather than as a writer. I must emphasise that very strongly. I am not an 'anti-apartheid writer'. I did not come to writing through a strong political sense. I was writing from the age of nine, when I didn't know what politics was.

Now the other part of your question, the real part of your question, can you repeat it?

Ulrike Ernst: *What importance do you ascribe to your non-fiction work in the time of transition, now, in the new South Africa?*

Nadine Gordimer: Well, it follows on whatever it was worth in the time of the struggle, the liberation struggle, when I not only spoke, and wrote, and I'm not by nature a public person at all. I think if I hadn't lived in a situation of great conflict about which I felt very strongly, I would probably never have appeared on a public platform, and would never have written articles. But you belong to the situation to which you are born and find yourself if you stay there, and I have stayed here. So whatever I contributed during the anti-apartheid struggle, life doesn't end when apartheid goes. The reconstruction period also requires some dedication on the part of anybody who feels that they belong and that they have a role as a citizen. And since I am a writer, then, for non-fiction purposes, I have used that as well, and continued to taking up issues that I think are tremendously important.

At present I am particularly engaged in the fight against AIDS, because I think that all the other things that concern me in the transition period, the lack of housing, the lack of work, the dreadful inheritance of - one can hardly call it education - from the apartheid era and the previous dispensations before that, which were also racial. They all can be undermined, no matter what you do, if you have this terrible problem of people dying of AIDS and if one wants to be selective in terms of what happens to the governance of a country. The people who are skilled, who are necessary to keep things going, they are very high in the number of people who die of AIDS. So that is one of the things that I have taken up out of a sense of great concern, adding whatever voice I have to urge people to think about this. I have written about it. Last month I attended a big meeting at United Nations of the World Alliance Against AIDS in Africa - a great emphasis on Africa. I wrote a piece subsequent to that which was published in the New York Times and is now appearing in other countries.

But of course my other concerns remain, which are cultural - what is going to happen to our literature here while we have very, very high illiteracy in the country. We writers need readers, you know.

Ulrike Ernst: *As part of your continuing sense of political responsibility after the end of apartheid, you became a member of the ANC and in 1993 were elected as a member of a board of trustees obliged to oversee a proposed foundation for arts and culture concerned with the process of transformation and cultural reconstruction, under the wing of the ANC's Department of Arts and Culture. In 1996, you were appointed as trustee of the 'Arts and Culture Trust of the President'.*

Nadine Gordimer: No, this is not quite right. No. First of all, you are not elected to be a trustee, and (right) I was attached to the African National Congress; I was a member of the African National Congress long before you could have a card. So my active association with the African National Congress long predates the time when the change came. Secondly, the cultural organisation that you mention, it's one of many to which I belong. So I don't think there is much point in singling it out. I am one of the founders of the Congress of South African Writers, which, alas, is not in a state to be talked about at the moment. The cultural movement that you mentioned, yes, indeed I am a trustee, but I am also a trustee of the Windybrow Cultural Centre and attached to the BATSUMI Film Trust. I am concerned about us bringing culture to the forefront.

As you know, the position is, I'm sure others have told you, that we relied on funds from outside. We had very helpful people, particularly in Scandinavia and in Holland and to a lesser extent other countries, who funded our cultural movements, whether it was theatre, whether it was literary, whether it was publishing, whatever it was, they did this. Once we had our own government, our own government in a free South Africa, and a Department of Arts and Culture, then the answer from abroad was, no, now everything belongs to you, people of South Africa, so you must fund your own cultural movements. But of course there are so many, many other things, naturally, that are seen as of greater importance: to bring people electricity, to bring them water, to put a roof over their heads, people who are squatting everywhere. So culture has become rather a stepchild. Which means we have to keep awareness of culture to the forefront and find ways of raising funds at home and also of convincing people abroad that it is still essential. If they care about the reconstruction as they cared about the struggle, then we still need help from them when they can afford it and of course they can afford it. So that is the premise upon which I am active now.

Ulrike Ernst: *Some might argue that an organic development towards the establishment of a strengthened democracy in South Africa implies a separation of the previously necessary alliance between ANC, SACP and COSATU. How would this dissolution influence the development of cultural politics, or how would this process enhance opportunities for the independence of writers as a literary opposition?*

Nadine Gordimer: Are you talking about the Congress Alliance here?

Ulrike Ernst: *Yes.*

Nadine Gordimer: I can't see that this would make any great difference. Unfortunately, no matter who is in government at the time, if there were to be a change of government to the left, or heaven forbid, to the right, I can't see that we could come first; writers, artists, before defence. I think that is the story all over the world. There is always money for the defence budget, and the cultural budget, even in countries that are more culturally aware; this comes very, very far behind.

But I think what people overseas and in South Africa, particularly in South Africa, need to understand, brought to realisation of, is that arts are part of education. You see, when you apply to various government agencies shall we say, or parts of government here, and you have to fill in forms and give in your mission and your 'raison d'être' you are not regarded as part of education. You cannot say, well, we have a school, and we take this exam now and that exam then. We don't have that kind of regular formal education curriculum - how can we have it! So it is not understood that arts are indeed an essential part of education. That you cannot simply have formal education without a very strong contribution from the arts. Studying a few books in a language class or in a literature class, that isn't really nurturing the arts in the way that they should be. So I think unless we can get it understood that arts are absolutely integral to education, we are going to be in trouble.

Ulrike Ernst: *Now I would like to turn to your recent documentary film, 'The Wall in the Mind'[8], which Hugo Cassirer produced in collaboration with you. At the beginning of the film you explain your interest in the comparison. "[B]oth cities have experienced the consequences of extraordinary social engineering, the wall that divided Berlin by ideology, and the wall that was apartheid that divided Johannesburg by colour. In each city there has been a forced distortion of human relationships."*

Where elsewhere a similarity is only claimed between apartheid and fascism, rather than between apartheid and the East German dictatorship, you underline the similarities, which seem to manifest themselves especially in the comparable aims of the opposition. As an example, you cite writers as oppositional thinkers and representational figures in each interregnum, as shown in your interviews with Wally Serote, or Christa Wolf or your fellow Nobel laureate, Günter Grass.

You show in the film that beyond the shared celebration of the new order what calls for specific cultural political intervention are not only the economic discrepancies but also the historically developed mentality gap.

What task of intellectuals would you ascribe to writers in these two societies of transformation?

Nadine Gordimer: It is always the same: to tell the truth as they see it. Nobody gets the whole truth. But to paraphrase, I think Goethe said somewhere, if you thrust your hand deep into the social fabric around you, you will bring up something of the truth. And I think that is what the writers should do. That is the writers' task. It's not something that one writer can do, or two writers can do, it is something that is put together by the sensibility of writers, by their questing minds from all over the world. So whether it is Günter Grass and Christa Wolf in Germany, whether it is Susan Sontag in America, whether it is myself and others here, it is all part of trying to understand how we live, why we live, and now, of course with the way this great talk of globalisation, where we fit in with the rest of the world.

So I think that is the task. Simply to approach our writing in the same way as we did before the 'Wende', that we are seeing how social forces affect people in their most intimate lives. Sometimes you are not even conscious of what you are doing; you are telling an intimate story, and when you look at it afterwards you realise that part of the reason why people behaved as they did, part of the reason why they looked for the solutions they did, comes from the society, from the societal values and mores that enclose them.

This last novel of mine, *'The House Gun'*[9], is to me the most glaring example of this. I began to write the book, interested in the relationship between the son and parents, and coming out of that, the wider theme: what are the responsibilities of life? If you say 'I love you' to a lover, to a friend, to a parent, to a child, especially a child, because you are responsible, you brought that child into the world - how far does the responsibility of that love go? Does this mean that no matter what that person does, no matter how reprehensible the behaviour that they exhibit is, that you always must stand by them, that you cannot withdraw that love in some kind of distaste or horror? So that was what I thought, that to me was what my book was going to be about.

But when I got deep into it and looked back at how the young man in a sense of absolute outrage or despair picks up the gun and goes and shoots the man, his former lover, who is now making love to his present, the woman he is living with, then I thought, well, why was that gun there? If the gun hadn't been there, he might have gone over and they might have had a fistfight, he might have punched him. But the gun is there because the gun is part of many, many households, certainly in this country, but also in many households in the rest of the world. Otherwise you wouldn't read, as you do, of these incidents in America, in France, I haven't heard about any in Germany, but they may happen, where a school child is annoyed with a teacher or has a row with a fellow pupil and takes daddy's gun and goes and shoots. It is happening virtually now every day. So this is a gun-happy world, where the gun is, as I have remarked in the book, like the household cat; it is there. So this is the way we are shaped by and influenced by the society in which we live.

Ulrike Ernst: *To return to the film: the East German Christa Wolf participated in the 'Wende', the changes, as a public person with her speeches, through her fictional and non-fictional work. She caused a heated debate about the role of literature and the writer and society in the unified Germany. How do you see the role and reception of Christa Wolf in the initial stages of German transformation and after the incorporation of East Germany into the West German constitution?*

Nadine Gordimer: First of all, you must remember that I am an outsider, so I only know what I read in the press. I haven't spent my time talking about these things when I have been with Christa. We've got more interesting things to talk about since we both live in the present. She certainly has put it behind her, but it has been very painful for her.

I see her certainly as a victim of circumstances of a particular kind. I am thinking particularly of two things. First of all I think she was accused of why didn't you publish 'this book' while the East German regime was still as rigid as it was. I can't give a judgement really on that, but I could see that she was first of all writing, saying perhaps the same things in a different way. The censorship was so incredibly rigid that it was very difficult to get away with saying anything outright. But I only read her writings in translation, of course - I can see in other writings of hers, which were not didactic, that they were against what the regime was doing.

Her position was very difficult because, as she has told me, and as she has said again and again, she was born and brought up as a communist, and she believed that this was the way that society should evolve if you wanted justice. To a certain extent, I think she still thinks so. She and I both believe - we meet there - that the left isn't dead. The left as it was practised, as it deteriorated in the Soviet Union and its satellites, that was indeed a tragic and terrible failure, but if you look at the communist period in Europe and Russia it didn't even last a century. And I cannot believe that some of the best of the ideas behind it, which were abused then by the people in power - that they don't have to be looked at again. You've only got to look at previous revolutions - if you think what came out of the French Revolution for example, which is part of the democratic idea today, long absorbed into totally accepted democracy among people who are only liberals, certainly not left. And if you look at 1848, again we have a revolution, and so it goes on. Right up to the Russian Revolution, to the October Revolution. Something good has come. Even though these revolutions were followed by terror, either the terror or subsequent terrors. So that unfortunately human beings learn very much the hard way, but society is, it is not immobile. It has to change all the time, it has to select, it has to throw away what has turned out to be a tragic failure and adopt what is still worthwhile.

And what people perhaps don't want to recognise is that the same thing applies to capitalism. Capitalism is regarded as the foundation of democracy. Well, what about the other foundations that I have mentioned? Capitalism is very reluctant to discard what it sees doesn't work, the inequalities that still exist in the most advanced and wealthy capitalist societies. We've only got to look at America - it is democratic, it is capitalist, and it still has a great many very poor people, it has a lot of illiteracy or semi-illiteracy, so that we have to be open-minded, but at the same time not open-minded in the sense that we don't believe in anything.

Now I think that Christa, to get back to her, right, she was brought up to be a communist. She really believed that a just society was going to come out of it, and I think that in her writing she dealt with it as she thought she could. Perhaps she could have been bolder, but perhaps that would have stopped her completely from writing at all as happened to writers in South Africa. And then your answer is exile. So we understand her position vis-à-vis this better than other people do, who live in democracies, where they just don't know that this could happen to you.

Then there is the question that she was accused of being an informer, isn't that so? On a very low level. But she was approached, and she was asked if she noticed anything. I think she was very young then, she was a student. Well, the very word informer makes anybody shudder.

So those of us who lived here - South Africa - whose organisations, we are talking about now, NGOs, cultural and otherwise, were infiltrated constantly by people who were spying. That was on the one side. On the other hand, if not in just my loyalty to a movement, the African National Congress, but to my conviction that apartheid was totally wrong and that the pursuance of apartheid's aims were indeed evil, so that if it didn't happen but if I had noticed among the circles in which I moved somebody who indeed was pushing these ideas, or who was a danger to the liberation movement - I would have had no hesitation, even though that person had been sitting next to me as you are sitting now - going to my comrades in the African National Congress or to other parts of the anti-apartheid movement, and saying look out for so-and-so. Now, is that informing? Indeed, on that level in the anti-apartheid movement we have all of us done it. Look, we mustn't talk openly in front of X, I don't know about that person. And very often you were right, but sometimes you were totally taken in. Like this terrible man, Williamson. You know, the arch-spy. He became a great friend of everybody in the liberation movement, especially among whites. It turned out he had been working for the government all the time.

So that if Christa among her friends heard people, or suspected, or heard things said that seemed to be against the movement she believed in, which was the success of the communist state, and she did mention this to somebody I can understand that! You have to live through, in, that kind of climate to understand that this could happen. I wouldn't call that an informer. Here you are doing it out of idealism, you are not being paid. Of course, there is another question - how serious will it be for the person? Suppose you are wrong and you are getting that person into trouble. These are the terrible questions that face you in the kind of situation that she lived in and to a lesser extent the kind of situation that we lived in here.

Ulrike Ernst: *What do you think about her direct role in the in the transformation period of East Germany?*

Nadine Gordimer: Well, I have talked to her, and I was rather moved because she was very idealistic. The crux of her belief was that by getting rid of the oppressive leaders of the regime, who had done really everything to make a totalitarian society of the worst kind, they had reintroduced a fascism of their own. She still believed that you could reform - you get rid of them, and you return to the old ideals of what that state should be. But there weren't enough of them, her supporters, and perhaps it was... I think that perhaps it was something that, given what had happened right up until then, given the fact that this would have kept the division of Germany, it would have split them for the unforeseeable future, god knows how long and how much protection there would have been. It was unrealistic.

But you see, there it links up with Günter, Günter Grass. Because many people think he was totally against reunification. He wasn't. He just thought that it was done in a rough and hasty way.

Ulrike Ernst: *A democratic society requires a defined official system of representation, but apart from that it also needs a critical voice of the independent intellectual who represents those who are misrepresented or silenced. How would you compare your own role to that of Christa Wolf in the light of this requirement in the new South Africa and in the new Germany?*

Nadine Gordimer: Oh, I think very different. There is no comparison. There are parallels but basically quite different. She has had to fight being discredited and being indeed reviled. She had to go, she went away to America, I think, for six months. She has had a very hard battle.

I have been fortunate. I am not in the position that she was. I threw in my lot with the liberation struggle; I threw in my lot with the African National Congress long ago. And whatever the South African government chose to do to me or wanted to do to me, that is completely over. And there is no question that I am distrusted by one side or another because there are supposed to be no sides in law. I am not in a position of having to fight distrust in whatever I do now. I am simply part of people who are working for reconstruction. Whereas I think her position is difficult, because these old accusations cling to her.

Ulrike Ernst: *However, talking about representation of certain groups in societies who are misrepresented or silenced, as Christa Wolf has taken the side of the 'weaker' East Germans in the process of the unification. (Some even see her as an idol.) How would you find your own role in comparison to that?*

Nadine Gordimer: Well, as I say, there is no comparison. I first of all I didn't know that the East Germans find her an idol. This is something new to me, because some factions of them gave her a hard time when she was suggesting that the system could be reformed. So, have they forgiven her, or do they idolise her, I don't know. But you see, you are stretching very hard to draw us together. There is no comparison. I wish that she had a better and an easier time and more support. As far as I know she doesn't. But I may be wrong. Perhaps it's grown since I talked to her in the last eighteen months.

Ulrike Ernst: *You see, there are very different groupings in former East Germany.*

However, part of the overcoming of the historical consequences on the 'morning after' as you called the new South Africa's experience in the film is an application of the concept of the African Renaissance, evoked by Thabo Mbeki and promoted through Mongane Wally Serote's installation of the South African Chapter of the African Renaissance Institute.

You "interpret the meaning of renaissance in Mbeki's context not as reviving the past [...], but of using it only as a basis for cultural self-realisation and development in an Africa that never existed before because it is an Africa that has come through..."[10]. On the other hand you widely identify how the "political ambitions of the former good black man of the apartheid government, Buthelezi, recklessly stir the power brew of ethnic differences"[11].

How can one reconcile a repressive neo-traditional Africanism with the African Renaissance?

Nadine Gordimer: Well, first of all, one has to do away with the repressive aspect of it. That does not mean to say that you've got to throw out the baby with the bath water, as we say in English. You haven't got to get rid of the whole thing. There are many aspects, I think of traditional organisations in society that are important and worth reviving. I think the recent moves of Mbeki and others to talk to the traditional leaders are a good thing because it is very good, I think, to have an element of what one might call natural authority. It may not be natural to you and me, because speaking for myself, the people that I helped to vote into power, I commit myself to their authority, and they commit themselves to be challenged by me if they don't live up to what I have voted them into the positions for. But in traditional authority, it is total acceptance, it is a kind of faith. Yet I think it can be useful, giving people some kind of psychological support, especially in tremendous times of change like the time of transition.

So I think we have to have a balance. The law must regulate their traditional authority, but that authority must not be pooh-poohed and discounted. Of course it is difficult in our country because it was built up as an alternative to freedom. You know, that is how the 'Bantustans' came about, and that is how there were many of these little tin-pot dictators in the 'Bantustans'. So now we've got to unravel this. Again the same problem - keep the best, and get rid of what is oppressive or what is retroactive.

Ulrike Ernst: *The film shows once more that you are a connoisseur of life in the city, which is what you have proved many times in the realisation of the 'Jim comes to Jo'burg' theme. However, already in his "Turkish Tales", Njabulo Ndebele asks the South African writers not to neglect rural culture[12]. Without solving rural problems the urban civil society could not consolidate itself, he said.*

Must 'Jim leave Jo'burg' for a while? In what sense would it be useful for writers to shift their focus to the rural?

Nadine Gordimer: You mustn't ask writers to become direct agents of change in this way. That is not our purpose. You are asking then for propaganda. And this is something that I personally would never write. I never wrote it even in the darkest days of my loyalty to the struggle. I certainly wouldn't begin to do it now, and I wouldn't like to see writers asked to do this. This is for politicians, journals, journalists, newspapers. And writers must write what they want to write about. And they must write about what they know. If a) most of the work is set in the city, that is because that writer knows it, if b) he/she comes out of the country or a small town background and writes from within that, that is what that writer knows. The best writers have always done this. If you look at Naguib Mahfouz he writes mainly in his wonderful books, his current trilogy, out of Cairo, which he knows. And there are other examples of this. Chinua Achebe from his country, from Nigeria. You know, there are examples, many examples, in Europe and America.

This writing about what you don't know is dangerous. You must know it from inside. Writers do project themselves, but there is a limit beyond which I think you could reject yourself. For me, if we turn to me again, I have written about rural people. You may not remember a novel of mine called '*The Conservationist*'. That was within the orbit of my experience, or experience I have gone after. There is a story of mine called *"The Ultimate Safari"* where not only is it told in the person of a child. The child is black, and the child has walked as a member of a refugee group coming through from Mozambique. That I was able to write because I had personal access to that experience.

I think for anybody to say that writers must stop writing about the city and write about the rural areas, that brings the other question, where are the writers from the rural areas? They are pushed into the background economically, educationally. The ideas may be there but the ability and even minimal education to express these things is not there. So we come back again to the broadening of cultural opportunity, beginning with education and going out into the arts.

Some of the things that I have been connected with have been trying to do this for instance the little BATSUMI Film Trust, where I am working with Mongane Wally Serote. And with Professor Mushe Nkondo in Venda. We've had several successful film festivals there. People coming to the university and then later to the town, the offer was extended to the town and people saw movies, films, African films. Not what they see on television. There are very few places now where there isn't some access to television. So that they see on television American sitcoms and American violence and serials and so on, but they hadn't seen a real film. On a big screen, and relating to our own country. So this is one of the ways of broadening the cultural experience of people.

To do it through literature is harder, but there again comes one of my hobby-horses, and that is that somehow we must fund publishing in African languages. Not of books written for schools, you know, 'educational', which was the only outlet for writers in African languages before. And then these, of course, had to be very carefully censored by the writer to get by: that it wasn't sexy, that it wasn't politically this that and the other. But let's have detective stories, romances, anything in African languages. I don't believe that there is not a reading public out there. I'm sure there are a lot of people who would love to read if the books were available. Entertaining books. But somehow it is difficult. It hasn't been done, there isn't money and there isn't the distribution, there are no bookshops, there are no libraries in these areas.

Ulrike Ernst: *The active role of the writer in his or her society has always been of great concern to you. When, in 1987, the Congress of South African Writers was formed as a representative national political platform for writers in the anti-apartheid struggle, you became its elected patron and trustee. You were elected publicity secretary and furthermore became COSAW vice-president in 1992. The former president of COSAW, Njabulo Ndebele, suggests that writers' organisations in South Africa seem to be an inherently transient phenomenon. Which reasons are responsible for the transience of COSAW?*

Nadine Gordimer: Oh dear. One of the contributing factors to the unhappy demise of COSAW was again funding. We were told from our founders abroad, you now have got your own Ministry of Arts and Culture. And also told - this is very strange - this coming from Europeans and Americans - what about your members, what about your membership fees? Most of our members were so poor, many of them were out of work, very talented, making a lot of use of COSAW and indeed seeing their work published in *'Staffrider'*, which was a wonderful publication. It was a great sorrow to me that we couldn't keep *Staffrider* going. I hope we will be able to revive it. This was due to us being told you've got to raise your own money. And what about those subscriptions. Well, as I say, most of our members hardly had money to eat, never mind to pay a subscription.

Ulrike Ernst: *As you say, in the past, emerging writers found in COSAW a support base, but this base is vanishing. How do you personally promote young writers and according to what criteria do you select the young writers whom you promote?*

Nadine Gordimer: I don't select them, they select me, unfortunately. (Laughs) No, to be serious, this has come to an end, because it was done, I did it in COSAW. I was one of the people who held workshops. Good talents came out of workshops. Workshops, you have twenty people, and if you have two who you could nurture and have come something, that's a great success. Because people would be there out of the desire to be a writer but perhaps should rather be concentrating on journalism or should be what we call a weekend writer, just, you know, for their own amusement. But, there is always someone there who desperately needs just, just that push. But unfortunately that doesn't exist any more.

So, the answer is I'm really not doing this nurturing except individually here and there. And the criterion has always been and will always be that little spark of talent. You must blow on that little spark and get it to glow.

Ulrike Ernst: *May I finally ask you what are you currently working on?*

Nadine Gordimer: I never talk about what I am working on. Sorry. (Laughs)

Ulrike Ernst: *Thank you very much for the interview.*

References

[1] **Gordimer, Nadine. 1973.** The Black Interpreters. Notes on African Writing. Johannesburg.

[2] **Gordimer, Nadine. 1989 [1988].** The Essential Gesture. Writing, Politics and Places. Edited and Introduced by Stephen Clingman. London.

[3] **Gordimer, Nadine. 1994.** Writing and Being. The Charles Eliot Norton Lectures. Cambridge, Mass.

[4] **Gordimer, Nadine. 1999.** Living in Hope and History. Notes from our Century. London.

[5] **Gordimer, Nadine/Cassirer Hugo. 1999.** The Wall in the Mind. A Journey with Nadine Gordimer through Johannesburg and Berlin. (Documentary Film). New York.

[6] **Gordimer, Nadine. 1988.** "Living in the Interregnum". In: **Gordimer, Nadine. 1989 [1988].** The Essential Gesture. Writing, Politics and Places. Edited and Introduced by Stephen Clingman. London: 264.

[7] **Gordimer, Nadine. 1997.** "The Status of the Writer in the World Today. Which World? Whose World?". In: **Gordimer, Nadine. 1999.** Living in Hope and History. Notes from our Century. London: 23.

[8] **Gordimer, Nadine/Cassirer Hugo. 1999.** The Wall in the Mind. A Journey with Nadine Gordimer through Johannesburg and Berlin. (Documentary Film). New York.

[9] **Gordimer, Nadine. 1998.** The House Gun. London.

[10] **Gordimer, Nadine. 1997.** "The Status of the Writer in the World Today. Which World? Whose World?". In: Living in Hope and History: 25.

[11] **Gordimer, Nadine. 1995.** "Act Two. One Year Later". In: **Gordimer, Nadine. 1999.** Living in Hope and History. Notes from our Century. London: 165.

[12] **Ndebele, Njabulo. 1991.** "Turkish Tales and some Thoughts on South African Fiction". In: **Ndebele, Njabulo. 1991.** Rediscovery of the Ordinary. Essays on South African Literature and Culture. Johannesburg: 11-36.

Mongane Wally Serote

Mongane Wally Serote interviewed by Ulrike Ernst
on 25 May 2000 in Midrand (Johannesburg area)

"Ordinary People Are the Creators of African Culture"

Ulrike Ernst: *Dr Serote, you are a well-known writer and politician, and you have a special reputation as a cultural organiser and representative. For example, you were the initiator of the Cultural Resistance Conference in Botswana in 1982 and of the Culture in Another South Africa Conference in Amsterdam in 1987. Today your name is closely connected with the promotion of the African Renaissance. Parallel to the ending of apartheid, a literary discussion evolved which criticised the notion of 'culture as a weapon' in the struggle. How do you see the development and the importance of literature in South African society after the end of apartheid, after the Albie Sachs debate?*

Mongane Wally Serote: Personally, I think that Albie Sachs didn't know what he was talking about. If you look at the body of work of African literature, all of it tries to address the whole question of almost five centuries of oppression, all of it, to the point even that there is no literature that talks about the period before oppression started. Even as people sing, you will find that they sing about the fact that as human beings they must not be oppressed. If you look at the paintings that people have painted, there is nothing that says, oppression was good, or that people should succumb to oppression. You can go through all of the art forms and you don't find that. So I don't know what he is talking about. Perhaps he is talking from a point of view of sitting on a tower and watching. The people who were not watching were not, I don't think so.

Whether you talk about the conferences I've organised in the past, or if you talk about the question of African Renaissance today, the key is the historical context. The manner in which Europe became totally inhuman to us, the manner in which Europe completely, deliberately and consciously underdeveloped the whole of our continent, including removing 15 million people from this continent, following with taking all the natural resources - it is still happening even now. How can we talk about anything else when this conscious, deliberate programme was so devastating in us: how can we talk about anything else? I think when we said 'culture is a weapon of struggle' that is what we meant. Other people in the world didn't have to do that. They celebrated their lives - we couldn't celebrate: there was nothing to celebrate about our lives. Everything that we did was highly politicised. That is my view.

Ulrike Ernst: *A democratic society requires a defined system of official representation, but apart from that, it also needs the critical voice of the independent intellectual. With your poems, like the acclaimed "Third World Express"[1] or "Freedom Lament and Song"[2], you contributed to the new South Africa as a writer. What role and task of intellectuals would you ascribe to writers in a society in transformation? How do you see yourself in this context?*

Mongane Wally Serote: If you take South Africa - we are all caught up in a situation where we should be reconstructing our country. First, to do that we have to agree what is it we want to reconstruct, how do we reconstruct it, and who is going to reconstruct it. I can't see any other role for African intellectuals other than to be directly involved in answering those three questions. I am not talking only about a physical reconstruction, where you build roads and lay down railroads and so on, more to do about that. I am also talking about the poverty of thought that exists, because our people were deliberately and consciously undereducated. I am talking about the breakdown of moral fibre in our country, because everything that we knew was systematically destroyed. I am also talking about the fact that even as we are like that, we are expected by the world to participate in the 21st century. I think African intellectuals, together with any other person or structure or body must address this reconstruction, otherwise we will go nowhere. That is the role that I see for African intellectuals.

Ulrike Ernst: *And this is a role you see for yourself as well?*

Mongane Wally Serote: Of course.

Ulrike Ernst: *You have been involved in the work of the Congress of South African Writers, who also published some of your work. Now one does not hear much about the Congress anymore. How would you explain the demise of COSAW, and was this an inevitable development?*

Wally Serote: I wouldn't say it was an inevitable development. I think there were certain mistakes that were made. The first and devastating mistake was that we didn't understand that Europe would take the view that when the first day of a democratic process starts, they would then say, ask for resources from your government. Now our government can't support projects like that. As I told you, they have to reconstruct schools, reconstruct hospitals, everything. They have to reconstruct everything. So that was the first mistake that we did, that we thought there would be sustained support from European sponsors. Because we made that mistake, then we built this very big structure of writers, national in scope, a proliferation of structures at provincial level, regional level and so on. And of course, as we got the money, the money was spent. So at the point at which the Europeans stopped supporting COSAW, it collapsed.

We have now put in place a thing called the National Arts Council. Compared to other national arts councils in the world, it's a very poor arts council. But I'm aware that we think that we feel that council, there is a section that deals with literature. They try to find how they'll support in a very small way organisations of writers and writers themselves. I can only hope that we'll put our moneys to see how we'll ensure that whatever meagre money they have grows, so they can support more and more. I am pleased by the programmes that they are doing because they've gone back and looked at the older writer and they are placing them as writers in residence in different places. They try to give support to individual writers also and to some organisations. But yes, you're right, COSAW almost disappeared.

Ulrike Ernst: *Outside South Africa the literature of this country is largely connected with the name of Nobel Prize winner Nadine Gordimer, whom you know very well. In her 1999 documentary film, 'The Wall in the Mind'[3], which is a journey through the new Johannesburg and the new Berlin, you are one of her main discussion partners. What is your opinion about the comparisons made in the film?*

Mongane Wally Serote: I can see, I understand, there were certain mistakes that were made by the communists. Berlin, East Berlin then being a communist city. Certain mistakes were done, but I don't think it is correct to just say there were only mistakes that were done. There were very important things that were experimented on. For instance, you and I know that there was minimal unemployment, we know that everybody had access to education, we know that everybody had access to health facilities, we know that public transport was accessible to everybody. Inasmuch as it was possible, people had homes to live in. It was an ideal which all of us must cherish, that we like a situation like that to still exist.

But of course there were other mistakes which were done: overreaction to the West, which then made the different government systems there prevent people from travelling, prevent contact with the West, and so on. Mistakes. In that regard Nadine is correct to say that there is a comparison between that and the city Johannesburg.

When the city was gripped by the apartheid system, that's what it did to its people: it prevented people from travelling, there were no educational systems, no facilities like hospitals and so on. If you've been around South Africa you still see the deep scars of apartheid. Nadine is correct to compare the two cities in that regard. I don't know how eventually objectively one accepts the comparison, but it is correct to compare any two anywhere. Because what we really should be saying is that under no circumstances should any government, any country, operate with a basis of totalitarianism.

Ulrike Ernst: *However, it seems that at home Nadine Gordimer's work and her role are often not so well received. How do you explain this difference in the reception inside and outside South Africa?*

Mongane Wally Serote: There are two reasons to that. The first and most sad one is the fact that the majority of people in South Africa are illiterate. So they cannot read Nadine Gordimer's books. But another very sad one is that those who can read, especially white South Africans, would have taken a direct contradictory position towards Nadine. In the first instance, I think in their minds, in their psychology, their hearts, they regarded themselves as European. They also did not think that there was anything wrong with apartheid. Nadine thought there was something wrong with apartheid. So you'll find a very small handful of people within the white community in this country who would have affinity with Nadine. The other people, if they read Nadine, they would have been very troubled. So, the result is that the world acclaims Nadine; South Africa doesn't. To a very great extent that is the prevailing situation for writers of Nadine's calibre.

Ulrike Ernst: *But what about black literate people and black intellectuals, black people who could have read her, or can read her now?*

Mongane Wally Serote: Now, yes, it's a different thing. We should look and say are people reading Nadine now, black and white, I don't know? But you see, the other thing is that the press in this country, the media in this country, is extremely unlettered, extremely Eurocentric, extremely self-defensive and therefore it would be very troubled itself if it were to enter into a dialogue with Nadine. And therefore they avoid the dialogue.

Young people in this country grow up knowing nothing about Nadine, because the only way that they should know is through the media in this country. I am hoping that with the education system coming, Nadine will be prescribed, so that she can be read. Because she is a very important writer of our country and she took a very unfashionable stance, a principled stance, in the past, when everybody else was afraid, when everybody didn't want to do so. Unfortunately, the price that she pays is that. I have travelled with Nadine abroad, Brazil, Argentina, Uruguay, Europe and so on, and I was consistently amazed by the hundreds of people that Nadine moves. It says something very good about the Europeans but it says something very sad about the South Africans.

Ulrike Ernst: *As you say, on many occasions you represented the ANC abroad during your time in exile. You were the ANC Cultural Attaché in London between 1986 and 1989 and in the collection of your essays, 'On the Horizon'[4], it is impressively shown how cultural work was an important part of the national liberation struggle. What was your organisation and structure of the cultural* *work of the ANC in exile and how would you retrospectively discuss the theory or ideology of the cultural work of the ANC in exile?*

Mongane Wally Serote: You see, the ANC didn't start arts and culture in exile. As a young person, a little boy, I attended what the ANC called 'cultural schools' which were put in place to oppose Bantu education. If you see the manner in which the ANC has always operated, there has been very strong cultural expression, even during the mass actions of the 1950s. There was lots of song, there was lots of dancing, lots of poetry. There was a proliferation of writing. It is this then that informs the ANC when it extends itself into exile. Wherever you went, whether you were in the Soviet Union, in the GDR, in Angola, in Tanzania, in Botswana, you always found cultural committees within the structures of the ANC.

I think the watershed happened when we held the Culture and Resistance Conference in 1982 in Botswana, which made it very clear then that it was very important to mobilise culture to become part and parcel of the liberation process. Because culture addresses the mind, the emotion. It is very important but it is informed by the struggle as the struggle unfolds, also it informs the struggle as it unfolds. I feel a little apprehensive about the fact that since we've come here the momentum that we had built from outside South Africa has sort of ebbed. I feel a little apprehensive, but I think that the fact that government has put in place a ministry and department, including a portfolio committee in parliament of arts and culture, is an indication of an understanding that arts and culture has a consistent role to play. But as I say, I am very apprehensive about the manner in which we are approaching it now, and the result is that I think there is lots of dissatisfaction among cultural workers in our country. They feel under-utilised, they feel marginalized, they feel very exploited, they feel that they are not even recognised for the work that they are doing. It is a matter that we have to address very urgently and see how we do it.

Ulrike Ernst: *First I would like to ask you one more historical question, and then we could continue with what you have just mentioned about the cultural politics after 1990.*

What impact did the debates on populism and workerism and the stages of the South African revolution have on cultural activism?

Mongane Wally Serote: Populism...?

Ulrike Ernst: *... and workerism and the stages of the South African revolution.*

Mongane Wally Serote: Well, I don't know. Those are very foreign concepts to our revolution. We didn't have anything like populism and workerism. We always engaged in mass action, the key thing being how to mobilise as many people as possible to defend democracy, to oppose the apartheid system. Of course we always said that our struggle had two faces: there was a national revolution which we had, which had to gain political power for people, and of course after that we will enter the question of class.

I am not going to talk about the class one, but I think so far we have succeeded in the national revolution in the sense that of course the political power is in the hands of the people and we are very keenly becoming aware of the fact that that is not enough. What must complement it is economic power. So we are addressing that. How do we empower ordinary South Africans economically? That is an important question that we have to raise. The second phase, it is leaning towards the second phase. We live in a country where to a large extent Western countries still dominate us economically. We live in a country where society is sharply divided into two nations, one white, and one black; the white one being extremely privileged and rich, the black one being extremely poor and disadvantaged. This is a challenge for us. This is where all African intellectual power must be applied to smooth out this schism that exists.

Ulrike Ernst: *Now I am moving towards the cultural politics of the ANC after 1990 with the question - what happened to the cultural politics of the ANC after its legalisation and return to South Africa between 1990 and 1994 from your point of view?*

Mongane Wally Serote: My view is that the reason why we seem to be in a little slope at the present moment is because we have to redefine, because we are faced by new challenges. For instance, the first and key thing is that we have to raise a consciousness that says to us as a diverse people each part of the component parts has the right to exercise its own culture. It is a very difficult thing to put in place properly.

Let me give you an example: you have nine African language groups in the country. Each of those groups has their own praise poetry, their own songs, their own dances, their own theatres and so on. All of that was never recognised as South African. On the other hand, we have European cultural activity, which was funded, promoted and nurtured. The question is: what do we do with these two? So we have to unfold a policy, a policy directed at redressing the situation. As you redress the policy, you also direct it at promoting and giving expression and hopefully that the people who are creative people will be consistent in seeking the new things that must emerge from this new experience. And I think that is happening. If you look at dances, if you look at music, if you look at anything which is happening. But you see, we cannot only focus on South Africa. We have also to focus our eyes outside and see how does this policy which we are making here, relate to policy on the African continent? And then we should develop a consciousness that says how does African culture relate to any other culture in the world? What is it that we should bring to the human experience, which is original, which is new, which is vibrant. Our policy is directed at this, to create infrastructure, momentum, for creative people to explore these issues. So, it's a new thing. We have shifted from organising culture against apartheid to organising our culture for interaction with other human beings.

Ulrike Ernst: *If you do not mind, I would like to put forward a more provocative question. The Mail & Guardian published a series of articles on the future of the arts and cultural politics, indicating that they were being affected by ideology and power struggles when you were still head of the department of Arts and Culture of the ANC. In an open letter to you, former cultural activist Mike van Graan said (that was in 1993) "that the ANC was threatened by independence in the arts and [...]seeks to control and manipulate the arts in ways not too dissimilar to our past rulers"*[5]*. On the other hand, Nadine Gordimer renounced what she called 'Serote-bashing'*[6]*.*

How would you respond to these challenges in retrospect?

Mongane Wally Serote: First, let me backtrack a bit. Two things happened, and I stand to be judged by those two things. The first thing was that I went and met with Sol Kerzner, who then used to own Sun City. I said to Sol Kerzner: "You have been operating in the North West Province, you haven't supported culture; how are you going to support it?" We then sat down with his people that he sent to me to say how he does support this. In other words, I was negotiating with Sol Kerzner to support financially South African culture.

The other thing that happened was that I was at some times approached by a couple, the husband was an outstanding South African film maker, who asked me, if I wanted to contribute in terms of film skills among blacks. What did I do? I said: "Form a trust." And we proceeded to form this trust. This thing that you refer to as a controversy begins at that point.

The other thing that we used to do in those days, ... the ANC, ... my department, ... the department that I headed, we used to interact with all other cultural formations in the country. To say, what is the policy that we must formulate for South Africa in arts and culture? Now, by the wildest stretch of the imagination, I don't see those two things as domination or control. I see those things as facilitation, to find how we shift out of apartheid culture, how do we integrate with the democratic culture that is emerging. It was always very clear, I even said it in those days that there is a role that government plays in arts and culture, and government plays a role now in arts and culture. Whether it is an ANC government or not, it plays a role at the present moment. There is a role that organs of civil society must play in culture. The question is going to be who must then sit down and say what is the relationship between the two? This has been my view ten years ago, it is my view even now. And consistently we are doing that. So, this is what I should be judged on, whether I am wrong or right. The other things, I am not interested in them. They just waste my time, they waste my energy, and I have a very short life; I can't do that.

Ulrike Ernst: *Thank you. What is your opinion of the cultural discourse and the cultural policy of the ANC after its accession to power with the first free elections in 1994 and the instalment of the Ministry of Arts, Culture, Science and Technology? Does it play a role that the ministry was given to an Inkatha minister?*

Mongane Wally Serote: Ben Ngubane is a very outstanding person. You must understand that when he was appointed as a minister, he didn't come from arts and culture, he came from science and technology. And I think the manner in which he has consistently encouraged that science must inform arts and culture and that arts and culture must inform science and technology, he is very outstanding. It's a very deep understanding of dialectics. That the two, being creative tools, must be used with great skill. And I think he has done that. The problem is that you are doing that on a warped society, a society that was devastated by apartness, racism, prejudice and so on. It will take us a long time. But I think also the fact that Ben Ngubane and myself worked with each other very, very well, I from the legislation part, he from the executive side. And we are very keenly aware of deep-seated problems of our society.

I was telling you just now about the question of total breakdown of the moral fibre of our society. Culture has to address that. Science has to address that. The languages of our country have to address that.

I was telling you about the schism of the two nations. We have to find a solution through arts and culture, through science and technology. I am telling you about the manner in which our country has to relate to other countries outside of our country. Already I moved from the position that the manner in which those countries relate to our country is in terms that they do not understand their historical role and the history of this country. And, therefore, we are again encountering very serious problems even at that level. But I think it was a very outstanding vision on the part of the ANC government to combine arts and culture, and science and technology and languages. It is a consistent challenge for us to say here is one of the most updated tools, which we must use to shift our country into the 21st century. We make mistakes now and then, but in general I think there is this consciousness among us.

Ulrike Ernst: *In the preparation of the transfer of the presidency from Nelson R. Mandela to Thabo Mbeki, or with the shift from the 'Reconstruction and De-*

velopment Plan' to the implementation of the 'Growth, Employment and Redistribution Programme', the political and economic aims have been changing towards a (neo-liberal) market economy. What do you as a member of parliament think: does this change of direction manifest itself in official cultural politics?*

Mongane Wally Serote: I don't know what is changing. Of course, Mandela did a very important thing, which is exemplary to our continent: when the time came, he said, it is my time now to move, let other people take my place. And all of us must salute Mandela for that. One has also to understand the African National Congress. The African National Congress has always insisted on collective leadership. And Thabo Mbeki comes from that culture. Thabo Mbeki was nurtured by that culture. So for me it was very logical that that is what was going to happen. It was a very smooth change which also said while you do not forget the issues that we addressed in the past, there are new issues now that we have to address and move forward. And he is outstanding at doing this, you know, the manner in which he has handled, in my view, sometimes very illiterate and very ignorant Western countries. The manner in which he has addressed all the issues of the African continent, the manner in which he is trying to relate our country to Asia. I think you can see a vision that he is trying to locate not only South Africa, but also the continent, into the 21st century, within to stand equally with other continents.

If there is a change, that is the change that has happened, which is a change correcting wrongs of 500 years ago. It must be done. I view this very optimistically and very positively.

Ulrike Ernst: *Do you think that GEAR had an influence on cultural politics, for instance the emergence of the underlining of the importance of tourism?*

Mongane Wally Serote: We are addressing the question of tourism very sharply with its negatives. It is very important for us to find how South Africa can continuously increase its tourist capacity. At the same time, within the department it is very important for us never to lose sight of the fact that we have also to nourish quality productions in the area of arts and culture. So we have to combine the two. Of course, if we get it correct, to consistently increase input in terms of tourism we will be addressing the question of jobs, we will be addressing the question of development, we will also be addressing the question of social and economic upliftment. Very important. Which are the key things that GEAR needs to address. So, I don't see a contradiction.

Ulrike Ernst: *An emerging notion furthered by Thabo Mbeki has been that of the African Renaissance. The South African Chapter of the African Renaissance Institute, which was founded in 1990, was launched at the African Renaissance conference 2000, whose convenor you are. Why do you think the African Renais-*

sance is a useful concept to face the social, economic and cultural issues in African countries in transformation?

Mongane Wally Serote: First let me correct a common mistake that has happened. In 1990, a structure called the African Renaissance Institute was launched in Pretoria. That structure has its headquarters in Botswana. In the year 2000, we launched a thing called the South African Chapter of the African Renaissance, and I was a convenor of the conference. I think it is very important to make a differentiation between the two. The African Renaissance Institute is a continental structure; the South African Chapter of the African Renaissance is a national structure, which means it would affiliate with the African Renaissance Institute.

Please remind me what your question was.

Ulrike Ernst: *Why do you think the African Renaissance is a useful concept to face the issues in African countries in transformation?*

Mongane Wally Serote: Because the concept says, Africans must build Africa. Africans must find a manner in which they locate the African continent to be equal to any other continent. But more important also, that Africa must be able to contribute to the human experience. That is what the Renaissance means.

Ulrike Ernst: *When I read your "Come and Hope With Me"[7], I was intrigued to see how you identify not only racism but also tribalism as a threat to civil society in the new South Africa. How can you reconcile a repressive neo-traditional Africanism and the African Renaissance?*

Mongane Wally Serote: I spoke to you earlier on and said that one of the greatest challenges of African intellectuals is to understand the dynamism of diversity. The dynamism of diversity depends on two things: we cannot negate differences, we must not negate differences or want to do away with differences. At the same time, you must be skilled enough to identify commonalties. And then, further, you must be skilled enough to keep the two informing each other. That is the challenge that we have. If we do that, we will address the question of racism, we will address the question of tribalism. I think it is a challenge of the African Renaissance to do so.

I will give you an example. White South Africans, when you say African, they do not feel African. They stand aloof and I think it is always because of certain assumptions that they make. And assumptions are based on fear, insecurity, misunderstanding, and so on. So we have to address and say, how do we address their fears? How do we say to them, if you want to be white, you'll still be white, but you are African. A simple thing like that people don't understand. If you want to still practise your European culture, you can practise it here, there is nothing wrong with that. If you want to speak your English, you still speak it here, there is nothing wrong with that. But people are afraid that this is not going to happen. I think it is a psychological thing, because they think a lot about what they did in the past, and they are imposing the past into the present. They are surprised, why is it that black people are not cutting their throats. They are expecting every day that maybe we will cut their throats. We don't want to dirty our hands with nonsense like that.

We are intent on leading good lives. Life is very short. We would like to meet the challenges of our time, as we did, as the generations before us did. We would like to meet our own generation's challenge of nation building, of building our continent, to give it quality life, to make it liveable. That is key in our mind.

Ulrike Ernst: *As you say, the African Renaissance claims to be an inclusive Africanness. The rallying cry is 'Motho ke Motho ka Batho ba Bang', a person is a person only through other people. You say that you have an African thoughts initiative, and that you are collating indigenous knowledge systems.*

Could you elaborate on that very interesting part of the work of the Institute, which could enhance cultural theories?

Mongane Wally Serote: The African thoughts initiative is a structure that is slowly emerging, which the South African chapter is going to use to enter the area of arts and culture. African thoughts initiative has different types of projects within it. The key that it does, is it says what is the work done by African hands? What is the work created by African thinking? What is the work informed by African knowledge? And how do we take those and put them in the 21st century? That is the key concept of the African thoughts initiative.

Ulrike Ernst: *And could you mention any of the thinkers or thoughts that you are especially concerned about?*

Mongane Wally Serote: Thinkers?

Ulrike Ernst: *African thinkers.*

Mongane Wally Serote: Well, the key thinkers are going to be the ordinary people of this country. They are the creators of African culture. If you talk about seamstresses, you find them in the township and the rural areas. And when you talk about people who do beadwork, you find them here, woodcarving, those are the thinkers and intellectuals we are talking about, who are creating African concepts.

Ulrike Ernst: *How would you relate the assumptions of the African Renaissance to the philosophy of Black Consciousness?*

Mongane Wally Serote: Well, what was Black Consciousness? Black Consciousness was saying to black people, you are in trouble, do something about it. African Renaissance is much broader than that. It addresses the question of a rebirth of a continent, a rebirth of a people. With clear objectives. The objectives being that the people have quality of life, once people have created a liveable continent, they must then proceed to contribute to the human experience. Not just for the continent, but for the total human experience. To make the world a peaceful place, to make the world a liveable place. I don't think the world is liveable at the present moment. I don't think the world is peaceful. And that is the concept of African Renaissance. It has very clear objectives.

Ulrike Ernst: *There has been extensive discussion about the correct picture of history and the appropriate use of African tradition in literature. Closely connected to the question of tradition is that of language, as you said. For your writing and your poems you use the English language.*

How would you assess the ways in which African tradition is or should be represented in the South African arts? How do you locate the terrain of languages as part of cultural and literary politics in South Africa?

Mongane Wally Serote: One important challenge that we have - working in the arena of arts and culture - is that you have to find a manner of unearthing literature written in African languages. And say to ourselves, how do we put it out there for both South Africans and the world to understand what it says. If we did that, I really suspect that we will hear things that we have not heard from any literature. If we do that. But of course also there are certain very peculiar things about South African literature that are emanating from the uniqueness of the manner in which South Africa itself developed. I think that some of the literature coming from this country has something to say to the world.

Of course, my understanding has always been that before you address the question of literature or of language, you have to address the question of culture. And here my most simple definition of culture is that culture makes individuals part of communities. It is in that interaction that language emerges and out of that literature. Therefore literature is an extremely important contribution to the human experience. We must find a manner to ensure that literature survives the television, your Internet and so on. We must find a manner in which this literature survives all of this.

Ulrike Ernst: *What do you think about publishing in African languages in this country?*

Mongane Wally Serote: We must find a manner of unearthing literature written in African languages. Because if we did and we put it properly in centre stage, this country and the world would hear things what they had not heard from any literature. So it is very important, that literature.

Ulrike Ernst: *You say the South African Chapter of the African Renaissance will also make recommendations on the promotion of arts. Which arts will be supported in the future?*

Mongane Wally Serote: African arts.

Ulrike Ernst: *Could you elaborate on that a bit?*

Wally Serote: If you talk about any arts, you must first address the question of culture. That activity where individuals and the community interact. Therefore this is what we have to address on the African continent. How do the individuals interact with the society and how does the society interact with individuals? When we talk about letting emerging African expression that is what I am talking about. Europeans will do it to Europe, Americans will do it in America, and we will do it on the continent.

Ulrike Ernst: *And finally, may I ask you which pieces of art do you find most influential or interesting in South Africa at the moment?*

Mongane Wally Serote: Art?

Ulrike Ernst: *Yes, art or literature in particular.*

Mongane Wally Serote: I am presently reading Mandla's book, his most recent one, *'Memory of Stones'*[8], and I think it is very appropriate for now. It takes us back in time, it takes us into the future, to think appropriately about issues. At the present moment that is what is preoccupying me. I am thinking about the issues he is raising.

Ulrike Ernst: *Thank you very much for the interview. It has been very insightful.*

References

[1] **Serote, Mongane Wally. 1997 [1992].** Longer Poems. Third World Express. Come and Hope with me. Cape Town.

[2] **Serote, Mongane Wally. 1997.** Freedom Lament and Song. Cape Town.

[3] **Gordimer, Nadine/Cassirer Hugo. 1999.** The Wall in the Mind. A Journey with Nadine Gordimer through Johannesburg and Berlin. (Documentary Film). New York.

[4] **Serote, Mongane Wally. 1990. On the Horizon.** Fordsburg.

[5] **van Graan, Mike. 1993.** "We Want Culture, not Commissars". In: Weekly Mail. 7-13 May: 15+24.

[6] **Gordimer, Nadine. 1993.** "Investigation was 'Serote-bashing'". In: Mail and Guardian. 3-9 Sept.: 31.

[7] **Serote, Mongane Wally. 1997 [1992].** Longer Poems. Third World Express. Come and Hope with me. Cape Town.

[8] **Langa, Mandla. 2000.** The Memory of Stones. Cape Town/Johannesburg.

Jeremy Cronin

Jeremy Cronin interviewed by Ulrike Ernst
on 27 May 2000 in Johannesburg

"The Cinderella Department"

Ulrike Ernst: *Jeremy Cronin, at the latest since the publication of your prison poetry 'Inside'[1] you have been known as South Africa's uncompromising political activist writer par excellence, fighting for the end of apartheid. Today you are still very prominent in the SACP, and you are Member of Parliament for the ANC. Let us begin with some historic political theory considerations.*

The basis for the ANC/ SACP alliance and the theoretical background for the importance of cultural work during apartheid was the two staged revolutionary theory. First, a multiracial 'native republic' would be established in a national democratic revolution, second the socialist revolution would follow. This two-staged struggle was systematically elaborated in the theory of a 'Colonialism of a special type', claiming that South Africa combines imperialism and colonialism, since the indigenous population experiences the features of a colony. According to the self-perception as being nationally oppressed, the formation of a national identity was requested and became the task of cultural work.

Some argue that when in opposition to the 'dominant culture' of the oppressor, a 'national culture' should be formed, this was simplistically equalised with 'resistance culture' or 'revolutionary culture'[2]. How do you respond? How would you theoretically dispute on the notion of protest or revolutionary cultural expressions?

Jeremy Cronin: I think that the struggle against apartheid, which obviously came in waves and had successes and defeats and so forth, but then grew very powerfully in the course of the decade of the 1980s, that what for me was very interesting to observe was that culture was very integrated into those waves of mobilisation and of struggle in several ways. First of all, certain forms of culture were more important perhaps than others - singing was perhaps the most important cultural expression. It occurred at all the mass rallies, the mass marches and so forth. It was a way of unifying people, of giving them a certain courage in the face of heavy repression, and it was manifested at massive funerals for political activists who were buried and so forth.

But of course, there were other cultural forms including poetry, pamphlets, graffiti, where the line of division between a more cultural and a more directly political form was very blurred. I think what was very interesting about many of those cultural forms was that they were drawing upon older cultural forms, in other words a tradition, a continued tradition of anti-colonial resistance, but also of peoples' popular cultures. So many of the songs that were overtly political, for instance, in the 80s had their roots in wedding songs, or warrior songs, or hunting songs and so forth. The existence of a majority indigenous population with its own indigenous culture, I think, was a very important asset in the struggle and remains an important asset. But I think that obviously the challenges have changed a little bit and cultural forms are battling to adapt.

Let me stop there.

Ulrike Ernst: *In an interview in 1987, you said you had a tentative concept of a national culture, saying: "[I]t is certainly not consolidated at all, there are a lot of unevennesses and disparities as a result of the apartheid system, but nonetheless there is an emergent national culture"[3]. However, the notion of the nation that became a rallying point in South Africa is widely rejected in theoretical discussions throughout the world.*

How would you discuss the concept of a national culture today? Does it hold, or are there other considerations to be made?

Jeremy Cronin: I think the question of a national culture will be needed to be linked to other imperatives as well, and is linked to them. A country like South Africa, on a continent like Africa, has to develop a capacity to exert some kind of national self-determination, some kind of national sovereignty, in a global situation, which is not designed to foster particularly the development and growth of Third World societies, not least, societies in Africa.

The cultural task in my view is linked to that, building up a sense of national self-confidence, a sense of South African identity, linked to the region and the continent. I think that is and remains very important, and perhaps we sort of understood that in the resistance period, lost focus on that in the middle 1990s, and I think there is a growing reassertion, which is uneven now again, towards the end of the decade of the 90s and at the turn of the century.

That then has cultural implications as well, but I think that (I am probably plunging into other topics), but I think that in a way South Africa benefited from a huge solidarity movement, a global solidarity movement, which was not always there; I mean, the reinvention of that solidarity is that there was this consistent solidarity with the oppressed people of South Africa. It really came to the fore with the development of social movements and solidarity movements in the North in the late 60s through the 70s and 80s. But certainly the breakthrough in South Africa, a very significant contributing factor, was that global solidarity which was particularly strong in Western Europe and in North America as well. But also obviously present in other parts of the world.

Precisely that sense of support for the democratic breakthrough created many confusions and illusions in South Africa, because the solidarity which had been spearheaded by progressive forces, social movements and so on was then adopted by the ruling governments as well, governments of the North. That was a great advantage to us, that the democratic breakthrough in South Africa was not treated in the way that the 1973 left-wing election outcome in Chile was treated or the way in which the Sandinista victory in Nicaragua was treated. The agenda of Washington, for instance, wasn't to immediately undermine the ANC government but was to lend support and so forth. That was an asset. But it was a confusing asset and what was a general political moral support for the deracialisation of South Africa was not the same thing as a commitment of major resources, especially economic resources, to underpin the political breakthrough and democracy. There was an illusion in South Africa that the two things would come together, and there was an expectation of a major flow of Marshall aid and of reconstruction and foreign direct investment into the economy. I think South Africa embarked into the negotiations around an EU-South Africa free trade agreement, for instance, with those kinds of expectations and hopes that there were many promises coming. I think those expectations have worn thin a bit and there is a sense that we have to assert a much greater [than only] South African [perception] ... We are part of the South, like the rest of the South. Globalisation offers some possibilities, but by and large has seen the deepening of inequality between North and South, and the inequality in the North as well. We are not just an underdeveloped country that has to catch up and that all we have to do is to join the freeway to the North, by applying the Washington Consensus. That we have actually got to try and charter a South African path and an African path and a Third World path in co-operation with progressive forces in the North of course.

I am saying all of that because I think that is starting to impact once more on the need to affirm a South African identity and an Africa identity, and that has cultural implications. But I think all of that got lost quite substantially in the confusions of the complicated world, because apart from the support that we got that was then confused with other things, obviously the decade in which we finally achieved our liberation was the decade that more or less began with the collapse of the Berlin Wall. It ended in a slightly different place, with Seattle, so I think something happened in the course of the decade. In the middle of the decade it looked like it was just, the traffic was running one way, which was a kind of Washington Consensus triumphalism, which dominated everything. That has been politically confusing, economically confusing, but also culturally confusing in South Africa. Now things are a little bit clearer, and it's starting to impact on a cultural practice and perspective as well.

Ulrike Ernst: *The importance of cultural struggle as part of the anti-apartheid struggle had found its expression in several ANC documents since the establishment of the Youth League and was furthered through the establishment of the ANC's Cultural Department in exile (1983), the foundation of COSATU's Cultural Unit and the UDF's own Cultural Desk. Which importance did cultural work have inside the SACP itself and how was it organised and how would you retrospectively discuss the workerist or populist stance of cultural work?*

Jeremy Cronin: The SACP in the period between its banning in 1950, because it as you know was outlawed ten years before the ANC was outlawed. Between 1950 and the unbanning in 1990, the SACP was a very small organisation and of quite deliberately vanguard character and became quite influential, was probably at the height of its influence in the ANC in the '70s up to the mid-1980s. So there wasn't a separate SACP focus, for instance, particularly on cultural questions. There were some SACP cultural activities, but SACP members, including someone like myself, were active less, culturally active less insofar as we were culturally active less within a sort of SACP framework, but much more as part and parcel of the various mass movements and ANC in which we were participants. In my particular case, my cultural activism in the 80s was very much integrated into the United Democratic Front period and so forth and the events and so on. The weaknesses and the strengths of all of that were shared by the SACP, and the SACP didn't have particularly an independent practice, or institution or desk or whatever.

Ulrike Ernst: *The workerist and the populist stance, do they still have their roles?*

Jeremy Cronin: Ja, I think what's very interesting about South Africa, which has parallels perhaps with a country like Brazil to some extent, but also with important differences, was that the 'old left' which would have been the Communist Party and a kind of Third World national liberation movement, the ANC, suffered a major defeat in the early 1960s, were badly beaten basically and suffered a major strategic defeat. What we saw was the emergence of a new left, really, which had parallels with many other countries, including let's say in Germany and so forth, were associated also, it started a bit later in South Africa, if you take 1968 as the sort of watershed year in which you started to see the flourishing of new social movements and associated with a new left. In South Africa, it goes really back to about 1973 with the first Durban strikes and the re-emergence of a progressive radical trade union tradition. But also the Black Power tradition associated with the youth, student movement, reaching a high point in 1976 with the Soweto uprising. If one stepped back, one could see that they were part and parcel of a global ferment of new workers. In the case of South Africa they were [and these new workers were those first organised]. What had happened was that the liberation movement had been badly smashed in the '60s, and the apartheid regime succeeded in attracting major investments, including from Germany, West Germany obviously, into chemicals, auto industry and so forth and there was - as in Brazil at a very similar time - so there was a kind of new industrialisation. In Brazil, as in South Africa round about at that time, investors were coming in because the old left had been repressed.

You started seeing the organic emergence of a worker's movement. What was very interesting was that in the course of the 1980s, the energies that emerged from the social movement and the workers' movement here in South Africa began to score victories and force the regime into a kind of what we characterise as a repressive reform which we saw happening in different ways in Eastern Europe as well. A little bit later, similar attempts were made to deal with the popular ferment through reform measures, which also had an edge of repression. In that situation the old left was able to connect with the new left - which was different from Brazil, where the divisions remain quite strongly.

There was a tremendous cross-fertilisation, which took place in a variety of ways. I think the ANC in particular was able to provide a kind of strategic leadership to these emerging movements, with the party playing an active role in that as well. But it was a contested thing and the debates in the 1980s between the so-called populists and the so-called workerists was part of this engagement of a very organically emerging trade union movement and its potential relationship to the broader national liberation struggle. I think we've come way beyond those debates, but I think there were important things inside of them that we shouldn't throw away, namely that a trade union movement mustn't become subservient to a political party or to a political [wing]. It needs to be a robust independent trade union movement. But it needs to connect its workplace struggles to a broader political agenda.

Yes, that's what we were debating, and I think, I hope, that we've learnt the lessons of that and that the best of both traditions are still present within the ongoing transition in South Africa.

Ulrike Ernst: *Even before the end of the apartheid era, Njabulo Ndebele spoke out against the limitations of so-called protest literature. When Albie Sachs criticised the idea of 'culture as a weapon', a huge controversial debate emerged. However, these rounds of discussions were only secondary to what had been disputed after the appearance of your review of 'Black Mamba Rising'[4].*

Cultural work had played an immense part in the struggle. Which place was it given in the transformation process?

Jeremy Cronin: I think it got lost in the transformation process. Well, it depends. I think that the structures that had been associated with this ferment of ideas and of culture in the 1980s got somehow to be displaced. In the 1980s possibly because of that it was associated with protest very often, and successfully so, and with resistance, successfully so, and the new imperatives of reconstruction and of development and of governing and so forth meant that there was a kind of pause and hesitation and uncertainty. The pursuit of new forms perhaps and so on.

Song has continued to be the one that has succeeded in easily making the transition. So there is a lot of song that continues to happen in ANC, SACP, and COSATU as well. But I think the poetry voices, for instance, were less vibrant. For me the most vibrant moment of poetry was actually the earlier Black Power, Black Consciousness period, where the sort of form and the political project coincided quite strongly. The lyrical form, using the lyric to assert a lyrical 'I', the use of English, but the appropriation of English to black rhythms are often quite explicit black [voices].

Ulrike Ernst: *You tried it yourself...*

Jeremy Cronin: Ja. But it was more successfully done, clearly, by those [black poets] I think in the 1980s. Mzwakhe Mbuli was a very successful poet in that period. I think some of those earlier Black Power voices had either been killed or were in exile. In so far as I was present, I think it was no longer this individualistic expression. I think others, like Kelwyn Sole, and some others have understood that. Some of that, already there was a kind of loss of energy a bit, with poetry and it didn't quite find its voice in the 1980s period quite as strongly as it had earlier on. All that remained and is a quite dynamic reality still. But the 1990s definitely much less. I think there has been a kind of diminishing of energy there. Partial poets just can't continue in the same vein and need to respond adequately to the new situation.

There were tendencies that remained quite strong, of a kind of bureaucratisation, and a managerialist kind of ethos to move in. I suppose that happens when political parties get into power. The evolution of the left victory in Eastern Europe over several decades is one example. As one commentor recently joked, he said, only the last few years, the only time you hear the word 'culture' it's 'culture of non-payment' or 'culture of unrealistic expectations'. And that is a kind of managerialist view of the masses and their culture. So I think that has been another factor contributing.

But at the same time there have been major cultural phenomena occurring and I think the most profound one has been the Truth and Reconciliation Commission process, which is, it depends on how one defines it a cultural process. Everyone is talking about texts and discourse and culture and ideology. I think that has been an amazing cultural reality, that whole TRC process. I include myself. Poets have tried to write poems about it; Antjie Krog has written a whole book about it and so on. The cultural reality of it is obviously much wider than the generic forms of the genre of high literature. I think that there has been a very dynamic cultural thing happening in South Africa which is not necessarily found in a novel, but is in this very interesting, unique, I think, nation involved in a talking cure. Talking to each other, past each other, in an amazing process, which were hearings that went on for two weeks in tiny, little isolated villages in which the whole community filled the hall. The white part of the community and the black part of the community shared their experiences of the decades in the past and so on. The high profile things have been the Hani assassination or Winnie Mandela and so on, but a very profound cultural process has been happening facilitated by this TRC programme.

Ulrike Ernst: *In your new collection 'Even the Dead'[5], you are concerned with issues of the complicated transition of the country. You capture a time span of about the last ten years in your poem "Running Towards Us" ending thoughtfully: "He is running, sore, into the new South Africa. Into the rainbow nation, in desperation, one shoe on, one shoe off. Into our midst. Running"[6].*

What happened to the cultural politics of the ANC after its legalisation between 1990 and 1994? What is your opinion of the cultural discourse on the cultural policy of the ANC after its accession to power with the first free elections and the establishment of the Ministry for Arts, Culture, Science and Technology?

Jeremy Cronin: I think, sadly, there is very little to report. If one is looking at the political institutions and particularly the ANC, since it's the predominant political formation, and a thoughtful institutionalisation of cultural realities - it simply has not happened. The Department of Arts and Culture has been a serious disappointment. The fact the ANC when it went to a power-sharing arrangement first with the National Party and the IFP and now just with the IFP, it is interesting that one of the Cinderella departments, ministries, there has been Home Affairs and the other one is Arts and Culture, has been given, along with science, has been given to an Inkatha minister. The current incumbent is not such a bad person, but it indicates a lack of prioritisation from the side of the ANC of that particular function. In the last year, couple of years, Mbeki has tried to develop this notion of an African Renaissance, which I think is the beginnings, a confused beginnings, but a beginnings of some kind of attempt to think about moral and cultural realities. It is very late and not particularly organically linked to anything in the ANC or to anything in government. I could go on and on, but in short I think that it has been neglected. The politics of culture has been neglected. The institutional facilitation of culture has been generally neglected.

Ulrike Ernst: *With the shift from the 'Reconstruction and Development Plan' to the implementation of the 'Growth, Employment and Redistribution Pro-*

gramme', the political and economic aims have been changing towards a (neo-liberal) market economy. In your poem "Joe Slovo's Favourite Joke", you deal in a rather light-hearted manner with plan and market, socialism and capitalism.

What do you as an SACP member think: a) does a market orientation manifest itself in the official cultural politics; and b) has this brought new cultural mobilisations on the scene?

Jeremy Cronin: Yes, the answer to the first part of the question is yes. I think that if you look at the policy papers of the Department for Arts and Culture for instance, they are all about trying to align what they are doing with the GEAR document. First of all, arts and culture are portrayed as an industry, which is the first step. Largely an export-oriented industry, designed to attract foreign capital and so forth, linked to tourism and so on. While undoubtedly that needs to be a dimension of any coherent governmental cultural policy, what is absolutely missing - when you look at the policy papers I have read from the Department of Arts and Culture - almost missing is the sense of assisting mass inequality, poverty, those issues. Missing is any word like values, never mind words like aesthetic values. It reflects a terrible reductionism of a kind of market orientation with regard to culture.

Happily, that is not the totality of the picture. But it certainly reflects a major problem, which is not just in the domain of culture but also exemplifies it there. Since mid 1996 when GEAR was unveiled, and it had a sort of heyday for a couple of years, I think it has failed ... although it is implemented quite harsh - restrictive measures, macro-economic measures and so on, a kind of self-imposed structural adjustment programme and although the leading minister is responsible for it now today. What I am saying is that even though the fundamentals are in place, they are all agreeing that in spite of the fact that the fundamentals are in place, the growth that was hoped for, the foreign investment that was anticipated, never mind job creation and redistribution, none of those things are being fulfilled. They are somewhat plaintively saying, we don't know what else to do.

So I think that that is the beginning of the re-acquisition of some wisdom in this matter that at least the admission that we have done everything, and it is not really working. So one hopes there is growing space now for a reassessment of many things, including therefore the cultural policy.

I said earlier that I think that the African Renaissance is a very vague one frankly, but certainly, and understanding that South Africa is not somewhere halfway between Europe and Africa, but is in Africa, and that any policies that we implement must be linked to a development for Africa. Therefore culturally we have to orient ourselves in those ways. That marks, potentially, a shift away from GEAR and its very narrow market type philosophy.

Ulrike Ernst: *Some might argue that the organic development towards the establishment of a strengthened democracy in South Africa implies a separation of the previously necessary alliance of ANC, SACP and COSATU.*

How would this dissolution influence the development of cultural politics? Would this process enhance opportunities for the independence of writers as a literary opposition?

Jeremy Cronin: That's not my perspective, and it's not the perspective of the SACP for instance. We are not working for the dissolution of the alliance. We think that those who are working for the dissolution are basically those who want to install a low-intensity democracy in South Africa. That in itself is not going to work, because multi-party dispensation with a good constitution, and we're proud of the good constitution that we've got simply existing on a sea of massive poverty, and something like 57% of our population are poor; 98% of those are African, so that the racial issue persists as a dominant feature of our society. Unemployment is about 35%, it's contested, exactly the figure, but it's about one third of our people are unemployed, not to mention the new crises of HIV-AIDS. All of those huge challenges that we have will undermine the constitution and democratic breakthrough that we've secured unless they are addressed simultaneously, unless we see that the consolidation and defence of the political democracy depends upon social and economic transformation - that the things are linked.

The agenda to break the alliance is basically an agenda to say, well, South Africa is now changed; we have a non-racial dispensation, and the struggle is over. That's what the agenda is. And to try and lure the ANC into being satisfied with the sharing of some powers, privileges and wealth with the old white privileged minority block. While the majority of people remain basically in the same predicament that they found themselves. So I think that the poems that you referred to, the *'Even the Dead'* collection, I would write a collection ... I am busy with poems now, which are slightly different; but that was at the height of the GEAR basically triumph. Culturally, for me, the endeavour was to create cultural spaces, which were in opposition, not to the ANC, but to that set of policies. To try to puncture that Washington Consensus basically. Which I think had a lot to do with the kind of colonial mentality in South Africa as well. There is a lack of often self-esteem; what colonialism does is to make people very insecure and uncertain about their own capacities, and I think this is what happened in that period. I think we are starting to move away from it, but the kind of sense that we had to prove ourselves to the big boys, and that if we talked the right language and implemented the policies that they said we should implement we would be justly rewarded. There was that profound illusion which had to do with the power of neo-liberalism, but it also had to do with a certain loss of faith in ourselves and our own capacities. So at that point that collection was trying to be an intervention into that kind of reality.

Ulrike Ernst: *In your poem "Even the Dead" you talk about the role of art in the new South Africa. You say: "I am not sure what poetry is. I am not sure what the aesthetic is. Perhaps the aesthetic should be defined in opposition to anaesthetic. Art is the struggle to stay awake. Which makes amnesia the true target and proper subject of poetry"[7].*

How do you see the development of literature in South African society after the end of apartheid? How would you theoretically discuss the political importance of literature today?

Jeremy Cronin: I'm not sure. I don't think I have some 'grande' theory, and maybe that is because I don't have a good bird's eye view on South African literature at present. That is partly because my intellectual activism is not focused, as I would like it to be, on, say, literature. But maybe the reality is also a whole lot more fragmented but perhaps that is just my excuse for not having the kind of oversight one should have.

Let me engage with the question in not quite the way that you were hoping. I detect two dangers in some of the interesting, some of the significant literature that is emerging. One is a tendency to move into a kind of oppositionism manifested in say a very fine writer like Breyten Breytenbach - I think the most interesting lyrical voice in South Africa in some respects. Kelwyn Sole would be another, different example, or John Coetzee, in a different kind of way. It is often white writers as it happens, it is not only them, but it is tending to be white writers, and it represents a kind of disillusionment of a certain segment of the intelligentsia in South Africa. It's not just a literary intelligentsia, but there is also that dimension of it. Including an intelligentsia that historically has been broadly associated with the liberation movement, often had been critical a little bit of the actual organisations and so on, but broadly in sympathy with it.

The paradigm that is operated with is, it is all a sell-out. We had high hopes and now there is a sell-out. The new regime is corrupt, it's venal, it's typical of a banana republic, and I reject it. Politically I think it is an incorrect understanding of the situation. There is certainly corruption, there is certainly confusion, there is certainly bureaucratisation, and there is certainly the confused appropriation of neo-liberal values and things like that. That is definitely part of the picture. But I think the danger of voices doing that in my view, of going into a narrow opposition, is that they end up isolated from the debates and are not heard by the political activists, etc.

I am just now coming out of a strategy meeting of the SACP. There are about 260 delegates, there are also some from the ANC and COSATU. There is a very vibrant criticism of corruption, of the economic policies and so forth. But it is a criticism that is engaged with the political movement. I think one danger, one temptation, is for intellectuals to isolate themselves from those realities in a kind of comfort zone of security and intellectual isolation and a kind of holier than thou position. It is a temptation for intellectuals to end up there. I think it is a wrong temptation; it is not a helpful one. The poetry needs to be read into, or the novels or the short stories or the journalism, needs to talk into the movement, which remains, I think, a popular and vibrant and fundamentally progressive movement. Not without many confusions and blemishes.

But the alternative, which is exemplified by my friend Wally Serote, is a poetry, which was very powerful in the early 1970s, remained somewhat powerful, if nostalgic, in exile - it was a poetry of deep nostalgia for South Africa and which has now become very vacuous, I am afraid to say. A poetry that sort of cruises at cruising altitude, and that is a kind of repetition of the liberation past. A critic once said, I think it was Colin Gardner, professor of the University of Natal talked about it as a poetry that is in the aspirational mode. Which I think again is not engaging with contradictions of reality.

If I look at my own poetry, I can recognise both - so I am not myself trying to be holier than thou - I can see poems that are veering in one or another direction. I think it's the challenge in the present for me, cultural, political, to keep the actual and the aspirational in a tense and dialectical dialogue with each other. We're in power, but power is much more limited and restricted than we thought. We intended to do many things, but we find that the budget is quite tight. There are thousands of things, but suddenly 'Realpolitik' becomes a huge responsibility and one can't just fly in the face of those difficult choices that have to be made. But the danger is that you sink into a sheer pragmatism.

On the other hand, you need to pepper that up with aspirations, hopes; it is wrong to reject people's culture as a culture of unrealistic expectations, because people's expectations are absolutely a key asset. That people want better houses, they want jobs and so on. But you have to bring those into a dialogue with the actualities of power, of government, of having to assume responsibility, of bureaucracy and an army and so forth. That is a political challenge and it is a cultural challenge. One finds cultural practices, which opt out of the real change, which is that kind of challenge.

Ulrike Ernst: *Now I would like to turn to another question concerning writing and representation. In a provocative essay, Peter Anderson compared Nadine Gordimer and you, describing her as "a writer self-conscious and self-righteous about her mission" and you as "a learner writer rather than an imposer of cul-*

ture". Your poetry "involves the home audience in a sharing of an experience", her novels are identified on the contrary as "self-justifying literary acts".[8]

How could you compare the representation at hand in your work and in that of Nadine Gordimer, and how do you explain the great difference in the reception of Nadine Gordimer's work?

Jeremy Cronin: Well, I think she is a much better writer than me. Let me say that, and I think it is very generous of Peter Anderson to say those things. I don't want to get into a comparison about achievement and merit and so on. I think she's outstanding and has devoted her life as a novelist and her achievements are very significant. I should also say that I had a very fulfilling correspondence with her when I was in prison, which was very helpful. She is a very generous person to young learner writers.

But, I think that she is a writer that is not known in South Africa other than in a small intellectual circle, and read by an even smaller circle of South Africans than even those that know her. That has to do with one of the colonial realities of the South African past, and I think also perhaps the particular cultural choices that she took, but which perhaps were the only cultural choices available to a progressive young white woman in the 1950s. That's not strictly true - let's not forget someone like Ruth First who was also a writer and had a different practice of writing.

Gordimer took on the challenge of the high novel, the Western 19th century novel basically, 20th century novel and used it as a genre to reflect in a very progressive, I think, consistently progressive way about the South African reality. But her principal readership was always an external readership, outside of South Africa, particularly in North America and in Europe. I'm sure she contributed. When I spoke earlier about the huge wave of solidarity, I am sure that her political practice had a resonance and played an important role in developing a solidarity and an understanding of the realities and dilemmas of South Africa.

The treasure that her writing represents is a treasure that has still to be discovered in South Africa. And it is not going to be discovered in the next ten or twenty years because the infrastructural realities that require an understanding and an engagement with that body of writing which she has produced are not in place. Again, the literacy rate is contested, but something like half of the adults of our country are not functionally literate. English is just one of 11 official languages.

The novel form is a little bit less accessible, no matter how accessible it might be written. I am sure that the Gordimer contribution is something that is awaiting us as a nation down the line. As a country we will come to appreciate and value her contribution and value and debate her novels in ways that we don't yet. I hope that part of the 'Cultural Revolution' that has to happen in South Africa is actually to make this kind of body of work available.

Obviously the kind of - on a much lower key - political poetry, the literary practice that I have tried to engage in has tried to connect much more immediately with a local audience and a sort of popular black audience as well. I've reached a very small audience, but there have been opportunities where there have been some possibilities - the rallies, mass funerals and so on. The 1980s had their moments. Insofar as there has been some interests in developments in the new South Africa there are fewer rallies and so on now and thank heavens. One doesn't, one resorts to the streets because there are serious problems. But I am doing lots of readings in schools, of poetry, and libraries and civic spaces like that, which weren't available and also in new community radios and even on the national broadcaster. Those spaces either didn't exist or were absolutely closed. Now there are some more possibilities. We need to do a whole lot more, as South Africans, to open up all of those spaces to a kind of cultural engagement and debate. There are the small beginnings of that, so that has been quite exciting.

Ulrike Ernst: *With your review already mentioned, of 'Black Mamba Rising', a discussion emerged about the correct picture of history and the appropriate use of African tradition in literature. How would you assess the ways in which African tradition is or should be represented in the South African arts?*

Jeremy Cronin: For me, what is most interesting about African traditions is the way in which they are able to, they are appropriated by popular forces, whether in churches through the tradition of choral singing and hymns and so on, or in the political movement and so forth, where hunting songs, wedding songs, are appropriated and turned into political songs. That dynamic exchange between the past and the present is what for me is most interesting. There is always a danger of having a different view of African tradition and of traditionalising it.

One of the debates inside the notion of the African Renaissance is precisely that: is an African Renaissance about going backwards and also sealing ourselves off as South Africans or as Africans from the world, or is it a dynamic, building on the positive from the cultures of humankind but with our own confidence and traditions as well? That is one of the tensions in the notion of an African Renaissance, which plays itself out in political tensions.

For me, ja, African traditions are a very powerful and persistent reality in South Africa. It's in the poems, in that collection *'Even the Dead'*, on Mandela I am trying to reflect something of that in the strange persona of Mandela who is this iconic figure.

Ulrike Ernst: *And yet you mention his hands as down-to-earth ...*

Jeremy Cronin: ... yes, his hands. What does he represent? He says in his own book, his autobiography, that he grew up in a Tembu royal court, so he was designed to rule, he was part of an emerging feudal class, but of course a very backward, underdeveloped Third World - it wasn't Versailles where he grew up in, it was a little rural village basically, but which embodied certain aristocratic values. An aristocracy that was just emerging out of primitive communalism.

You have this Mandela at the end of a cynical 20th century, striding the globe as he does, with this nobility which comes out of this tradition, but also a tradition of daily communication with people, because it was such a weak and barely emergent aristocracy, it was a kind of benevolent aristocracy which knew all of the problems and took responsibility for ordinary people. Although those are arcane and even anachronistic values in some respects, coming as they do in the midst of liberalism, market values and so on, they create an interesting vibration. So there are some very honourable things that need to be held on to and built into the new millennium if you like.

For me, Mandela embodies something about the African tradition, and at the same time he is quite a modern person. He married, divorced his wife, married another wife, married a strong person, married a Mozambican, not a South African, he lived with her without getting married for a long while which was disapproved of by conservative circles. So he is very interesting, and I think that is one of the interesting things about South Africa, that there is tremendous telescoping of times and of values and of cultures. One can go in all kinds of directions but I think there is something that can be quite powerful and progressive in that as well, provided we manage it all right. Somehow for me Mandela embodies a lot and the poem is trying to work some of that through, that Mandela embodies some of that interesting, vibrant telescoping.

Ulrike Ernst: *Part of the question of tradition is that of language and identity. Different Nguni languages were promoted to serve the colonisers' ruling order, as for example Mahmood Mamdani showed in his 'Citizen and Subject'[9]. In "Time of the Prophets", you work with a traditional theme, the incidents of the so-called 'Xhosa cattle killing' that had been provoked by the prophesy of Nongqawuse. You connect the old diviners with the new soothsayers of the global market.[10] How do you locate the terrain of languages and tribal politics as part of cultural and literary discourse in the new South Africa?*

Jeremy Cronin: You ask me nice and easy questions. (Laughs)

Again, I am not sure I'm going to give you a comprehensive answer to any of those questions. Another important reality is that Mamdani has another nice phrase, it's a lovely phrase in the book that you refer to. It is: what colonialism perpetuated was not the force of tradition, but the tradition of force. So it latched on to an emerging aristocracy, traditional leadership, but transformed that to be a kind of form of indirect rule to implement its policies. In order to do that it deepened gender oppression, it deepened the distance between what had been old traditional leadership and the communities and so forth. It tried to use language and to divide people along linguistic and other grounds in order to better maintain control. I think that in the new South Africa there are again areas where we got things right rather than wrong. We've not suppressed traditional leadership. We've tried to create a lingering space for it in the new democratic and progressive constitutional order, but recognise that in deep rural areas traditional leaders continue to have some authority and respect and are seen as the embodiment of certain traditional values and so on.

There are positive and reactionary elements in that reality. We haven't sought simply to suppress it as they did in 1917 say, or post-1917 in the Soviet Union particularly and those Asian areas where there were traditional leaders. We've tried to engage that reality but draw it into a new democracy - not without contradictions and so on, but that's the agenda. I personally think that is the correct agenda. The same with language. We've obviously understood that although language divisions were enforced by apartheid for its own purposes of manipulation, our task is therefore not to impose one single language or one single culture on people, but to try to liberate languages, and to ensure that languages that had been marginalized, but codified in particular ways to separate Nguni-speaking people into different segments. To work with that reality; but to understand that language and the ability of people to talk, to discuss, to experience the world, to be citizens of South Africa, that is, we require unifying elements but unity has to be a unity developed through diversity, which would include cultural, ethnic, language diversity. That is a cultural dimension that is proceeding relatively well. Again, there are unevennesses, but I think progress has been made on those fronts.

Ulrike Ernst: *But, which problems would you see as still remaining? You were mentioning Mamdani's book. He was saying that deracialisation has taken place, but detribalisation is lacking. The focus has been too much on the urban and has not been on the rural. Would you connect this with the emerging land issues, land distribution issues?*

Jeremy Cronin: I disagree a little bit with Mamdani. Maybe because I have an urban perspective on these things, I think that the countryside in South Africa is not the same as the countryside even in Zimbabwe, which is the next most developed Southern African country. At the time of independence in Zimbabwe the reserves, it was called the Native Trust Lands, constituted some 50% of the terrain. Here in South Africa since 1913 the reserves were 13% of the terrain. By

1980-1990 they were virtually unable, except in some deep KwaZulu-Natal, deep Northern Transvaal as it was called, generally they were basically areas designed to supply migrant labour into the urban centres. So the connection between the urban and the rural [has been there], particularly in South Africa, but because South Africa was at the hub of a whole migrant labour system throughout South Africa, even to some extent in the rest of Southern Africa. Yes, people have tribal identities somewhat still in South Africa, but I think that those are much more tenuous than in some other African countries.

It is very obvious in urban places like Soweto - if you ask people then characteristically someone's father was Zulu speaking, mother is Sotho speaking and he speaks all the languages and so on. It is obviously different if you go into rural areas. The one attempt to ethnicise, or the one serious attempt to ethnicise politics which had some kind of mass base was the Inkatha political party. It is interesting to note that it's a project which has not succeeded in mobilising. I think it's in decline. Its partial success had to do with the size of the Zulu speaking population, the relative backwardness of the rural areas of KwaZulu-Natal compared to some other rural areas. Although the tribal card is still played by Inkatha, it is a card that has less and less resonance, frankly.

Obviously it's something that one needs to watch. It could become a danger if we fail to maintain the momentum of development and of reconstruction. If there's deepening poverty, deepening inequality and dislocation and if the ANC breaks up and fragments and so forth. If the kind of national project loses its way then the demagogic use by elites of the tribal mobilisation becomes a possibility. You find it even inside the ANC from time to time that intra-elite competition to be nominated for a key position and so on. It is heavily disapproved of in the ANC, but there are elements of a kind of use of tribal linkages to promote individuals or groups or whatever, occur, so it is not a problem that has absolutely vanished, nor will it probably vanish for many, many decades.

If anything, huge progress has been made, even in the short space of ten years. For me, one good example would be the declining fortunes of Inkatha insofar as it still exists. We've managed to pull it into the national project rather than to have it outside of the national project, mobilising a sort of rural tribal base.

Ulrike Ernst: *The title of your poem "Motho ke motho batho ba bang" (1983) became also the rallying cry for the African Renaissance you already mentioned. Some fear that the African Renaissance is no more than a mere slogan and a bureaucratic haven for strugglati.*

How do you understand its concept and potential? How can one reconcile a repressive neo-traditional Africanism with the African Renaissance?

Jeremy Cronin: I think it has the potential dangers that you've mentioned. Also the idea of a renaissance is a Eurocentric notion that one is talking about. It is very much attached to the president, the new president, who has been very anxious to find a theme, like Tony Blair with the 'Third Way'. In the first place it needs to be understood like that here is a president who has to take over from this global icon, Mandela, and needs to find some kind of etiquette for his presidency. Therefore the notion has been actively promoted from the presidency itself and from a small group of intellectuals closely associated with the presidency. He then attempts to institutionalise it and set up African Renaissance chapters and institutions and so forth, which by and large have been colonised by an emerging black elite, an emerging black bourgeoisie in our country, who are not particularly progressive and who have a tendency to play kind of Africanist cards. The notion is often quite exclusive of other people in South Africa.

It can go in that direction and there are active attempts to shape in that kind of way. But broadly within the ANC, certainly in the SACP and other places, rather than simply rejecting this, we've said: what are the potentially positive things about it? One: it draws our attention that we are part of Africa. It draws our attention to the plight of Africa: AIDS, the debt burden, mass poverty, wars, the plight of women in Africa - so let's use the theme to try to broaden our understanding in solidarity with all those things. In South Africa we become very self-absorbed with our own transition in 1994 and negotiations and the applause and bouquets that we won internationally encouraged the narcissism that we suffered from. We neglected our African neighbours in Southern Africa quite considerably, who had often suffered tremendously as a result of apartheid. We need to do those kinds of things. Whether one would want to use the word African Renaissance or whether there will be an African Renaissance, and whether declaring this century the Africa century is not hopelessly voluntaristic which I think it is. It has often become a kind of superficial advertising campaign. There are all those dangers. But, the challenge is to give it a very substantial content. The president himself is increasingly doing that. In international forums and so on increasingly South Africa is trying to speak for the Third World in a more robust way than perhaps was the case just three or four years ago.

Ulrike Ernst: *Jeremy, thank you very much for the interview.*

References

[1] **Cronin, Jeremy. 1984.** Inside. Johannesburg (London 1987).

[2] **Kistner, Ulrike. 1989.** "Literature and the National Question". In: JLS 5(3/4): 302-314.

[3] **Welz, Dieter (ed.). 1987.** Writing against Apartheid. South African Authors interviewed by Dieter Welz. NELM interviews series 2, Grahamstown (reprinted 1988, 1989): 23.

[4] **Cronin, Jeremy. 1987.** "Poetry. An Elitist Pastime Finds Mass Roots", In: Weekly Mail 13-19 March; **Sitas, Ari (ed.). 1986.** Black Mamba Rising. South African Worker Poets in Struggle. Alfred Qabula, Mi S'Dumo Hlatshwayo, Nise Malange. Durban.

[5] **Cronin, Jeremy. 1997.** Even the Dead. Poems, Parables and a Jeremiad. Johannesburg/Cape Town.

[6] **Cronin, Jeremy. 1997.** Even the Dead. Poems, Parables and a Jeremiad, Johannesburg/Cape Town: 4.

[7] **Cronin, Jeremy. 1997.** Even the Dead. Poems, Parables and a Jeremiad. Johannesburg/Cape Town: 40.

[8] **Anderson, Peter. 1990.** "Essential Gestures. Gordimer and Cronin and Identity. Paradigms in White South African Writing". In: English in Africa 17. 2 October.

[9] **Mamdani, Mahmood. 1996.** Citizen and Subject. Contemporary Africa and the Legacy of Late Colonialism. Cape Town.

[10] **Cronin, Jeremy. 1997.** Even the Dead. Poems, Parables and a Jeremiad. Johannesburg/Cape Town. 36-38.

Ulrike Kistner

Ulrike Kistner interviewed by Ulrike Ernst
on 22 April 2001 in Johannesburg

"Underrated: A Critical Poetics of Knowledge"

Ulrike Ernst: *Ulrike Kistner, coming from an academic background of Comparative Literature, you have made yourself a name as provocative and creative scholar in a wide range of areas linking cultural, philosophical and political critique.*

Let us begin with some considerations of earlier political theory in South Africa. The basis for the ANC/ SACP alliance and the theoretical background for the importance of cultural work during apartheid was the two-stage theory of revolution. First a multiracial democracy would be established through a national democratic revolution, followed by the socialist revolution. This two-stage theory was systematically elaborated in the context of the notion of 'Colonialism of a Special Type', claiming that South Africa combines colonisers and colonised in one and the same country. Whites' colonial domination over blacks means that the indigenous population experiences the features of a colony. National oppression was to be combated through, among other things, the formation of national identity. The latter became the paramount objective and task of cultural work.

You argued in your essay "Literature and the National Question" that when in opposition to the 'dominant culture' of the oppressor, a 'national culture' was to be formed, this was simplistically equated with 'resistance culture' or 'revolutionary culture'.[1]

How would you theoretically discuss the notion of protest or revolutionary cultural expressions today?

Ulrike Kistner: The notion of a revolutionary culture has evaporated, for good and for bad reasons. For bad reasons, because it has been subsumed under the goal of latter-day nation-building or rainbow-nationalism, i.e. under the new version of the two-stage theory, which has ditched the second stage. For good reasons, because the notion of a revolutionary culture that featured in the anti-apartheid struggle, was theoretically suspect anyway. Its parameters were not specified: revolution judged by what criteria? Considerations of a 'revolution in poetic language', or a 'theoretical revolution' fell out of the ambit of those writers and cultural critics glibly marching behind a national-revolutionary banner.

Instead, they focused on the content and the thematic aspects of 'plot' or 'story' that are most easily naturalised. Themes such as sex across the colour line made for favoured novelistic writing and reading. Or the 'protest' of 'protest literature' was pinned to a proliferation of struggle icons, emblems, slogans or phrases, and to some supposedly anti-hero gaining moral high ground. The sterility of 'struggle literature' has been well described by Njabulo Ndebele in his critical essays, notably in those collected in *'Redefining Relevance. The Rediscovery of the Ordinary'*.

What has been less well outlined are the organisational possibilities arising from practices of cultural production understood as processes of articulation. These are often not evident in the consideration of the mere products. Although such process-work was fundamental to the role of organisations such as COSAW, this does not find statement in the publications featuring cultural 'products'.

And what has been least well outlined in the talk of 'revolutionary culture' are the possible routes for a 'revolution' in literature, and in theory, which attains its status as such precisely through its counter-inductive, counter-experiential, counter-intuitive relation to what is taken as natural, in founding something new – new orders, models, concepts, ways of seeing, or a new rationality. A critical poetics of knowledge has probably been the most underrated revolutionary force. If we were to retain the notion of a 'revolutionary culture', it is here that I would want to locate it.

Ulrike Ernst: *During the last few decades, constructs of the nation have been rallying points not only for the ANC but also for many different groupings in South Africa. What kind of 'national imaginary' has been at hand? What function and role would you attribute to 'the nation' and 'national culture' today?*

Ulrike Kistner: The rhetoric of national culture notwithstanding, nationhood comes to South Africa today as a belated gift from above that might turn out to be empty on its unwrapping. While the rhetoric of 'national culture' reminds us that secular culture has been tied to the nation-state, which it helped to imagine, enthrone, unify and legitimate, it remains rhetoric precisely inasmuch as its conditions have been overtaken by globalised capital and consumer culture.

In South Africa, various versions of the notion of national culture are currently being invoked in a desperate attempt to halt and possibly heal the proliferating and widening rifts that are threatening to tear this society apart. This attempt, I think, has to be taken very seriously. It calls for rethinking the relationship between state, nation and ethnos, between state and civil society, society and community, class and race, nationalism and racism. However, to believe that national culture and nationalism can address these issues positively, rests on the idea that racism and nationalism are antithetical: that the legacy of racism can be healed by national unity, national identity, national culture, and various forms of nationalism. This, I think, is misleading; for the very construct of national identity, national unity and national culture rest on prior exclusions. As the nationalisms of liberation are being converted into hegemonic nationalism, new forms of racism and xenophobia emerge.

The jury, I believe, is still out on the widely proclaimed obsolescence of the nation-state under conditions of capitalist globalisation, information and communications technology, and other means of conquering space by time. It has been argued that the power of the nation-state has even been enhanced in certain areas, such as labour control, fiscal discipline, and infra-structural investments.

In South Africa, the relationship between the state and international flows of capital and information is an uneven, contradictory one. It manifests itself in, among other things, a contradiction between developmentalism (the imperative of providing for 'basic needs') and competitiveness (labour flexibility, reduction of public spending, financial efficiency).

Within these contradictions, I think, lie some critically circumscribed conditions for the assertion of a new kind of 'national imaginary' that I would prefer to call a 'civil imaginary': holding the state to safeguarding civil, political, and social rights, while at the same time extending the bounds of citizenship.

Literature could have an important role in fostering this imagination (in the Kantian sense of making sensible in advance of concepts).

However, I think, South African literatures and their teachers and critics have not heeded this kind of wake-up call as yet, caught, as they are, in the process of a reorientation from a largely national-democratic-realist mould to what will hopefully become an imaginary-aesthetic one (in the above mentioned sense). In the meantime, I think, critics can usefully engage in a productive reading of those realist texts, showing their historical pretexts and discursive contexts.

Ulrike Ernst: *Outside of South Africa, the literature of this country is connected with the name of Nobel Prize winner, Nadine Gordimer. Inside the country, her achievements as a writer and a political figure have been the subject of heated controversy. However, she has always been close to the ANC. Suddenly, in April 2001, some of Nadine Gordimer's writing was taken off the literature teaching syllabus by a regional schoolbook committee. How do you explain the general difference in the reception of Nadine Gordimer's work? What do you make of the 'new censorship' of the committee?*

The differential reception of Gordimer's work attests to the kind of sensibility that was frequently mobilised for the anti-apartheid struggle. The solidarity that it inspired from outside of South Africa has, to some extent, reference points different to those of political activism inside the country.

The fact that her work was recently censored, as it were, for teaching purposes, only attests to the effective realisation of her realist narrative strategies (designed for easy naturalisation) by her schoolbook committee readers. So she can be proud to have found her 'ideal readers'.

Ulrike Ernst: *Let us turn to a related field that you were recently working on - the media. You were following the publication of the 'Interim Report of Inquiry into Racism in the Media' at the end of November 1999, and were observing South Africa's first public hearings on racism in the media in Spring 2000.*

The hearings were preceded by a lengthy conflict, leading to a standoff between the daily press and the Commission, and between editors supporting and rejecting the procedures initiated by the Commission. The process was designed to produce elicit, voluntary compliance and the Human Rights Commission used its power of subpoena to force newspaper editors and broadcasters to appear before the Commission. The press understood this to be an infringement of freedom of the press and of statement more generally.

You warned that "the new approach to practices of cultural regulation harbours some pitfalls that could potentially catapult [South Africa] into post-democracy".[2] How do you respond to the discussion of the issue of racism in present-day South Africa?

Ulrike Kistner: There are some tendencies in current public discussions of racism that I find disconcerting. 'Race' is fore grounded in a way that social theorists in South Africa in the 1970s and 1980s would have described as 'race reductionism'.

The relationship between race and class that has exercised the minds of historians and social theorists dealing with the specificities of racial capitalism in South Africa, has been factored out of the current public discussion. While this scholarship could possibly be said to have assumed too automatic a correlation between race and class and has disregarded the lived experience of racial categorisation, I believe that it had important insights and findings to offer. I would concede that we have to rethink our understanding and explanation of racism, as the category of 'race' is losing its status as instituted social fact in the new dispensation, so that we have to consider various possibilities of 'racism without 'race'.

Nevertheless, I think, ignoring the conceptualisations and explanations offered by social-historical and theoretical scholarship on race and racism in South Africa means that non-historicized notions of 'race' and 'racism' are made to bear a disproportionate explanatory burden, which deprives them of much of their explanatory power.

Unmoored from historical and socio-political co-ordinates, the new talk of racism is harnessed to a discourse of human rights, which is relatively new in South Africa. With the lack of theoretical, historical and political understanding of the role of human rights, I perceive the danger of conflating human rights and law. Subordinating human rights to legal protocol, in turn, runs the risk of closing down spaces for political debate. In the absence of political contestation, and with a weakening social service delivery through which some of the political and social rights could be actualised, postulates of human rights run the risk of becoming quality control measures designed to achieve international legitimacy. In that sense, then, I think that the public discourse of race and racism, much as it claims to address the horrific legacy of apartheid, has its own modes of forgetting.

Ulrike Ernst: *Is 'multiculturalism' a useful concept in describing cultural formations at work in South Africa?*[3]

Ulrike Kistner: 'Multiculturalism' has, I would say thankfully, never caught on in a big way in South Africa, except maybe in the current efforts launched within the heritage and tourism industries and in talk of the rainbow nation, which is a relatively recent import. It conjures up apartheid models of ethnic pluralism, which have remained highly suspect. It also resonates with practices, widely understood as racist in gesture, of translating racialist categories into markers of cultural difference. I would consider such suspicion healthy.

Ulrike Ernst: *Now I would like to turn to a different area, i.e. your intervention in the HIV/AIDS debate.*[4] *Insofar as the public AIDS debates reached a high profile, they have been dominated by the controversy around the causal link between HIV and AIDS. President Thabo Mbeki's statements on the subject (most prominently in the article in Time Magazine and in his speech at the 13th International AIDS Conference in Durban in July 2000) have served to catapult the issue into the limelight. In my view, the facts and fictions surrounding HIV/AIDS - touching on issues like post colonialism, developmentalism or, neo-liberalism - are indicators that brutally show that South Africa is undergoing a cultural crisis. How do you respond? What cultural challenges does the debate entail?*

Ulrike Kistner: If I were to confine myself to the specifically 'cultural' challenges, I would say that the President's and the AIDS Advisory Panel's pronouncements highlight the contradictory nature of South Africa's globalisation. Within a global pandemic, involving movements of labour migration, co-ordination of research, drug policies (including trials, patenting, production, marketing and financing) and health services and interventions internationally, the President and his advisors are advocating a uniquely (South) African intervention and solution. In assessing this stance critically, it has been pointed out that there is a terrain of struggle emerging here that is symptomatic for constellations in post-apartheid South Africa: a newly configured state power (the ANC transforming itself from a movement to a party to government) countering attempts by activists and scientists within new social movements to influence the policy terrain.

For AIDS awareness and education campaigns, is imperative to come to understand patterns of those social relations and cultural practices that shape exposure and responses to the epidemic, in particular the social relations of sex. Vulnerability to risk and risk aversion has to be studied in much more differentiated ways, so as to be able to mobilise peer groups and other social networks in prevention. A particularly socially pressing 'cultural' issue in promoting the prevention, and understanding the incidence and the effects of HIV infection is that of power imbalances in gender relations, calling for challenges to the understanding of masculinity.

The 'witchcraft paradigm' also remains to be addressed, when HIV/AIDS is frequently interpreted, along the lines of the understanding of the action of invisible forces, as a form of witchcraft. The possibility of re-significations within that paradigm would need to be investigated. The cultural barriers to 'community-based' care of people living with HIV/AIDS would need to be analysed and addressed. At the moment, such care is hampered among other things by stigmatisation, fear, conflicts within households, and local beliefs about the transmission of HIV.

Ulrike Ernst: An emerging notion furthered by Thabo Mbeki has been that of the African Renaissance. Do you regard the African Renaissance as providing a useful conception of renewal? How can one reconcile a repressive neo-traditional Africanism with the African Renaissance?

Ulrike Kistner: I do not think I can fully answer this question. A part-answer possibly lies in outlining one of the most fundamental divisions that remain not only from apartheid, but also from a specifically colonial legacy. This division concerns the relation between ethnic and civic citizenship. It is based on the countering of (potential) popular anti-colonial resistance through fragmenting the colonised into tribal minorities. The essence of indirect rule lay in the dualism of colonial power whereby civil society became racialised, while native authority became tribalised. The new constitution, the recognition of tribal authorities as civic structures, the redrawing of municipal boundaries, a new electoral system, and the recognition of customary marriages have been designed to address this issue.

Nevertheless, structural limitations, shortcomings, blind spots, and bottlenecks in various reform processes have led to a partial re-ethnicisation of social relations. If one were to give the African Renaissance any credibility, one could see it as a plan to bridge this divide between ethnic and civic citizenship.

However, its proclamation from above, in the absence of a basis within a social movement or civil society, would mean that it is doomed from the start in meeting this objective.

Ulrike Ernst: *You have been teaching literary theory, cultural and media studies and related subjects at the University of the Witwatersrand for a long time. You invested a lot of energy into the establishment of an all-inclusive university system, with all its implications for teaching and learning. Today, many of your colleagues have left South Africa for better teaching opportunities elsewhere. At a recent international conference you were introduced as a 'peripatetic intellectual' (Gunter Pakendorf) because you seem to have to find your way as a critical intellectual outside the established academy.*

How would you describe the relationship between intellectuals, scholars, and activists in South Africa over the last two or even three decades? What is the role of a public intellectual in present-day South Africa? Where would you locate her or his challenges/responsibilities in a time of transition and after the establishment of a democracy? How do you see yourself in this context?

Ulrike Kistner: In the past, though they were not confined to the university, intellectuals were assured of a ready and prepared base in the universities in more ways than one. Research interests and projects of activists could find themselves actualised in the movements, with firm backing from colleagues and resource bases within the university. The university was a resource base for many activists who might otherwise have had only tenuous links with the institution. Since the latter half of the 1990s, this 'Personalunion' between academic, intellectual, and activist has disintegrated. They all go into different directions now. Judged by job security and livelihood, it is the activists and the intellectuals who are the losers - so much so that they have become an endangered species at a time when a precarious democracy requires them most. In the great tertiary education shake-up that attempts to hide its neo-liberal adaptations behind a developmentalist and a bureaucratic 'transformation' jargon, scholars have emigrated to universities offering them more congenial conditions, or alternatively, they have re-invented themselves as adult basic education teachers; intellectuals have transmogrified into fast-lane hi-tech or IT business or HR consultants; activists in the mainstream national liberationist tradition have become disgruntled government officials, ministers, or bureaucrats. Universities have been left intellectually stymied finishing schools with the tatty polish of snob-value.

Education for active citizenship is happening elsewhere now. It is happening in newly emerging social movements contesting macro-economic policy, urban living conditions, land reform, and the poverty of education, privatisation, job losses, home losses, and health care delivery. The articulation of a new social and political project from these fragmentations – that is where I see the role of intellectuals as activists.

Much of this means an 'ou-topic' place that is the place of no place, which exists for as long as its name and its hope. It is the place from which a lot of work needs to be done, and it will never be 'business as usual'.

Ulrike Ernst: *Thank you very much for the interview.*

References

[1] **Kistner, Ulrike. 1989.** "Literature and the National Question". In: Journal of Literary Studies 5(3/4): 302-314. See also **Kistner, Ulrike. 1991.** "The Politics of Canon Formation in Literary Theory - for example: Realism and the Popular Front". In: Journal of Literary Studies 7(3/4): 217-227.

[2] **Kistner, Ulrike. 2000.** "The Elided Performative. The Human Rights Commission's Inquiry into Racism in the Media". Johannesburg (Forthcoming in **Kistner, Ulrike. 2002.** Commissioning and Contesting Post-Apartheid. Hamburg/Münster/London).

[3] See **Ernst, Ulrike. 2001.** "Cultural Politics in South Africa in Transition. Or, Multiculturalism and the Logic of South African Macro-Economics". Paper presented at the conference 'Africa and Europe: Myths, Masks and Masquerades'. Johannesburg (Forthcoming).

[4] **Kistner, Ulrike. 2001.** "Necessity and Sufficiency in the Aetiology of HIV/AIDS. The Science, History, and Politics of the Causal Link". Johannesburg. Paper presented at the WITS History Workshop (Forthcoming).

Highlights of Interviewees' Literary-Political Contexts

These short biographical notes aim at helping the reader understand many of the questions and responses in this book in the light of the interviewees' particular personal experience. The notes therefore concentrate on issues concerning the personal/political and academic life of the writers and critics in relation to their cultural and literary contexts .The formal end of apartheid serves as the point of intersection between Past and Present. Publications cited are limited to the period after 1990.

The aspects highlighted in these notes can only present a fragmentary impression of the individuals' achievements. For further information on the writers see e.g. *Killam, Douglas/Rowe, Ruth. 2000.The Companion to African Literatures.* Oxford. Additionally, *Coldham, G. 1968-[ongoing] Dictionary of South African Biographies. Pretoria*, is useful for more information on the more prominent personalities.

Michael Chapman (1945)

Michael Chapman was educated in South Africa (University of Natal and UNISA) and England (London). Today he is Professor of English and Dean of the Faculty of Human Sciences at the University of Natal, Durban, South Africa.

Chapman entered the South African literary scene during the late 1970s. The ideas and philosophy of Black Consciousness Movement were the main vehicle for the statement of Black aspirations at this time. Chapman advocated a socially responsive, contextual criticism in literature and the arts. Having offered the first extended understanding of New Black Poetry of the 1970s (or, as he called it, Soweto Poetry), Chapman published two monographs *'Douglas Livingstone: A Critical Study of his Poetry'* (1981) and *'South African English Poetry: A Modern Perspective'* (1984), as well as an anthology of essays *'Soweto Poetry'* (1982) and the collection *'Voices from Within: Black Poetry from Southern Africa'* (1982). His anthology of short stories, *'The Drum Decade: Stories of the 1950s'* (1989; 2001), was followed by the 600-page literary history *'Southern African Literatures'* (1996), a book which suggested that a new South Africa required not a reversal of white/black polarities, but ongoing interrogation of the concepts of Africa and the West. Chapman's current projects include the anthology *'The New Century of South African Poetry'* and a book of essays *'South/North'*, postcolonial revisions of African/Western literary-cultural relationships.

1988. "The Liberated Zone. The Possibilities of Imaginative Expression in a State of Emergency". In: English Academy Review, 5.
1989. "The Critic in a State of Emergency. Towards a Theory of Reconstruction". In: Theoria no.74.
1992. Perspectives on South African English Literature (eds. together with C. Gardner and E. Mphahlele. Johannesburg.
1996. Southern African Literatures. London/New York.

Jeremy Cronin (1949)

Jeremy Cronin was born in Durban, the son of a naval officer, and grew up in the Western Cape. He studied philosophy at the University of Cape Town and the Sorbonne in Paris. Returning to Cape Town in 1974, he lectured in the philosophy and politics departments. He was arrested in 1976 and was charged under the 'Terrorism Act' for carrying out underground work for the then banned ANC. He spent his prison sentence in various security prisons in Pretoria, including three years among death row prisoners in the notorious Pretoria Maximum Jail. During his sentence, his wife died unexpectedly. He was released after seven years. After his release in 1983, he was in exile in London and Lusaka, Zambia.

Cronin returned to South Africa in 1990. He has been prominent in South African Communist Party politics and has worked as its Deputy General Secretary. He has since become a Member of Parliament for the ANC. One of the challenges of this position is to reconcile the inevitable political differences between the SACP and the ANC government. Today, he lives with his family in Johannesburg and Cape Town.

Cronin's first volume of poetry, *'Inside'*, written illegally while he was in prison, was published on his release. It was a great success, translated into many languages and winner of the Ingrid Jonker Prize in 1984. In this collection of poems, he deals with the relationship between public and private existence and with the challenge of expressing sentiments of political struggle versus personal emotions. As a critic, he made several important and thought provoking contributions to the South African discourse on culture and politics. After the political changes in South Africa, Cronin continued to write poetry. *'Inside'* was created during the struggle against apartheid. A very 'different Cronin' (Leon de Kock) now looks back to re-examine that past struggle. In his collection *'Even the Dead'* (1997), severe poetry with ambiguous poetic meaning toys with new forms and expressions of language. At times, Cronin becomes a prophet who warns of the dangers of historical amnesia.

1975. The Ideologies of Politics (with A. de Crespigny). Cape Town.
1985. Thirty Years of the Freedom Charter (with R. Suttner). Johannesburg.
1987 [Enlarged edition of 1983/84. Johannesburg]. Inside. London.

1997. Even the Dead. Poems, Parables and a Jeremiad. Johannesburg/Cape Town.
1999. Inside Out (compilation from previous volumes). Cape Town.

Nadine Gordimer (1923)

Nadine Gordimer was born in a small mining town near Johannesburg. The daughter of Jewish immigrants, she started to write at a very early age. Her education as a writer was gained from extensive reading and from a growing awareness of societal issues.

Gordimer consistently opposed racial injustice in her writing and aligned herself politically and ideologically with the ANC. Although not directly involved in political activities beyond her writing, her work was at times banned during the apartheid era. Gordimer has been a prominent activist in the Congress of South African Writers. Today, she is engaged in human rights work and holds various positions in international bodies. She is, for example the vice-president of International PEN. Gordimer continues to support the ANC in government.

Her immense body of work as a novelist, short story writer and essayist spans the period from the beginning of formal apartheid (1948) to its end (1990) and thereafter. She has received many major awards, among them the Booker Prize in 1974 for *'The Conservationist'* as well as honorary doctorates abroad. In 1991, Gordimer was awarded the Nobel Prize for Literature. After the end of white minority rule in her country, she remains a highly productive writer, focussing on issues of post-apartheid South Africa. In 1999, Gordimer also produced a documentary film, *'The Wall in the Mind'*, comparing Johannesburg and Berlin after their respective political changes.

Gordimer has attracted a fair amount of controversy throughout her writing career in South Africa: ranging from the supporters of the apartheid system that she criticised, to those who opposed apartheid, many of whom felt that her involvement was not far-reaching enough. Some oppositionists resented being represented by a white, 'middle-class', full-time writer. Gordimer, in turn, did not shy away from criticising the quality of writings of some 'struggle propaganda' writers. On the other hand, critics questioned whether her realist writing and her use of the conventional novel genre were the appropriate form to not only inform but enhance the transformation of the reader or to project new worlds. Internationally, a different perception of Gordimer prevailed. Here, she was appreciated for her ongoing awareness-raising of South African apartheid issues and her ability to write compellingly in forms readily accessible to overseas' readership. Gordimer claims that she had always aspired to write and act as a private person outside the political-public sphere. However, in terms of the responsibilities of the intellectual, not only did her international fame force her to reconsider this aspect of her writing self, Gordimer herself in some of her nonfiction writing, makes reference to Antonio Gramsci, thus tacitly conceding the challenge of this position to writers. The question, whether or not she fulfils these responsibilities in a post-apartheid South Africa dominated by strictly market-oriented ANC cultural and literary policies, remains open.

1990. My Son's Story. London/Cape Town.
1991. Crimes of Conscience. Oxford.
1991. Jump and Other Stories. Cape Town/London.
1994. None to Accompany Me. London/New York.
1994. Writing and Being. The Charles Eliot Norton Lectures. Cambridge, Mass.
1998. The House Gun. London/New York.
2001. The Pickup. London/New York.

Stephen Gray (1941)

Stephen Gray was born in Cape Town and was educated at the University of Cape Town, at Cambridge and in Iowa. He taught for a short period in France and held the Chair of English between 1987-1992 at the Rand Afrikaans University, Johannesburg.

Gray, who welcomed the political changes, values his independence as a writer. Since withdrawing from formal academic life, he has worked as a fulltime poet, novelist, editor and critic, writing primarily for a South African readership. He has remained a proclaimed 'non-joiner' who carries out his social responsibility, which he expresses through his position as an independent public intellectual.

Gray was the first academic writer to compile a literary history of modern South Africa, *'Southern African Literature. An Introduction'*. This study included black writers at a time (1979) when African literature was not yet considered a legitimate branch of English Literature. Gray has edited many South African writers (among others Solomon Plaatje, H.C. Bosman, Stephen Black and Athol Fugard), three anthologies of South African stories and poems in the Penguin series and four volumes of South African drama. His play, *'Schreiner, A One-Woman Play'* (1983), was highly successful.
In his writings,

Gray constantly explored South Africa's political landscape whilst examining the role of a poet in a restricted society. In the late 1980s, his response to an increasingly brutal environment was expressed in *'Season of Violence'*. Gray's novels have been highly experimental and diverse in form. Two of them deal with homosexual relations as a political issue. *'Time of Our Darkness'* (1988) is a provocative political contextualisation of a love affair between a white schoolmaster and a black schoolboy. *'Born of Man'* (1989) derides South African attitudes towards sexuality. *'War Child'* (1991) is an account of a Cape childhood during the Second World War. Much of Gray's literary preoccupation centres around the re-presentation of (African) history, reclaiming it from its apartheid interpretations.

1993. Human Interest and other Pieces. Johannesburg.
1993. Accident of Birth. Johannesburg (Autobiography)
1994. Selected Poems. 1960-92. Cape Town.
1994. Drakenstein. A Novel. Johannesburg.
1998. Gabriel's Exhibition. Belville.

Peter Horn (1934)

Peter Horn taught German and Literary Theory at the University of Cape Town, where he remains an Honorary Fellow. Horn's wide-ranging academic interests encompass research on the Enlightenment (Schiller, Goethe), on Kleist as well as on the philosopher Hegel and the Frankfurt School. In 1974 he won the Pringle Prize for his work on poetry. Responding scholarly to the political change in South Africa, he published a volume of essays on South African literature *'Writing my Reading'* (1994). In the essay *"Wendezeit"* (1997), he compared South African and German literature of transition. Today, he lives in Cape Town and Berlin where his wife presently works.

As a leftist thinker, he was supportive of activities against the apartheid regime; he nonetheless held some reservations about certain ANC policies. Horn has been a prominent figure in the Congress of South African Writers, although he has distanced himself from some of their undertakings. A firm supporter of political change in South Africa, Horn finds the present cultural politics of the ANC government 'totally confused'.

Horn has published seven volumes of poetry, of which *'Poems 1964-1989'* (1991) has earned him an honorable mention in the Noma Awards for Publishing in Africa. He edited and translated a collection of South African poetry in struggle: *'Kap der Guten Hoffnung. Gedichte aus dem südafrikanischen Widerstand'* (1980). The collection of short stories, *'The Kaffir Who Reads Books'*, earned him the Alex La Guma/Bessie Head Prize 1993. Today, Horn deals in his fiction with the apartheid past in an angry but imaginative manner, as in his award winning short-story collection *'My Voice Is Under Control Now'* (1999). He investigates the fear of the defenders of the past and shows problems and absurdities of a society in transition.

Horn has tried to be accessible to a wide readership. His poetry has been published and translated into French, Italian, Portuguese, Spanish, German, Polish, Xhosa and Tagalog. Horn also put a great effort into making South African poetry available on the internet.

1991. Poems 1964-1990. Johannesburg.
1992. An Axe in the Ice.
1993. Derrière le vernis du soleil, poèmes 1964-1989. Choisis et traduit de l'anglais sud-africain par Jacques Alavarez-Péreyre.
1995. The Rivers that Connect Us to the Past. Survivors. Poems. Cape Town.
1997. "Parallels and Contrasts - Wendezeit in South African and German Literature". In: Literator 18 (3) Nov: 25-40.
1999. My Voice Is Under Control Now. Cape Town.
See also Noyes, John K./Pakendorf, Gunter/Pasche, Wolfgang (Eds.). 2000. Kultur, Sprache, Macht. Festschrift für Peter Horn. Frankfurt a.M./Berlin/Bern et al.

Ulrike Kistner (1954)

Ulrike Kistner was born in Greytown, Natal. She was educated in South Africa and Germany. During the 1980's, she was actively involved in organisations active in the fields of health care reform, worker education, and in addressing violence against women. Kistner gained her doctorate at the Witwatersrand University Johannesburg, where she has taught Comparative Literature, Cultural Studies, Gender Studies and Media Studies. Today she works as a freelance lecturer, writer and researcher in Johannesburg.

Her teaching goals have been shaped by emancipatory projects and visions of theoretical revolutions and social and political transformations internationally. She finds herself at some critical distance from current (South African) education policies which, while proclaiming a developmentalist agenda (the imperative of providing for 'basic needs') tend to entrench educational poverty. In her own work, she attempts to create the conditions for active citizenship.

Consistently a left-wing critical intellectual, Kistner was detained for some time during apartheid. With the political change in South Africa, she has remained an independent thinker and continues her societal critique.

Kistner is presently involved, as co-editor of the journal *Debate*, in reconstituting a forum for the independent left, and in bringing together forces of new social movements which have not found a political home in the existing party-political landscape, including the Tripartite Alliance (ANC-SACP-COSATU).

1989. "Literature and the National Question". In: Journal of Literary Studies 5(3/4): 302-314.
1991. "The Politics of Canon Formation in Literary Theory - for example: Realism and the Popular Front". In: Journal of Literary Studies 7(3/4): 217-227.
2000. "The Elided Performative. The Human Rights Commission's Inquiry into Racism in the Media". Johannesburg (Forthcoming in Kistner, Ulrike. 2002. Commissioning and Contesting Post-Apartheid. Münster/Hamburg/London).
2001. "Necessity and Sufficiency in the Aetiology of HIV/AIDS. The Science, History, and Politics of the Causal Link". Johannesburg. Paper presented at the WITS History Workshop (Forthcoming).

Mandla Langa (1950)

Mandla Langa was born into a Zulu family in Durban and grew up in Kwamashu township in Natal. He received his BA at Fort Hare University, the well known college for black South Africans. In 1976, he was arrested for political activities. Skipping bail, he went into exile in Botswana and subsequently lived in Lesotho and Mozambique. In Angola, he underwent military training in the camps of Umkhonto we Sizwe (MK), the military wing of the ANC.

Langa has held various ANC posts abroad, including that of the Cultural Representative in Great Britain and Western Europe. After the political changes in South Africa, Langa was given international and national positions in various cultural-political spheres. He was, for example, the vice-chairperson of the afrika95 Exhibition in London and the last chairperson of the Congress of South African Writers. In 1996, he became the convener of the task group on government communications. He has been involved in the hearings by the Human Rights Commission on 'Racism in the New Media'. At present, he is chairperson of the Independent Broadcasting Authority.

Besides his work as a cultural organizer, Langa became well known through his weekly columns for the magazine New Nation.

In 1991, he was the first South African to receive the Arts Council of Great Britain Bursary for Creative Writing. In his earlier writings - even though they were preoccupied with the experience of battles and exile - he has never applied struggle propaganda or a claim to 'one truth' only. In his thoughtful work after the end of apartheid, Langa deals with the legacy of racial division as well as the (physical and psychological) 'scars' left by the liberation movement's human rights violations in the course of the struggle. One of the themes of Langa's present writing is his attempt to reconcile pre-modern tribal traditions with modern life.

In 1996, he produced a 13-part series of local short stories for TV, aiming at making South African literature widely accessible even to the high number of illiterate South Africans.

1987. Tenderness of Blood. Zimbabwe.
1989. A Rainbow on a Paper Sky. London.
1996. The Naked Song and other Stories. Cape Town/Johannesburg.
2000. The Memory of Stones. Cape Town.

Nise Malange (1960)

Nise Malange was born into a 'Xhosa-Coloured' family just outside the city of Cape Town. She spent her childhood in shelters and shacks in the racially segregated areas of Clovelly, Vrygrond and Guguletu. Her education began in a so-called 'coloured' school. It was affected by the disruption caused by fighting among the local hostel-dwelling population. Malange was sent by her family to the Transkei (a designated 'black' area in the Eastern Cape) where she experienced the effects of the 1976/77 Soweto uprisings. These were followed by class boycotts, school burnings and police-attacks, which rapidly spread all over the country.

Returning to Cape Town in 1977, Malange lived through the full force of the student rebellion, during which many young people were killed. Malange experienced a life that is symptomatic of the entire 1976 'black wandering youth generation', who in the aftermath of the Soweto political turmoil fled their township homes. (Many of these subsequently left the country thus swelling the ranks of MK.) After resuming her studies in the Ciskei for a short while, Malange returned to Cape Town in 1981. In 1982 she moved to Howick, Natal. It was in Natal that Malange started to work with the trade unions where she became an organiser for the Transport and General Workers Union. Trade Union work soon became the central concern of her life.

Malange's preoccupation with cultural production - plays, poetry, dancing - started in the Cape. Together with working class cultural activists, such as Alfred Qabula and Mi Hlatshwayo, she was involved in the formation of the Durban Worker's Cultural Local and the Culture and Working Life Project. Malange wrote, directed and facilitated many projects in the Workers' Cultural Locals in Durban. In Natal, she recites her own poetry at mass-meetings and political gatherings.

Malange, together with Nadine Gordimer, has been the vice-president of the Congress of South African Writers. After the political changes in South Africa, she became the chairperson of the Natal Provincial Arts Council. Malange is highly critical of the cultural policy of the Department of Arts, Culture and Science and Technology. At present, she is the director of the BAT Cultural Center in Durban. Through her involvement in Kwela Publications, a Cape Town-based publishing company, she tries to promote the work of younger writers. Malange also runs creative writing workshops.

Nise Malange's poetry writing and performance continues. In accordance with her perception of the lack of improvement in the living conditions of the majority of the population, Malange's old themes, now, become the new themes of exploitation, unemployment and social hardship. Still a political activist and campaigner, she continually criticizes the corruption and bureaucracy of some of her former struggle allies. Malange is the down-to earth writer who feels compelled to address the burning issues, which continue to undermine the lives of working men and women. She has, however, also developed other aspects of herself, and her writing now often reflects the beauty of life itself.

1986. Collected Poems. In: Sitas, Ari (ed.). 1986. Black Mamba Rising. South African Worker Poets in Struggle. Alfred Qabula, Mi S'Dumo Hlatshwayo, Nise Malange. Durban.
1989. "Women Workers and the Struggle for Cultural Transformation". In: Meintjes, Frank/ Hlatshwayo, Mi et al. (eds.). 1989. Worker Culture. Special Issue of Staffrider 8 (3/4). Johannesburg: 76-80.

Mongane Wally Serote (1944)

Serote was born in Sophiatown and brought up in Alexandra township (Johannesburg). After completing school, he worked in journalism and advertising. After being detained without trial for anti-apartheid activities in 1969, he left (1974) for the USA where he studied fine art and creative writing at Columbia University in New York.

Returning to southern Africa in 1979, Serote chose self-imposed exile in Botswana. From 1986-1989, he acted as the cultural attaché for the ANC's Department of Arts and Culture in London. He has become well known as the organiser of the important international 'Culture of Resistance' conferences (e.g. Conference for Another South Africa in 1987).

Serote returned to South Africa in 1990, after the unbanning of the liberation movement and continued to play a leading role in the ANC's cultural department. He has been criticised for carrying out cultural work along the line of a one-party discipline (see discussion in Weekly Mail 1993-1994). In 1994, he was elected ANC Member of Parliament and was nominated as chairperson responsible for the parliamentary Committee on Arts, Science and Technology. Serote has continued his work in the legislature of the Department of Arts, Culture, Science and Technology. After the second democratic elections (1999), he became involved in the formation of the African Renaissance Structures, including the South African Chapter of the African Renaissance Institute. In 2000, he convened the African Renaissance Conference in Johannesburg.

Serote has published several volumes of poetry and received numerous literary prizes. In 1981, his novel *'To Every Birth Its Blood'* was published in Johannesburg. His writing bore an active commitment to the liberation struggle, becoming increasingly militant as the struggle against apartheid strengthened. After 1990, Serote's writing began to address the issues arising out of the transition in South Africa. His current literary work has, however, been criticised by old struggle comrades (for example, Cronin) for displaying a certain indulgence in 'struggle nostalgia'.

1990. On the Horizon. (essays)

1992. Third World Express. Cape Town (Winner of Noma Award)
1994. Come and Hope with Me. Cape Town.
1997. Freedom Lament and Song. Cape Town.

Ari Sitas (1952)

Ari Sitas was educated at the Witwatersrand University in Johannesburg where he received his PhD in Sociology. Sitas became a professor of Sociology at the University of Natal, Durban and was previously Vice-Chancellor of the University. He has written prolifically on trade union work and on cultural issues in KwaZulu Natal. Today, Sitas is very sceptical of the Department of Arts, Culture Science and Technology's demand that art should 'nation build'.

Sitas's career in cultural work started in the 1970-80s in Johannesburg, where he and others founded the Junction Avenue Theatre Company. He was involved in all its important projects up until 1982. These included *'The Fantastical History of a Useless Man'*, *'Will of a Rebel'*, *'Dikhitsheneng'* or *'Marabi'*.

Since 1980, he has been occupied with trade union work. Sitas was one of the main initiators of the worker theatre movement in South Africa. After his move to Durban in 1983, he was involved with COSATU and other trade unions in Natal. He was the intellectual head of the groups, developing and directing many plays, such as *'Ilanga Lizophumela Abasebenzi'*, *'The Dunlop Play'*, *'Khoze Kuphe Nini?'*, or *'Bambatha's Children'*. Sitas participated in the formation of the Durban Worker's Cultural Local, where he played a key role in the development project Culture and Working Life, attached to the Department of Sociology at the University of Natal.

Sitas, a poet himself, was also involved in the foundation of the Congress of South African Writers in 1987 and was a Natal executive member of COSAW. He became known as the editor of the worker poetry book *'Black Mamba Rising'* that induced a wide discussion on popular art, the question of Eurocentric standards of literature versus struggle sloaganeering, and the appropriate use of African tradition in progressive art. Sitas remains a writer and critic but finds it increasingly difficult to have critical poetry published.

1984. African Worker Responses on the East Rand to Changes in South Africa's Metalworks, 1960-1980s. Johannesburg (WITS).
1985. Productive Mythologies.
1989. Tropical Scars.
1991. William Zungu. A Xmas Story.
1999. The Autobiography of a Movement. Trade Unions in KwaZulu-Natal 1970s-1990s. In: Zegeye, Abebe/Kriger, Robert (eds.) 1998-99. Cultural Change and Development in South Africa. Culturelink Special Issue. Zagreb.
Forthcoming. The Flight of the Gwala-Gwala Bird. Essays on Politics, Culture and Labour in Natal (Madiba Press).

Abbreviations/Acronyms

ANC	African National Congress
AZAPO	Azanian People's Organisation
BCM	Black Consciousness Movement
CASA	Conference for Another South Africa, Amsterdam 1987
COSATU	Congress of South African Trade Unions
COSAW	Congress of South African Writers
CST	Colonialism of a Special Type
DACST	Department of Arts, Culture, Science and Technology
DP	Democratic Party
GEAR	Growth, Employment and Redistribution Programme
FOSATU	Federation of South African Trade Unions, predecessor of COSATU
IFP	Inkatha Freedom Party
IMF	International Monetary Fund
MDM	Mass Democratic Movement
MK	Umkhonto we Sizwe, the military wing of the ANC
PAC	Pan Africanist Congress
RDP	Reconstruction and Development Plan
SACP	South African Communist Party
Soweto	South Western Townships
TRC	Truth and Reconciliation Commission
UDF	United Democratic Front
UWUSA	United Workers' Union of South Africa

Photographs

Front Cover: *'The Gumboot Dance'* 2000 taken in Lesedi Cultural Village near Sterkfontein Caves.

Back Cover: Ulrike Ernst photographed by Malick Sidebe.

Portraits:
Peter Horn
Mandla Langa
Stephen Gray
Michael Chapman
Ari Sitas
Nise Malange
Nadine Gordimer
Mongane Wally Serote
Jeremy Cronin
Ulrike Kistner

The photographs were taken on the day of the individual interview.

All photos, including cover, are copyright © Ulrike Ernst.

A Note on the Author

Ulrike Ernst was born in 1964 in (East) Berlin and grew up in the north of Germany. She was educated in Berlin, Rostock and at Cambridge/UK and became a fellowship-holder of the Friedrich-Ebert-Foundation.

After receiving her M Theol and CELTA and working as a freelance lecturer, she is currently finishing her PhD at the Faculty of Cultural Studies at the Humboldt University Berlin. Her wide range of interests include cultural and literary theory. At present, she is especially engaged with issues of globalisation and its effects on national identity in the African context. Her thesis is dealing with the challenges this bears for intellectuals and writers in South Africa after the end of apartheid.

At the time of the publication of this collection, Ulrike Ernst lives alternately in Berlin and Bamako, Mali.

FORECAAST
(Forum for European Contributions to African American Studies)

Maria Diedrich; Carl Pedersen; Justine Tally (eds.)
Mapping African America
History, Narrative Formation, and the Production of Knowledge
Bd. 1, 1999, 256 S., 30,90 €, br., ISBN 3-8258-3328-3

Stefanie Sievers
Liberating Narratives
The Authorization of Black Female Voices in African American Women Writers' Novels of Slavery
Bd. 2, 1999, 232 S., 25,90 €, br., ISBN 3-8258-3919-2

Justine Tally
Paradise Reconsidered
Toni Morrison's (Hi)stories and Truths
Bd. 3, 1999, 112 S., 17,90 €, br., ISBN 3-8258-4204-5

Dorothea Fischer-Hornung; Alison D. Goeller (eds.)
EmBODYing Liberation
The Black Body in American Dance
Bd. 4, 2001, 152 S., 20,90 €, br., ISBN 3-8258-4473-0

Patrick B. Miller; Therese Frey Steffen; Elisabeth Schäfer-Wünsche (eds.)
The Civil Rights Movement Revisited
Critical Perspectives on the Struggle for Racial Equality in the United States
The crusade for civil rights was a defining episode of 20th century U.S. history, reshaping the constitutional, political, social, and economic life of the nation. This collection of original essays by both European and American scholars includes close analyses of literature and film, historical studies of significant themes and events from the turn-of-the century to the movement years, and assessments of the movement's legacies. Ultimately, the articles help examine the ways civil rights activism, often grounded in the political work of women, has shaped American consciousness and culture until the outset of the 21st century.
Bd. 5, 2001, 224 S., 24,90 €, br., ISBN 3-8258-4486-2

Fritz Gysin; Christopher Mulvey (Hrsg.)
Black Liberation in the Americas
The recognition that Africans in the Americas have also been subjects of their destiny rather than merely passive objects of European oppression represents one of the major shifts in twentieth-century mainstream historiography. Yet even in the eighteenth and nineteenth centuries, slave narratives and abolitionist tracts offered testimony to various ways in which Africans struggled against slavery, from outright revolt to day-to-day resistance. In the first decades of the twentieth century, African American historians like Carter G. Woodson and W. E. B. Du Bois started to articulate a vision of African American history that emphasized survival and resistance rather than victimization and oppression. This volume seeks to address these and other issues in black liberation from interdisciplinary and comparative perspectives, focusing on such issues as slave revolts, day-to-day resistance, abolitionist movements, maroon societies, the historiography of resistance, the literature of resistance, black liberation movements in the twentieth century, and black liberation and post colonial theory. The chapters span the disciplines of history, literature, anthropology, folklore, film, music, architecture, and art, drawing on the black experience of liberation in the United States, the Caribbean, and Latin America.
Bd. 6, 2001, 280 S., 24,90 €, br., ISBN 3-8258-5137-0

Justine Tally
The Story of *Jazz*
Toni Morrison's Dialogic Imagination
Ever since its publication in 1992, *Jazz*, probably Toni Morrison's most difficult novel to date, has elicited a wide array of critical response. Many of these analyses, while both thoughtful and thought-provoking, have provided only partial or inherently inconclusive interpretations. The title, and certain of the author's own pronouncements, have led other critics to focus on the music itself, both as medium and aesthetic support for the narration. Choosing an entirely different approach for *The Story of Jazz*, Justine Tally further develops her hypothesis, first elaborated in her study of *Paradise*, that the Morrison trilogy is undergirded by the relationship of history, memory and story, and discusses "jazz" not as the music, but as a metaphor for language and storytelling. Taking her cue from the author's epigraph for the novel, she discusses the relevance of storytelling to contemporary critics in many different fields, explains Morrison's choice of the hard-boiled detective *genre* as a ghost-text for her novel, and guides the reader through the intricacies of Bakhtinian theory in order to elucidate and ground her interpretation of this important text, finally entering into a chapter-by-chapter analysis of the novel which leads to a surprising conclusion.
Bd. 7, 2001, 168 S., 20,90 €, br., ISBN 3-8258-5364-0

L**IT** Verlag Münster – Hamburg – Berlin – London
Grevener Str. 179 48159 Münster
Tel.: 0251 – 23 50 91 – Fax: 0251 – 23 19 72
e-Mail: vertrieb@lit-verlag.de – http://www.lit-verlag.de
Preise: unv. PE